The Public Lands in
Jacksonian Politics

THE PUBLIC LANDS IN JACKSONIAN POLITICS

Daniel Feller

The University of Wisconsin Press

10711428

Published 1984

The University of Wisconsin Press
114 North Murray Street
Madison, Wisconsin 53715

The University of Wisconsin Press, Ltd.
1 Gower Street
London WC1E 6HA, England

First printing

Printed in the United States of America

For LC CIP information see the colophon

ISBN 0-299-09850-8

For

Paul Conkin
Richard H. Jones
Richard H. Sewell

scholars, teachers, gentlemen

CONTENTS

TABLES

INTRODUCTION

The date was January 19, 1830. The first Congress under President Andrew Jackson had been sitting just six weeks. Robert Hayne of South Carolina was addressing the Senate:

> Every gentleman who has had a seat in Congress for the last two or three years, or even for the last two or three weeks, must be convinced of the great and growing importance of this question. . . . No gentleman can fail to perceive that this is a question no longer to be evaded; it must be met—fairly and fearlessly met. A question that is pressed upon us in so many ways; that intrudes in such a variety of shapes; involving so deeply the feelings and interests of a large portion of the Union; insinuating itself into almost every question of public policy, and tinging the whole course of our legislation, cannot be put aside, or laid asleep. We cannot long avoid it; we must meet and overcome it, or it will overcome us.[1]

Hayne was not speaking of the tariff, or nullification, or slavery, or internal improvements, or the Bank of the United States, or Indian removal. He was talking about federal public land policy.

Americans of the Jacksonian era well understood the importance of the public land issue. Two years after Hayne, Henry Clay told the same Senate that "no subject which had presented itself to the present, or perhaps any preceding Congress, was of greater magnitude than that of the public lands." Politicians and voters knew that public land policy addressed certain fundamental problems of American development, problems that affected not only the West but the whole society, problems that even touched the integrity of the Union itself.[2]

Before the War of 1812 the United States had faced seaward. American commerce girdled the globe, while interior resources lay untouched. But the war reoriented Americans from the seaboard to the frontier. Shipping went into eclipse, while settlers poured into the trans-Appalachian West, bringing five new states into the Union in six years. Everywhere nationalistic sentiment flourished, and with it the spirit of enterprise. Americans contemplated grand designs for roads, canals, factories, schools, colleges, asylums, and hospitals.

xi

Yet the nation lacked capital and labor to match its boundless energy and enthusiasm. New frontier communities competed for population with established farms and cities. Neither state and local governments nor private entrepreneurs could finance the anticipated improvements in transportation, education, and social services. Promoters of development therefore turned to the federal government for help. Frontiersmen begged for aid to emigrants, manufacturers for a protective tariff, road and canal enthusiasts for federal subsidies, state governments for aid to education.

Upon the government at Washington fell the responsibility for ordering developmental priorities in a diverse and rapidly expanding Union. The ensuing debate over national economic policy did not merely concern the distribution of current wealth. It looked far into the future, addressing the question of what kind of country the United States was going to become—rural or urban, localized or cosmopolitan, commercial, industrial, or agricultural. Seen closely, those broad alternatives translated into specific questions that touched every community and every household: whether a canal would open distant markets to an Ohio farmer, whether a Missouri settlement could attract the emigrants it needed to prosper, whether new industry would revive a dying Massachusetts seaport town.

The federal government, far more than state or local authorities, seemed to hold the keys to the nation's economic future. Its revenues dwarfed those of even the largest states, and Congress controlled the disposal of millions of acres of public land. With cash and land the federal government could, and did, subsidize education and internal improvement. Only the government at Washington could shelter infant industries with tariffs; only it could provide a uniform national currency.

Yet established political traditions and constitutional interpretations often frustrated those who sought federal economic assistance. The Jeffersonian legacy of frugality and strict construction in government survived the Republican party's organizational collapse in the postwar Era of Good Feelings. After the war the treasury ran a regular annual surplus, liquidating a national debt of $127 million in twenty years. By 1817 Congress had repealed all the wartime internal taxes, limiting federal revenue to the tariff on imports and the proceeds of public land sales. The combination of reduced revenues and balanced budgets left few funds for discretionary spending. And strict constructionists challenged Congress's right to promote economic growth through protective tariffs, a national bank, and subsidies for transportation and education.

But beyond these impediments stretched the vast federal public domain, in the words of President James Monroe a "resource of great extent and duration."[3] Unencumbered, immensely valuable, it shimmered on the horizon of America's vision like the pot of gold at the end of the rainbow, ensuring a future of national greatness and limitless economic growth. Monroe, like most Americans, saw the national domain as a capital fund for improvements, which replenished the fund in turn by augmenting the value of unsold lands. The congressional prerogative under the Constitution to "make all needful Rules and Regulations respecting the Territory or other Property belonging to the United States" even seemed to exempt the land revenue from constitutional restrictions on federal spending. Precedent sustained that interpretation. Congress had given land away for schools since confederation days, and in 1802 Jefferson himself signed legislation creating a permanent transportation fund from the land proceeds.

Through the public domain Congress also directly influenced the movement of population. The lure of the frontier was land, and in all the new Western states the federal government still owned nine-tenths of the land in 1821. Congressional land policy could entice or deter new emigrants, and shape patterns of settlement and tenure for generations to come.

Hence the postwar competition for capital and population centered on national land policy along with the tariff and internal improvements. In politics that competition found expression through sectionalism. The brief Era of Good Feelings, buoyed by an inflationary prosperity, masked the gathering of sectional constituencies behind alternative programs of economic development. The panic of 1819 and the Missouri crisis over slavery shattered the illusions of economic abundance and political harmony. For the next decade the clash of sectional interests dominated national politics.

Sectionalism in the halls of Congress mirrored sentiment in society at large. The emergence of a new section in the West and the growing social and political diversity brought on by regional economic specialization served to heighten geographical consciousness everywhere. Sectional pride and sectional loyalty were displayed in distinctive ways of working and playing, in manners and dress, and in song and story. Still sharing a common cultural inheritance and refusing to acknowledge class distinctions, many Americans identified themselves not by their church or occupation or country of origin, but by their section. Westerners were, beyond all else, Westerners, and they celebrated in themselves the frontier virtues personified by Andrew Jackson and the heroes of New Orleans. Southerners displayed their graciousness and code of honor; Yankess proudly exhibited their sobriety and thrift. Sectional identity embraced a whole complex of shared traditions, aspirations, and prejudices.[4]

Sectionalism in the 1820s was partly a product of political and economic geography, partly a distinctively flexible state of mind. Unlike sectionalism a generation later, it did not fasten on a single political issue or polarize the nation into two warring camps. Politically, the sections were not fixed geographic entities but shifting combinations, arraying themselves according to the subject at hand. In Congress, the slavery question precipitated one sectional division, the tariff another, land policy a third. Still, in national and state and even local forums, sectional rhetoric pervaded political dialogue. Officeholders, candidates, editors all phrased their aspirations—and antagonisms—in sectional terms. Westerners talked of Western programs, Southerners of Southern interest, Yankees of New England policy. Yet they could differ as to means; while all Westerners demanded Western measures, they sometimes disagreed on what those were, and the word "Western" meant something different in Indiana than in Alabama, though it was used in both places. Divided loyalties also complicated sectional identities. Ohioans were both Western and Northern, Mississippians Western and Southern, Carolinians Southern and Eastern. Sectional perceptions were not static; they evolved in response to changing circumstances. Easterners became Westerners when they moved to the frontier; Westerners became Easterners when the frontier moved away from them. New Englanders, retaining their sense of sectional identity, over time found new policies through which to express it.

The dialectic of sectionalism controlled national politics through the 1820s. Sectional blocs and coalitions collided first over slavery and economic policy issues, then, beginning in 1824, over the presidency. But the politics of sectionalism soon yielded to a politics of partisanship. By the 1840s straight party divisions in Congress replaced sectional bloc voting. In election campaigns, Democrats and Whigs competed closely in every section and nearly every state in the Union. Sectionalism seemingly vanished from national politics, supplanted by the most geographically balanced party system in American history.[5]

The transformation from sectionalism to partisanship, the simultaneous mobilization of a mass electorate, and the subsequent collapse of the party system and reversion to sectionalism in the 1850s, are the fundamental facts which all scholars of Jacksonian politics have puzzled to comprehend. The problem embraces the identity and character of the Whig and Democratic parties, for to explain why national parties rose, flourished, and fell is also to explain what they stood for and who they appealed to.

The modern debate over Jacksonian politics, as over much else, began with Frederick Jackson Turner, who stressed the persistence of sectionalism through the party period and indeed through all of American history. In Turner's view the parties at best mitigated but never thoroughly suppressed sectionalism, and themselves often served as instruments of sectional interest.[6]

In 1945 Arthur Schlesinger, Jr., countered that "more can be understood about Jacksonian democracy if it is regarded as a problem not of sections but of classes." His *Age of Jackson* accordingly described the Whigs and Democrats as the respective representatives of the business community and the working classes.[7]

A third generation of historians, dismissing both Turner's and Schlesinger's formulations as products of "economic determinism," sees Jacksonian politics as the vehicle for cultural conflict between hostile ethnic and religious groups.[8] Their work, which questions the relevance of national issues (especially economic issues) to local party organization, receives indirect support from studies suggesting that the national parties themselves avoided meaningful policy controversies, and that the government at Washington was thoroughly isolated from the citizenry.[9]

This new orthodoxy—for such it has become—takes as axiomatic the primacy of local over national and of ethnocultural over economic concerns; sectionalism as a political force it skirts altogether. But its premises merit scrutiny. Historians have found abundant evidence of ethnocultural conflict following the dramatic rise in Irish and German immigration around 1840, but much less in the 1820s and early 1830s, the gestation period of the Jacksonian party system. And Washington politicians in the decades after the War of 1812, though physically removed from their constituents, were in some ways closer to them than they ever have been since. The houses of Congress functioned as public forums, their debates reported at length in the Washington press and, much abbreviated, in papers througout the country. Important speeches were struck off as pamphlets and distributed by the thousands. Dozens of newspapers, subsidized by Congress, published the laws in full. On important roll calls, editors displayed the record of what Hezekiah Niles called "the yeas and nays—that glorious republican invention, the yeas and nays."[10]

The brevity of congressional sessions and the crudeness of the capital city rather facilitated than obstructed contact between representatives and their constituents. Unlike their modern successors, Jacksonian congressmen really lived in their districts; the dearth of amenities at Washington propelled them home promptly at session's end. In the 1820s representatives ministered to constituencies of only 40,000, smaller than those of many state legislators today.

Washington politicians did not slight such national questions as the tariff, internal improvements, or public land policy when they went before the voters. Rather they discussed them almost incessantly; even candidates for state and local office commonly took positions on national issues. State legislatures debated and adopted resolutions on national affairs, and the opinions they expressed were faithfully reflected on the floor of Congress. In return, national controversies provided an essential rallying standard for state and local party organizers.[11]

My purpose in this book is to show how one national policy controversy, that over federal public land policy, originated and evolved, how it interacted with other issues, and how it figured in the transformation of political alignments from 1815 to 1840. Secondarily, I also offer some suggestions regarding the impact of changes in land policy upon the actual distribution and settlement of the public domain. My larger goal throughout has been to essay a contribution toward understanding what Jacksonian politics were all about—to show how sectionalism operated and why it gave way to partisanship, and to make it plain how events at Washington and the state capitals related to the concerns of citizens at home.

The Public Lands in
Jacksonian Politics

CHAPTER 1
THE NATIONAL LAND SYSTEM
BEFORE 1815

Origins of the federal public domain

Political controversy about the public land policy of the United States began with the American Revolution. In fact, even before independence from Britain was won, it became clear that resolving the dilemmas surrounding the public domain might prove necessary to preserve the Union itself.[1]

At the peace negotiations with Britain Americans demanded, and got, a western boundary at the Mississippi River. Thus the new nation secured for its birthright a vast internal empire rich in agricultural and mineral resources. But under their colonial charters, seven states—Massachusetts, Connecticut, New York, Virginia, North Carolina, South Carolina, and Georgia—claimed portions of the western wilderness. Virginia's claim was the largest, stretching north and west to encompass the later states of Kentucky, Ohio, Indiana, Illinois, Michigan, and Wisconsin. The language of the charters was vague and their validity questionable, but during the war Virginia reinforced its title by sponsoring Colonel George Rogers Clark's 1778 expedition to Vincennes and Kaskaskia, which strengthened America's trans-Appalachian pretensions at the peace table.

The six states holding no claim to the transmontane region doubted whether a confederacy in which territory was so unevenly apportioned would truly prove what it claimed to be, a Union of equals. Already New Jersey, Delaware, Rhode Island, and Maryland were among the smallest and least populous of the states. While they levied heavy taxes to repay state war debts, their larger neighbors might retire debts out of land-sale proceeds. Drawn by fresh lands and low taxes, people would desert the small states for the large, leaving the former to fall into bankrupty and eventually into political subjugation. All the states shared in the war effort, said the New Jersey legislature; how then could half of them "be left to sink under an enormous debt, whilst others are enabled, in a short period, to replace all their expenditures from the hard earnings of the whole confederacy?" As the Revolution was a common endeavor, so ought its fruits, including the western lands, to be a common property.[2]

Efforts to write a western boundary for the landed states into the Articles of Confederation failed in the Continental Congress. Notwithstanding, twelve states ratified the Articles in 1778 and 1779, New Jersey and Delaware accompanying their ratifications with renewed appeals for a federal domain in the West. Maryland, brooding under the shadow of the Virginia colossus, refused to join the new government. Maryland's recalcitrance (apparently also inspired in part by the machinations of certain land speculators) delayed the implementation of the Articles for two years. But in February 1780 New York promised to cede its western claims to the United States, and later that year Congress "earnestly recommended" that the rest of the claimant states follow suit. Thus assured, Maryland finally ratified the Articles on March 31, 1781.[3]

The cessions took another two decades to complete. Virginia's, by far the most important, was completed in 1784, others during the 1780s, Georgia's not until 1802. In their final form, most cessions conveyed jurisdiction and property, meaning that the United States became both the direct governing authority and the owner of the soil. But there were exceptions. Both Virginia and Connecticut withheld large tracts in present-day Ohio, the latter for a time retaining both property and jurisdiction in its "Western Reserve." Virginia never ceded its territory south of the Ohio River at all, and in 1792 it became the state of Kentucky. North Carolina ceded the Tennessee country, but only after dispensing virtually all the land therein to soldiers, settlers, and speculators. Like Kentucky, Tennessee never came under the federal land system; the United States finally abandoned its scattered holdings there to the state in 1841. Georgia's cession was encumbered with the embarrassing Yazoo claims, the product of a 35-million acre land sale which the state legislature authorized in 1795 and repudiated a year later. Congress also agreed to pay Georgia $1,250,000 from land-sale proceeds, the only such payment to any ceding state.

Far more important than the idiosyncracies of the individual cessions were the general principles that underlay them all. In 1780 Congress pledged that the ceded lands

> shall be disposed of for the common benefit of the United States, and be settled and formed into distinct republican States, which shall become members of the Federal Union, and have the same rights of sovereignty, freedom, and independence, as the other States.

Virginia's Act of Cession, which became a model for those following, repeated the guarantee of statehood, and stipulated that the ceded lands

> shall be considered as a common fund for the use and benefit of such of the United States as have become, or shall become, members of the Confederation or federal alliance of the said States, Virginia inclusive, according to their usual respective proportions in the general charge and expenditure, and shall be faithfully and bona fide disposed of for that purpose, and for no other use or purpose whatsoever.[4]

Congress and the ceding states thus asserted two principles at the outset: the public domain should be managed for the benefit of the whole Union, and should be eventually carved up into states admitted on an equal basis with the original members. Apparently it did not occur to anyone that the two conditions might be contradictory.

Yet the broad generalizations of the Virginia Act of Cession contained the seeds of a controversy that would trouble the Union decades later and that still continues, though in muted tones and under very different circumstances, today.[5] Managing the public lands as a "common fund" meant retaining them in federal hands, at least until they could be profitably sold. But in the original states there was no federal domain. Massachusetts, New York, and Georgia retained vast open tracts within their redrawn borders, and managed them precisely as they pleased. In some Atlantic states little public land remained, but in none of them was all the vacant domain in the hands of an absentee landlord that was also a government. Nothing was more important to new frontier states than control of the terms under which land was opened for settlement. Whether federal ownership of their public domain could be reconciled wtih their guaranteed rights of "sovereignty, freedom, and independence" remained to be seen.

From the date of its creation, the federal domain was a potent agent of nationalization. The authority of the Confederation Congress over the western lands contrasted sharply with its other limited powers. Congress could not tax. For revenue it relied on requisitions from the states, which they were required to supply but Congress was powerless to compel. Exercise of the most important congressional functions pertaining to diplomacy, war, and finance required the assent of nine out of thirteen state delegations. But congressional authority over the public domain was virtually plenary. In the West Congress could govern directly, raise a revenue, and create new states. Financially and administratively, the public domain was the government's greatest asset—indeed, its only asset—and offered it the opportunity to test and expand its powers.

In early legislation for the West, Congress reaffirmed the dual doctrines of the Virginia cession, while clarifying its intention to retain ownership of the public domain even after the creation of new states. A congressional ordinance of 1784, prescribing a territorial government and a statehood process for the western regions, stipulated that new states "in no case, shall interfere with the primary disposal of the soil by the United States in Congress assembled," and also "that no tax shall be imposed on lands the property of the United States." The Northwest Ordinance of 1787, superceding the earlier legislation, repeated both prohibitions, but also provided that upon reaching a population of 60,000 each new state would be admitted "on an equal footing with the original States, in all respects whatever." By fiat, the ordinance proclaimed its own provisions as "articles of compact" between the existing and future states, to "forever remain unalterable, unless by common consent."[6]

Everyone understood from the beginning that Congress would use the lands to pay off the public debt. In 1783 and again in 1784 Congress urged the recalcitrant landholding states to cede their claims "as a further mean, as well of hastening the extinguishment of the debts, as of establishing the harmony of the United States." In the words of a resolution of 1784, "Congress still consider vacant territory as a capital resource." The assumption that land receipts would go to debt service also underlaid Virginia's requirement that the domain be employed as a "common fund" for the states "according to their usual respective proportions in the general charge and expenditure." Logic demanded the application of the government's only tangible resource to cancel its greatest liability.[7]

The Confederation Congress approved, in May of 1785, an ordinance establishing a federal land system. Its essential features have never been changed. The public domain was to be surveyed into townships six miles square, subdivided into square-mile (640-acre) lots numbered from 1 to 36 in each township and later called "sections." The lands were to be sold at auction at a minimum price of one dollar per acre. Half the townships were to be offered whole, the others by individual sections.[8]

The Land Ordinance of 1785 also reserved one section (number 16) in each township "for the maintenance of public schools." Congressional authority to subsidize education was unknown to the Articles of Confederation or, for that matter, to the Constitution. But the school grants quickly became embedded in federal land policy and furnished a plausible precedent for similar grants for other purposes.

The rectangular surveys, the auctions, and the school sections survived many subsequent revisions of the land laws. But the revenue from the first sales was disappointing. It took two years to complete the initial surveys in eastern Ohio, and the auction at New York in 1787 yielded only $117,108 in depreciated securities (accepted at par) for 72,974 acres. Not for another nine years would the United States again offer land at public sale.

The thirst for revenue drove Congress to circumvent its methodical sales system before it had been fairly tested. In 1787 Congress sold a million and a half acres to the Ohio Company, a New England venture, for one million dollars. A year later John Cleve Symmes made a similar but smaller purchase. These bulk sales held certain advantages. They avoided the expense and delay of surveys, and though the purchasers got their tracts below the nominal price by paying in depreciated government securities, the United States was still retiring obligations it would otherwise someday have to redeem at par. Both Symmes and the Ohio Company defaulted on their later payments, however, and in the 1790s they had to be rescued with commutations and outright grants of land. The experience soured Congress on large sales, and none were ever authorized again.

Federal land operations ceased for several years under the new Constitution of 1787. The Constitution itself granted Congress "Power to dispose of and make all needful Rules and Regulations respecting the Territory or other Property belonging to the United States," confirming without clarifying authority already exercised under the Articles of Confederation. The new government also inherited responsibilities and obligations from the state deeds of cession and the Northwest Ordinance, fortified in 1790 and again in 1795 by specific congressional pledges of the land revenue "solely" to the payment of the national debt and the newly assumed state debts.[9]

At first Congress neither implemented nor superceded the Land Ordinance of 1785, so no land was sold. But successive land laws of 1796, 1800, and 1804 revitalized the earlier arrangements and established them, with certain alterations, on a permanent basis. Prior survey into townships and sections, auction sales with a designated minimum price, and school grants all were retained. The domain was marked off into districts, each containing a land office staffed by a register and receiver. After several attempts to sell in the East, Congress thus fixed the place of sale in the West itself, where settlers would have ready access to the auction. The act of 1800 also provided for continuous sales after the auction by stipulating that unbid land could be "entered" privately at the land office at any time afterward, at the minimum price.

In 1796 Congress fixed the minimum price at two dollars per acre, double the minimum ordained in 1785. Since government paper had risen in value in the interim, the true increase was even greater. However, two other innovations counterbalanced the higher prices and greatly facilitated sales. The basic purchase unit was halved from 640 acres (a section) in 1796 to 320 acres in 1800 and again to 160 acres in 1804. Beginning in 1796, Congress also offered credit. As revised in 1800, the terms were as follows: 5 percent down, 20 percent more in forty days, and the remainder in three equal installments due two, three, and four years from the date of sale, plus 6 percent per annum interest. An 8 percent per annum discount for advance payment of the later installments (which included full interest, no matter when the payments were actually made) reduced the actual price for cash purchases to $1.84 per acre. In 1804 Congress waived all interest except on arrears, in effect lowering prices and reducing the cash rate to $1.64 per acre.[10]

The admission of Ohio, the first state carved (though only partially) out of the federal public domain, put the finishing touches on the land system. It also provided the occasion for a major expansion of federal power, a milestone on the road to nationalization.

The federal title to the public domain in Ohio was secure, guaranteed by the Virginia Act of Cession and the Northwest Ordinance, which had since been reaffirmed by Congress under the Constitution. But following the contractual precedent set by the ordinance, Congress offered the nascent state an additional bargain, or compact, the terms of which were as follows: Congress would grant Ohio some sections containing salt springs, donate one section in each township for schools (already reserved for that purpose), and spend 5 percent of all future Ohio net land proceeds to build roads to and through the state, provided the state constitutional convention refrained "by an ordinance irrevocable" from taxing any lands sold by the United States for five years "from and after the day of sale." Ohio accepted the compact with the condition that the road fund be divided, 3 percent of the net land proceeds to be spent by Ohio on roads within the state, and the other 2 percent by the United States on roads leading to its borders.[11]

With this Ohio Enabling Act of 1802, the administration of Thomas Jefferson, inaugurated barely a year before on principles of states' rights and strict construction, irrevocably committed itself and all future administrations to a program of federal internal improvements within the states. The agreement once made was "obligatory upon the United States" until Ohio consented to abandon it, which Ohio would never do. The arrangement deftly sidestepped the constitutional question of the federal government's right to build roads within the states by creating a contractual obligation to do so. In later years John Quincy Adams correctly paired the Ohio Enabling Act with the Louisiana Purchase as destroyers of the original Jeffersonian creed.[12]

The ostensible purpose of the compact with Ohio was to protect credit purchasers of government land from state taxation until they completed their payments and acquired full title. But Secretary of the Treasury Albert Gallatin, who proposed the arrangement, believed that the Northwest Ordinance already barred Ohio from taxing land before a patent was issued. As an incentive to purchasers, he had suggested that the state forebear from taxing lands for ten years, not after the sale, but "after the completion of the payment of the purchase-money," in return for a road fund of 10 percent of the land proceeds. The Ohio bill originally included Gallatin's provision, but somewhere in its progress through Congress the language was changed. Thus, according to Gallatin's understanding, the concession required from Ohio in the bill that came to Jefferson's desk was really no concession at all. Yet the secretary did not object. Unlike Jefferson, Gallatin did not doubt federal power to build roads and canals; he thought them economically beneficial and politically essential as a bond of Union between dissimilar sections. His original proposal would have worked a real financial hardship on Ohio and might well have been rejected. The suspicion is strong that Gallatin and perhaps others in Congress acquiesced in its amendment because their real purpose was not to exact concessions from Ohio, but to commit the federal government to an internal improvements policy. Gallatin later endorsed his original proposal "Origin of National Road."[13]

The compact with Ohio served as a precedent for the admission of other new states. Louisiana, Indiana, Mississippi, Illinois, Alabama, and Missouri all came into the Union under similar terms. Each received the 16th-section school lands, some salt spring sections, two townships for a seminary, and the 2 percent and 3 percent road funds, in return for pledging not to tax federal lands for five years after their sale or to tax lands of nonresidents higher than those of residents. In addition, Louisiana, Mississippi, Alabama, and Missouri, which were not covered by the "articles of compact" in the Northwest Ordinance, had to renounce any claim to the ownership or taxation of the public domain, which should be "at the sole and entire disposition of the United States."[14]

Early land operations

After a desultory beginning under the Land Act of 1796, surveying began in earnest under the provisions of 1800, and land sales finally got under way. But down to the War of 1812 sales remained modest, partly because of Indian troubles on the frontier and partly because of competition from private land companies and several states, all of which offered better terms. Along with Kentucky and Tennessee, portions of Georgia and New York and the Maine district of Massachusetts still beckoned to the emigrant. Federal land sales from 1801 to 1813 averaged about 350,000 acres a year, ranging from a high of 619,266 acres in 1805 to a low of 181,068 acres in 1803.[15]

For the most part the land system functioned smoothly in those years. The surveys spread from Ohio into the Indiana Territory, the huge Georgia Cession, and the new Louisiana Purchase, though in the latter the task of adjudicating vague French and Spanish grants long delayed the opening of public sales. Federal land rarely sold for much above the two-dollar minimum per acre, but in a glutted market with the minimum deliberately pegged near the supposed real value of the lands, this was to be expected and caused little concern.

Problems soon appeared with the credit arrangements. The system inaugurated in 1800, it will be recalled, provided for payment over a period of four years. Discounts and interest remissions encouraged promptness. A purchaser who fell behind could carry his debt, plus accumulating interest, for one year after the due date for the final payment, five years from the date of sale. After that he forfeited his land, which was to be resold for not less than the balance due. If the resale brought more than was due, the forfeiter received the excess; if not, he got nothing.

A few farsighted critics, most notably Albert Gallatin (who as Treasury secretary administered the system), predicted trouble from the start. They pointed to the purchaser's natural inclination to exhaust his funds on the first payment in order to secure the largest possible tract. Few buyers accepted the incentives for advance payment of the later installments. In the first four years of credit operations, the outstanding debt for land purchases swelled to more than a million dollars, a sum Gallatin foresaw "great difficulties" in collecting. The credit system postponed the day of reckoning and encouraged the buyer to take risks. Some no doubt expected to pay from the produce of their farms; Gallatin almost alone realized how difficult that really was. On the frontier, disease, natural disasters, Indian wars, fluctuations in crop prices, and lack of access to markets could ruin even sober calculations of finance. And many buyers perhaps did not think clearly about how they would meet their later payments. The frontier inspired dreams and visions, and five years is a long time.

By 1805 the final payments on the first sales under the Land Act of

1800 were coming due, and Congress faced an unpleasant prospect. Enforcing the forfeiture penalty meant expelling the settler into the wilderness, his years of privation and struggle set at naught. It was doubtful whether frontier communities, composed largely of purchasers in similar circumstances, would permit resales of forfeited land, or whether anyone would dare to bid if they did. If the land were not resold, the defaulter would likely remain on it as an illegal squatter. Failure to enforce the forfeiture penalty, on the other hand, would inspire contempt for the law and encourage other debtors to ignore the payment deadlines.

Faced with these alternatives, congressional committees sought Gallatin's advice. In response, the Treasury secretary formulated a trenchant analysis of the credit system that became a text for all its later critics. Gallatin advocated sales for cash only. Not only would the land debt be difficult to collect, but "its daily increase may ultimately create an interest hostile to the general welfare of the Union." Debt invariably estranged debtor and creditor, and when one owed allegiance as a citizen to the other the estrangement carried unpleasant political implications, especially when debtors were concentrated in a remote section of the Union whose loyalty to the national government was already questionable. The larger the debt, the greater the temptation for Westerners to repudiate their obligations en masse, forcibly obstruct the land system, or even secede, confiscating the public domain from the government in Washington as the Americans had seized it from Great Britain. With Spanish intrigues and the Burr conspiracy fresh in everyone's mind, the existence of what amounted to a multi-million-dollar bribe for Western disloyalty was disconcerting.[16]

For his reform recommendations, Gallatin returned to first principles. The purpose of the land system was to generate revenue and to promote a "gradual and equal distribution of property." By pegging the minimum price near the actual value, the government prevented "a waste of the public property" without shutting out purchasers of modest means. Lowering the price too much would mean "promoting migration beyond its natural and necessary progress" and "throwing the lands into the hands of a few individuals" who would hold them for speculation. Raising the price, on the other hand, would disqualify the poor. The ideal, then, was a system which offered everyone land for his own use without encouraging monopoly or speculation, a system which would "satisfy the demand for land created by the existing population" without artificially stimulating or narrowing that demand.[17]

Specifically, Gallatin recommended a threefold revision of the land system: eliminate credit sales, reduce the size of the purchase unit, and lower the minimum price from $2.00 to either $1.25 or $1.50 per acre. Sales for cash would prevent conflict between government and buyer, while lower prices and smaller tracts would aid poor purchasers. The sum of $120, previously a first payment on a quarter-section, could then purchase an eighty-acre farm free and clear. The new minimum price would still be high enough to deter speculation, and sales would probably speed up, holding the revenue constant.

Five congressional committees endorsed Gallatin's proposals between 1804 and 1812.[18] But none of the reforms were enacted; in fact, none even came to a vote. Despite repeated warnings, Congress felt no need to overhaul the land system, because the political and financial crises envisioned by Gallatin failed to materialize. Down to 1813, the United States sold 4,520,933 acres under the credit system at an average price of $2.11 per acre, and took in $7,316,615 in actual cash. Though $2,114,136 was still owed, receipts already in hand worked out to $1.62 per acre, probably more than would be realized under cash sales at a lower minimum price. Contrary to prediction, the land debt also quickly stabilized. After growing to more than two million dollars by 1805, it held virtually constant over the next eight years; indeed, it declined by 29 percent in the land districts of the Old Northwest as buyers completed old purchases faster than they made new ones.[19]

Prognostications of disunion and disloyalty proved visionary as well. Against the blandishments of Spain and the belligerence of Britain, the West was tested and found true. Disunionist schemes foundered for lack of followers. Land debtors petitioned for relief, but did not rise in revolt. Though land frauds and squatting on the public domain troubled officials as always, no army of angry frontiersmen gathered to seize the public lands or to block forfeitures.

Congress itself avoided confrontation by extending liberal relief to land debtors. Rather than abolish the credit system or enforce its penalties, Congress extended the payment deadlines and postponed forfeitures. Gallatin had warned against this policy, saying that "if credits shall not be allowed hereafter, some indulgence, in point of time" might be granted to delinquents, but "should the present system be continued, a more rigid enforcement of the law will be necessary." Nevertheless, a law granting additional time to complete payments passed in 1806. Another followed in 1809, still another in 1810, and by the outbreak of war the passage of an annual relief act had become routine. As the provisions of the laws were not uniform, and as occasional gaps appeared among them, a few forfeitures still occurred. Contrary to Gallatin's forebodings, the relief legislation does not appear to have inspired widespread contempt for the law. The stability of the land debt down to 1813 showed that most purchasers would rather finish paying and acquire sure title than count on relief from Congress.[20]

When war with Britain began in 1812 the national land system had been in operation for little more than a decade. Its sales were small but steady. Despite the warnings of Gallatin's disciples in Congress, there was little to excite controversy or to foretell crisis in the system in 1812. As measured by the annual Treasury statistics, the federal land business seemed remarkably stable. But with the war, all this changed.

CHAPTER 2
THE EMERGENCE OF THE NEW WEST, 1815–1821

Our country still presents the finest theatre in America. Our lands are yet cheap, and advance in price while sinking everywhere else. Our towns flourish while so many others are perishing. Our noble rivers are enlivened with commerce; and the tide of emigration flows in upon us with a force and steadiness which should announce to the old states that the power of this continent is gravitating to the borders of the Mississippi. Look back to what we were thirty years ago; see what we are today; tell what we must be in 1830. From that day the west will give law to the Republic . . .

Thomas Hart Benton to James Preston, November 14, 1819

The Great Migration

The War of 1812 loosed a flood of migration to the western fringes of the American Republic. Before the war powerful Indian confederacies, abetted by British allies, hindered the movement of settlers to the rich lands of the Ohio Valley and the Georgia Cession. But the campaigns of Andrew Jackson and William Henry Harrison broke the Indian resistance. Jackson's victory over the Creeks at Horseshoe Bend forced them to surrender southern Georgia and more than fourteen million acres of central Alabama at the Treaty of Fort Jackson in August 1814. Other capitulations followed. Within four years, more than thirty treaties swept away the remaining Indian title to western Ohio and Tennessee and most of Indiana, Alabama, and Illinois. Across the Mississippi River, Missouri and Arkansas now lay open to white penetration.[1]

Suddenly millions of acres of public land were available for settlement. Glowing reports of the region's soils and climate began to appear in the Atlantic press. Good prices for farm products also enticed emigrants westward. New Orleans cotton in 1815 soared from seventeen cents a pound to twenty-seven cents. By 1817 Ohio Valley wheat and corn brought double their pre-war values.[2]

14

Settlers by the thousands funneled through the Appalachian passes and dispersed through the valleys of the Ohio, the Tennessee, and the Wabash. Rude clearings appeared in the wilderness, while cities like Cincinnati and St. Louis laid the foundations of commercial greatness. Emigrants jammed the wagon traces. "Old America seems to be breaking up, and moving westward," marveled an Englishman, himself on the way to found a settlement in Illinois. Thomas Jefferson mused that "emigration to the West and South is going on beyond anything imaginable."[3]

The Old Northwest nearly tripled in population in ten years, from 272,000 in 1810 to 792,000 in 1820. In Indiana the increase was sixfold; in Alabama, where Indian cessions opened up prime cotton lands, it was twelvefold. Even Mississippi, still largely covered with tribal holdings, more than doubled its population.[4]

The political growth of the West matched its burgeoning population. Before 1815 the trans-Appalachian West, numbering only four states in a Union of eighteen, carried little weight in Washington. No Westerner had ever sat in the cabinet. In twenty years only one state, Ohio (and that only partially), had been carved out of the public domain. (Louisiana was a public land state, but problems in untangling Spanish land titles postponed the first sales until after 1820.) The Great Migration brought in four new states in as many years—Indiana, Illinois, Alabama, and Mississippi. By 1819 Westerners numbered more than a third of the United States Senate. In the House of Representatives the West was much weaker, but rapid population growth promised an early accession of strength. None of this went unnoticed. A Bostonian worried over the "influence, indefinable, but possibly terrible" soon to be exercised by "that *western world.*" A new Kentucky congressman discovered that his Carolina and Georgia messmates "seem to think that the W[estern] C[ountry] will receive the requisite population to acquire the ascendancy" in Washington. "I can assure them," he added, "that if the ability is ever possessed the power will be exercised."[5]

The sight of farms and cities springing up in the wilderness inspired many Americans to heady visions of continental empire. The Great Migration accompanied a powerful revival of patriotic spirit in the wake of Andrew Jackson's triumph over the British at New Orleans. But in the Atlantic states, other effects of the Western lure soon began to appear: abandoned farms, declining population, falling property values. "You, Sir, can't conceive of the anxiety and confusion that pervades all ranks of people in this section of country to remove to the Alabama," remarked one North Carolinian. "The consequence is that land here is deminishing in point of value, and the country loseing many of its most enterprising and respectable inhabitants." A Virginia legislative committee lamented the state's sorry condition: "How many sad spectacles do her lowlands present, of wasted and deserted fields! of dwellings abandoned by their proprietors! of Churches in ruins!" A similar committee in North Carolina found it "mortifying to witness the fact, that thousands of our wealthy and respectable citizens are annually moving to the West . . . and that thousands of our poorer citizens follow them, being literally driven away by the prospect of poverty." Alongside the glittering descriptions of Western plenitude in Atlantic newspapers, there began to appear complaints of lost population and wealth, and of Western publicists who exaggerated the attractions of the frontier.[6]

In the new states, editors and civic leaders eagerly charted the growth of agriculture, commerce, and industry. But the immediate key to prosperity was the emigrant. Commercial agriculture developed slowly, for bringing new land into production took time, and the wretched roads restricted access to Atlantic and European markets. With little to sell to the East, the West's trade ran a chronic deficit, draining the region of its already scarce cash. What redressed the balance and kept the economy booming was a constant influx of new settlers, who absorbed local farm surpluses and provided infusions of cash to grease the wheels of trade.

The newcomers also bought land. Before the war, annual federal land sales exceeded a half-million acres only twice, in 1805 and 1812. But in 1814 sales topped eight hundred thousand acres, in 1815 a million acres, and in 1816 a million and a half.[7]

The General Land Office, a bureau of the Treasury Department created in 1812 to administer the public domain, could not handle the new business. Its surveyors and auctioneers soon fell behind the wave of pioneers, who forged ahead despite a law of 1807 forbidding trespass on public lands. The law had always been honored in the breach, for unauthorized settling, or "squatting," was an ancient frontier practice. But before the war the Indians and the slow pace of migration had helped to restrain squatters. Now they flocked to the choicest locations, leaving the cumbersome machinery of the federal land system to follow along in their rear.

Westerners urged the government to eliminate the squatting problem by accelerating the surveys and sales. Some praised the squatters for opening paths into the wilderness; others condemned them for destroying precious timber. Either way, the arrival of public sales would force unauthorized settlers to purchase or clear out. One land official even suggested that auction gavels, like magic wands, could work wondrous reversals of character. Suddenly transformed from illegal trespassers to respectable freeholders, the pioneers would become "better citezens in every respect, . . . more Patriotic inteligent indoustrious & I believe more Honest & Virtuous" once their interests were "identified with that of the country."[8]

Pioneers could also assist the army by building roads and furnishing supplies and manpower to the frontier garrisons. From his headquarters at Nashville, General Andrew Jackson dismissed the fears of "short sighted politicians" that accelerated sales would "drain the oth[er] States of their population." The real danger, according to Jackson, was foreign invasion; against this a population of resident freeholders furnished the best defense.[9]

President James Madison attempted a peremptory solution to the squatter problem. In December 1815 he issued a proclamation warning "uninformed or evil-disposed persons . . . who have unlawfully taken possession of or made any settlement on the public lands . . . forthwith to remove therefrom" or face ejection by the army and prosecution for trespass.[10]

Frontiersmen were furious. Western newspapers railed at the "injustice, ingratitude and impolicy of this proclamation," inspired by "mischievious advisors." Petitioners insisted that the law against trespassing was a dead letter; squatters had always been tolerated and occasionally even rewarded with special pre-emption laws entitling them to purchase their "improvements" without competition and at the minimum price. Certainly the current crop of hardy pioneers, having beaten off the British and Indians and opened the territory for settlement, deserved the same privilege. Protests and demands for legislative relief poured in on frontier congressmen.[11]

In the end nothing came of Madison's proclamation. The military could throw the settlers off the public lands, but it could not keep them off. Congress, deciding as in the past to accept what it could not prevent, duly authorized squatters to remain as temporary tenants if they secured permission from local land officers. Few bothered to do so, but the squatting problem soon diminished as the General Land Office put its administrative house in order and hastened the surveys and sales. Still the episode was full of omens for the future. It revealed that along with their buoyancy and optimism, Westerners harbored an extraordinary sensitivity to what they perceived as Atlantic jealousy of their growth and prosperity. They saw settlement of the West as a national service, and they demanded federal cooperation not just as good policy, but as a matter of justice and right. They phrased their demands with a vigor which to Easterners smacked of insolence. A candidate for territorial office in Missouri demanded faster land sales, cheaper prices, and legalization of squatting so that Missouri could be quickly raised to statehood and "freed from the shackles of colonial dependence." An interpretation of a pre-emption law adverse to the claims of some Missourians by the commissioner of the General Land Office prompted a scorching legislative protest against the "illegal, arbitrary, and officious intermeddling of *Speculative land jobbing Executive officers.*" While misgivings over emigration gathered in the Atlantic states, frontiersmen cried for still greater encouragements. Both Easterners and Westerners eyed the land system as the instrument to control the flow of population. Already by 1817 ingredients were brewing for a sectional confrontation over the public domain.[12]

Land boom

In October 1817, Treasury secretary William Crawford noted that federal land sales were "increasing with a rapidity wholly unexampled." In fiscal 1817 they exceeded two million acres, a large increase over the record year of 1816. For the first time also, prices began to rise appreciably above the two-dollar minimum. For the entire period 1800–1815 the average sale price per acre was $2.10, but in 1816 it advanced to $2.20, and in 1817 to $2.35. Considering that the average included much land entered privately at the minimum price in the older districts, the increase was impressive.[13]

Prescient observers noted a new speculative trend in the Treasury statistics for 1817. Sale, settlement, and cultivation had never proceeded in lockstep. Always there had been investors who purchased without settling, and squatters who settled without buying. Still, a dramatic surge of population had backed the postwar land boom. But the Great Migration opened an intoxicating vision of interminable economic growth and escalating land values. For those who invested early, this meant sure profits. Henry Clay, purchasing two thousand acres on the Wabash at the minimum price, expected a tenfold return from "the growth of our population." Thousands made the same calculation. The speculative rush was on.[14]

Expanding credit promoted the boom. The suspension of specie payments and the wartime demand for funds had encouraged banks to issue notes based on little hard capital. After the war new banks continued to appear, some created expressly to finance land purchases. The federal government inadvertently added to the paper profusion in 1816 by issuing four million dollars of "Mississippi stock" in payment of the old Yazoo claims, receivable as cash in the land offices of Alabama and Mississippi.

Rapidly rising land revenues enabled the new president, James Monroe, to anticipate the early achievement of that hallowed Republican object, the payment of the national debt. But they also led him to wonder whether federal lands were perhaps being sold too cheaply. "The public lands are a public stock, which ought to be disposed of to the best advantage for the nation," Monroe reminded Congress in December 1817; therefore the nation, not private speculators, should "derive the profit proceeding from the continual rise in their value." Monroe asked whether some "further provision may be made in the sale of the public lands, with a view to the public interest." The language was oblique, but the meaning was clear. He was suggesting that Congress raise the minimum price of public lands.[15]

Monroe's suggestion brought howls of protest from the West. The Illinois Territory congressional delegate promised to fight the increase "with all my strength," for it would deter emigration and perhaps postpone statehood. Editorialists hinted of the president's secret hostility to the West. "Mr. Monroe commenced his career by a wanton disregard of the feelings and just expectations of the West," charged the *Kentucky Reporter*; "would such a recommendation have been made, if the west had been represented in the Cabinet?" The Illinois *Western Intelligencer* commented:

> It cannot be possible, that this measure has been dictated in a spirit of jealousy of the rising importance of the western country. The president we believe to be too magnanimous for that. But certain it is, that such a measure if effected, will tend much to retard the rapid population which is now experienced daily. That the western country will ultimately acquire an important stand in the government, is evident, and no restrictions, nor obstacles which can be thrown in its way, will prevent, that effect from being sooner or later produced. The government, therefore should aid in promoting this event, as it will tend to harmonize the two sections of the country. But if the western country finds a spirit of opposition prevailing in the national councils to its prosperity, when it shall acquire that stand which it will ultimately attain, a spirit of reciprocal opposition will perhaps be manifested, and give rise to those discontents which critics on our government have so often predicted. The government should pause before this step is taken.[16]

In the House of Representatives, Monroe's proposal went to the Public Lands Committee, five of whose seven members were Westerners. Chairman Thomas Robertson of Louisiana presently submitted a report deriding "golden dreams . . . of enormous revenue" and suggesting that land prices should rather be reduced than increased. That ended the matter.[17]

Meanwhile other incidents marked the growth of sectional tensions over the public domain. The efforts of the Treasury Department and the newly-created Bank of the United States to return the national finances to a specie basis prompted complaints from Western land buyers. To halt the accumulation of worthless paper in the Treasury coffers, Secretary Crawford moved in 1817 to ban notes of nonspecie-paying banks from the land offices. The Cincinnati *Western Spy* denounced the "*useless* and *unnecessary* oppression" of the order, which threatened to deprive Westerners of an acceptable medium for land purchases. The governor and legislature of Indiana protested, while the Ohio *Scioto Gazette* warned that Crawford's policy would "excite universal indignation; and must, unless this oppressive order be speedily rescinded, alienate the affections of the people from the general government." Crawford soon retreated, but the widespread suspicion that the Bank of the United States was behind his efforts earned it Western enmity even while prosperity continued.[18]

The anger evoked by Crawford's attempt to restore soundness to Western finances was curiously disproportionate to its success. For instead of returning to normal, the land office business ran wild in 1818. Farmers, planters, merchants, and politicians all threw themselves into land speculation. Few paid in full, despite the incentives to do so. With quick turnover assured, only the foolish tied up more than the necessary first payment in cash. "For nearly every sum of eighty dollars there was in the country, a quarter section of land was purchased," an Illinoisan later recalled. "Every one was to get rich out of the future emigrant." At Huntsville, Alabama, pandemonium reigned when rich Tennessee Valley cotton lands went up for auction. Choice tracts were bid off at $40 and $50 per acre. In the year ending September 30, 1818, as Crawford reported to Congress in December, the federal government sold two and a half million acres of land for more than seven million dollars, or $2.95 per acre.[19]

Crawford's statistics also showed a startling reversal of the prewar downward trend in the land debt. North of the Ohio, the indebtedness of federal land purchasers, from a nine-year low in 1813, had doubled by 1815 and again by 1818. In Alabama and Mississippi, it had grown nearly tenfold in those last three years. Altogether, land buyers now owed the federal government more than twelve million dollars.

Under the circumstances it was almost inevitable that someone should again question the wisdom of selling public land on credit. On December 18, 1818, Rufus King of New York moved a Senate inquiry into the abolition of the credit system.

Chairing the Senate Public Lands Committee was the highly respected Jeremiah Morrow of Ohio. A veteran of sixteen years in Congress, "Old Father Morrow" had inherited Gallatin's position as the recognized authority on land matters, and like Gallatin he was an opponent of the credit system. As chairman of the House Committee on Public Lands he had recommended its abolition in 1809 and 1812. In response to King's resolution, he now submitted a report reiterating Gallatin's old arguments and proposing sales of land for cash only, in tracts of eighty acres (half the current size) at a reduced minimum price of $1.50 per acre.[20]

Similar reports had languished on congressional tables ever since 1804. But this time the Senate moved quickly. The semi-official *National Intelligencer* swung its influence behind Morrow's bill, calling it the most important measure of the session. A week after Morrow's report, the Senate took up his bill, pushed it through a test vote by 28 to 6, and passed it the following day without a division.[21]

A single curious incident interrupted the bill's swift passage through the Senate. Senator Ninian Edwards from the new state of Illinois offered amendments providing for continued credit, pre-emption rights for frontier settlers, and further reductions in the minimum price. The Senate having disposed of his amendments by lopsided margins, Edwards took the floor to oppose the bill. He began calmly but soon fell into hysterics, losing both his temper and his manners. Finally, in what appeared to be an attack of apoplexy, he staggered and crashed to the floor. The horrified senators bore him to the lobby, where bleeding restored him to his senses.[22]

Edwards's performance made a vivid impression but won him no friends. Still, he had not fought entirely alone. His Illinois colleague (and political archenemy) Jesse Thomas stood with him on five of his six amendments, and he found backing on three of them from three other Westerners. On the six amendments together, the public land states cast 25 of the 34 aye votes. And on the bill itself, five of the six opponents were Westerners, including Edwards.

The *National Intelligencer* predicted swift passage of Morrow's bill in the House of Representatives, where two-thirds of the members were said to favor it. But the House did not act, and though the *Intelligencer* at first ascribed the failure to "accidental interruption," it shortly revealed that two Westerners, William Henry Harrison of Ohio and Francis Jones of Tennessee, had managed to scuttle the bill. The *Intelligencer* consoled itself that the subject was at least now "placed fully" before the public.[23]

The Fifteenth Congress adjourned early in March of 1819. Its successor would not convene for another nine months. Meanwhile the

postwar boom was coming to an end. By late 1818 there was trouble in
the money markets. The Bank of the United States, which had promoted the bubble with a carefree expansion of credit, now found itself
in difficulties and began calling in its loans. In January 1819 the Bank's
president resigned, and his successor, taking office in March, inaugurated a rigorous contraction. In the meantime word arrived of a sharp
break in Liverpool cotton prices. The panic of 1819 had begun.

Panic and crisis

The collapse, when it finally came, was the sharpest in the young
Republic's history. New Orleans cotton prices dove from thirty to
fourteen cents a pound in a few months. Prices of wheat, corn, and
other commodities fell. Banks failed, rents and property values plum-
meted, trade ceased, workers lost their jobs. In the West, the paper-
money structure remained standing just long enough to sustain a final
surge of buying before the collapse. By September 1819 land purchases virtually ceased, but in the final year buyers had snapped up
four million acres at an average price of $3.37 per acre. They now
owed the federal government the staggering sum of twenty-two million
dollars.[24]

Suddenly Gallatin's old prediction that the land debt would ultimately endanger the Union seemed about to come true. Obviously the
huge land debt, contracted in a period of soaring inflation, could never
be paid; but after years of relief legislation, could anyone believe that
Westerners would now tamely forfeit their lands? The "all-grasping
spirit" of the land buyers had "shaken the stability of the Union,"
warned the St. Charles *Missourian*; refusing relief now "might almost
breed an insurrection." The *Albany Register* thought it required "no
extraordinary stretch of the imagination" to conceive that forfeiture
might produce "a civil war, if not an ultimate dissolution of the federal
compact." In a widely circulated piece, "Franklin" labeled the land debt
"the most portentous evil that ever existed in America: *it threatens a
dissolution of the Union*":

> Will they [the land debtors] not very naturally become disaffected?
> Let nine-tenths of these persons reside in a particular section of the
> Union; let that section be pre-eminently well situated for the forma-
> tion of a separate government; let the existence of the debt depend on
> the continuance of the union; let the doctrine be advanced and
> enforced by every press and every orator in that quarter that the other
> states had no just and natural right to the property for which the debt

was incurred, while those states insist rigidly on an enforcement of the collection, and where will the bonds be found sufficiently strong to hold us together? They do not exist!

Nor was this all newspaper hysteria. "State Sovereignty is the cry," federal land surveyor Edward Tiffin confided to the commissioner of the General Land Office in October. "I much fear a Spirit of disaffection & & & towards the general government is arising in the West sufficient to alarm its fast friends."[25]

Tiffin's advice was to get rid of the credit system and "make no more Debtors." To many, the menacing land debt proved the need to abolish the credit system once and for all. An Ohio congressman concluded that cash sales at a reduced price "will be better for the people and certainly for the Government." "The Rubicon is not yet passed," declared "Franklin," "but we now stand upon the shore, and it depends on the measures to be adopted by the next Congress, whether we shall remain a peaceful, happy, and united people, or advance, with a steady and certain pace, to civil war and a dissolution of the Union." Editorials from every section of the Union, reprinted in the *National Intelligencer* and *Niles' Weekly Register*, urged the abolition of the credit system. The *Intelligencer* especially seized on articles from the West, saying that they refuted the supposition that Westerners would oppose any change in the current arrangements.[26]

Western opinion was, in fact, divided. From Ohio and Kentucky particularly came many expressions of support for a cash system. But the Western opposition made up in vehemence what it lacked in unanimity. Abolishing land office credit was "a measure calculated vitally to stab the future growth of this country," a Missourian charged. The *Kentucky Reporter* branded it "injurious to the interests of the west," while Illinois congressman Daniel Cook announced that as "it will seriously retard the settlement of our country, I shall be compelled to vote against it." The legislatures of Indiana and Louisiana remonstrated against changing the current system.[27]

To its Western foes, the proposition to sell public lands for cash only came freighted with sectional overtones. At any time, frontiersmen were bound to oppose tightening the terms of sale. That the credit system attracted purchasers Westerners freely acknowledged, and in that they saw only good. If land buyers got into trouble, the government should extend relief and liberalize the payment terms, not constrict them. Small tracts and lower prices were fine, but a bill like Morrow's would require $120 in cash for eighty acres, whereas under the credit system twice as much could be had for a down payment of only $80.

Of course, if one stressed the total price rather than the payment terms, cash sales appeared as an actual liberalization of the land system. Representative John Rankin of Mississippi saw it that way; so did some prominent Ohioans. Not coincidentally, those two states had been little affected by the great bubble of 1817–1819. It was in the places where land sold fastest during the boom—Indiana, Illinois, Alabama, and Missouri Territory—that opposition to cash sales was strongest. All Westerners wanted to stimulate migration. But in the states just named, politicians naturally evaluated prospects of enticing new emigrants from the viewpoint of those who had purchased during the boom. For them, cash sales meant catastrophe.[28]

Counting on continued emigration and rising land values, thousands of frontiersmen had thrown all their capital into land during the last three years. President Monroe's recommendation to Congress in 1817 had convinced them that federal land prices were more likely to go up than down. An abrupt conversion to cash sales would catch them in a vise. The value of the lands they had bought at inflated prices would drop with the government minimum, while their obligation to complete payment at the old price continued. Undercut by the government itself, they could not resell; and if, as they feared, abolition of the credit system discouraged emigration, there would be no one to sell to. They had gambled on continuing inflation, not on government-imposed deflation in the form of cash sales. Most severely hurt would be the squatters on unoffered lands who had managed to qualify under various special pre-emption laws. If cash sales became law, they would have to raise the entire purchase price before the public sale or lose their improvements. A cash system would do much to render the pre-emption privilege a nullity.[29]

But there was more to the Western resistance than speculative self-interest. The circumstances and timing of the cash proposition caused Westerners to question its motive. The plight of land debtors cried for relief, not for a reform that would actually worsen their situation. The idea of substituting cash for credit had been before Congress intermittently for fifteen years, without ever coming to a vote. Now, just when cash was almost impossible to come by, Easterners suddenly were eager for cash sales. Surely there was more here than met the eye. Atlantic advocates of a cash system said it would actually aid the emigrant; but behind their plausible arguments and logical demonstrations, many Westerners discerned a device to stifle the growth of the West and deprive it of its coming political hegemony.

It was easy to see the measure in such terms in 1819, for the panic had sharpened all the sectional tensions of the previous years. Spurred by the sudden collapse of prosperity, resentments between East and West as well as between North and South accumulated as the economic crisis deepened. The land question, the financial and commercial crisis, congressional inattention to Western transportation needs—even the treaty of 1819 with Spain, by which the United States acquired Florida but withdrew its claim to Texas—all contributed to a general sense of grievance in the West. "Jealousy of the rising greatness of the west" inspired Congress to deny Missouri the boundaries it wanted, according to territorial delegate John Scott. Some Westerners attributed the depression to government policies and the machinations of Eastern banks. "Many of our embarrassments spring from the ungenerous policy of the General Government towards the Western country, from either unpardonable ignorance or wilful neglect of our interests by the Atlantic half of the Union," charged an Ohio writer. "Their true policy, their *only safe* policy is to cherish the West, and as far as possible to relieve its embarrassments. . . . We ourselves should well understand when we ought to *solicit* and when to *demand.*" The *Kentucky Reporter* editorialized:

> Nothing has been done to promote our local interests; and every scheme to advance our local prosperity and give to us a fair participation in the benefits of the union, has been thwarted or defeated. . . . The truth is, that the western states and territories and the population in them, are considered at Washington as *inferior* to the states and the people on the other side of the mountains. We are regarded as a sort of colonies or distant provinces, that may serve to swell the pride of empire, but which can by no means be considered as entitled to the same privileges with the Good Old Thirteen United States.[30]

Contributing to Western apprehension was the Missouri crisis, which erupted in the same angry summer of 1819. In Congress the attempt to prohibit slavery in the new state of Missouri pitted North against South. But to many Missourians and other Westerners, the question of slavery or no slavery was less important than whether a new Western state could be denied a constitutional right of self-determination that all the old states enjoyed. More crucial still was the relation between slavery, migration, and land values. Since most of the settlers in Missouri, and in Indiana and Illinois as well, came from slave states, some construed the antislavery campaign as a veiled effort to discourage emigration—a blow aimed at the West as well as the South. The fact that Senator Rufus King of New York took the lead against both slavery and the credit system heightened suspicions. A St. Louis writer thought Eastern jealousy of the West lay behind those "obnoxious propositions," prohibition of slavery and elimination of land office credit. David Barton, first senator from the new state, traced the antislavery agitation to a Northeastern plan to preserve its congressional dominance "by crippling the growth of the West, and preventing the increase of new States," excepting "mere appendages" like Ohio, Indiana, and Illinois which "by their institutions, virtually exclude the immigration of their brethren and friends from the Southern and western states." The *Missouri Intelligencer* said of the antislavery men:

> They view with a jealous eye the march of power westward, and are well aware the preponderance will soon be against them; therefore they have combined against us; but let them pause before they proceed further, or the grave they are preparing for us, may be their own sepulchre! As well might they arrest the course of the ocean that wash their barren shores, as to check our future growth. Emigration will continue with a giant stride until the wilderness shall be a wilderness no more.[31]

Put in those terms, Missouri's freedom to choose or reject slavery vindicated not only the rights of the slave South, but those of the frontier West as well. In the United States Senate, Ninian Edwards and Jesse Thomas of Illinois defended Missouri's right of self-determination. Soon afterward Illinois fought its own internal battle over slavery, and there too the controversy focused on slavery's influence upon immigration and land values.[32]

In short, the West was not united in defense of the credit system of land sales. On its merits, many Westerners favored a change. The size of the debt piled up during the boom certainly indicated a need for reform. But Westerners felt the burden of Atlantic hostility bearing heavily upon them in the summer of 1819. Those who held a vested stake in the credit system perceived the demand for its abolition as one more manifestation of the sectional jealousy that nearly all Westerners saw radiating from across the mountains.

Reform: the Land Act of 1820

The Sixteenth Congress convened in December of 1819 in an atmosphere permeated with sectional bitterness. The land issue did not take first precedence. "The Missouri subject," Henry Clay explained in mid-January, "monopolizes all our conversation, all our thoughts and for three weeks at least to come will all our time. No body seems to think or care about any thing else." For a time the Union itself appeared in jeopardy. But Illinois senator Jesse Thomas's proposal to admit Missouri as a slave state and ban slavery elsewhere in the Louisiana Purchase north of 36°30′ opened the way for a settlement. In mid-February the Senate approved the Thomas compromise, then took up the land issue.[33]

The twenty-two million dollar land debt lent urgency to the discussion. It was, said Senator John Walker of Alabama, "a fearful sum," larger than the entire annual federal budget (debt service excluded), and owed by a small fraction of the nation's population, residing in an underdeveloped section where commerce was at a standstill and reputable currency had ceased to circulate. In Alabama alone, with a population of 128,000, the land debt was more than ten million dollars.[34]

Clearly another extension of payment deadlines for debtors was required to prevent massive forfeitures. Advocates of a cash system accordingly brought in Morrow's bill from the previous session and used the West's exigency as a whip to drive it through the Senate. Led by Rufus King of New York, they parried all efforts to stall the cash bill and take up the relief question first. Edwards of Illinois and Walker of Alabama offered amendments for relief, pre-emption, and continued credit; all received substantial support from the West but little from the East. The Senate fixed on $1.25 per acre as the new minimum price (a concession to the West) and passed the cash bill by 31 to 7; then it took up the relief bill postponing forfeitures for another year, passed it, and sent both together to the House.[35]

There defenders of the credit system won some tactical victories. The Public Lands Committee recommended striking the cash bill's main clause, and relief advocates succeeded in slipping that measure through the House first. Speaker of the House Henry Clay of Kentucky spoke long and passionately against the cash bill, while fellow Westerners threatened with "political ostracism" another Kentuckian who dared to defend it. But it was all to no avail. By the huge majority of 135 to 19, the House reinstated the provisions deleted by the Public Lands Committee, and passed the cash bill by 133 to 23. The small group of nay votes included half the Western congressmen (see table 2.1).[36]

President Monroe signed the measure on April 24, 1820. Henceforth federal lands would be sold only for cash, in tracts of eighty acres, at a minimum price of $1.25 per acre.[37]

Was the abolition of the credit system, as Ninian Edwards charged on the Senate floor, a measure "calculated . . . to retard the settlement and check the prosperity" of the Western country? Its advocates denied any such motive. But the real sectional interests at stake were

TABLE 2.1
ABOLITION OF THE CREDIT SYSTEM, 1820

	Senate		House	
	For	Against	For	Against
Kentucky		2	3	4
Tennessee	2		2	4
Ohio	2		6	
Indiana	1	1		1
Illinois		2		1
Alabama	2			1
Mississippi	2		1	
Louisiana		2		1
West	9	7	12	12
New England	10		37	1
Mid-Atlantic (incl. Del. and Md.)	7		61	3
South Atlantic	5	1	39	7
Total	31	8	149	23

Sources: Senate Journal, 16th Cong., 1st sess., pp. 219, 223; *House Journal,* 16th Cong., 1st sess., pp. 431–432, 436–437.

Note: Both House and Senate columns combine two roll calls, one on the bill's passage and one on its opponents' earlier attempt to strike out its main clause. This procedure is widely used in preparing "contrived items" for Guttman scalograms, which rank legislators on a continuum by comparing their responses over a series of votes (see Lee F. Anderson et al., *Legislative Roll-Call Analysis* [Evanston: Northwestern University Press, 1966], chap. 6). By correcting for absenteeism, combining substantively similar roll calls allows a fuller picture of the congressional division on an issue. For instance, though Senator Jesse Thomas of Illinois missed the final vote on the land bill, he almost certainly would have voted against it; for earlier he voted to strike out its main provision, and every senator who acted with him on that question later voted against the bill. I have combined roll calls only when: (1) their substantive issue was the same; (2) there was at least a 95% cohesion between them. I define cohesion as the number of members voting the same position on two roll calls divided by the total number voting. A 95% cohesion therefore means that 19 out of every 20 members present for both roll calls voted together on both. In the two cases presented here, cohesion was 100%.

obscured, on both sides, by a rhetoric that cast economic questions into moral modes. Both in and out of Congress, discussion of the land question fastened on two archetypes, as sharply contrasted in the public mind as night and day: the virtuous "actual settler" and the rapacious land speculator.[38]

The actual settler personified the Jeffersonian ideal. Honest, hard-working, loving liberty, he wanted only a small farm from which to support his wife and children. His poverty matched his virtue. Tragically unable to provide for himself on the wornout, high-priced lands of the East, he drifted westward in search of a home. Though he might fall on hard times and petition Congress for relief, his sufferings were always traceable to impersonal forces, or to the evil machinations of others. His character was pure, his patriotism invincible.

At the opposite end of the moral scale stood the speculator. Shrewd, shifty, fundamentally dishonest, he grew rich off the labor of others. To the development of the country he contributed nothing; he engrossed large tracts and left them idle until the improvements of neighboring settlers made them valuable. His financial leverage reduced the actual settler to poverty and tenantry. Not a farmer himself, he had no tie to the soil, no concern for the welfare of town, state, or country. He cared for nothing but his profits. He was, at root, a menace to free society.

In an America steeped in Jeffersonian agrarianism, deeply suspicious of finance and financiers, these images carried great political appeal. In addition, the boom and panic had inspired a kind of fundamentalist revulsion against paper money, banks, and speculation. Wherefore every discussion of land policy, then and for years afterward, focused on one simple question: what policy would protect the actual settler and proscribe the speculator?

The credit system's defenders complained that a cash system would place settlers at the mercy of speculators. The latter did not need credit; they had ready money, and could purchase under one system as well as another. But the actual settler had no cash; he had to have credit if he was to buy at all. A cash system would drive him to the speculator for the credit that government denied.

Cash advocates, on the other hand, claimed that the credit system invited speculation at every turn. It allowed the financier to turn profits on his purchases while paying only a fraction of their cost. It enabled him to control much more land than he could actually afford. Forced to narrow their operations under a straight cash system, speculators could offer the settler less competition. The settler could then calculate his costs precisely and purchase in perfect security. No panic or crop failure could steal his home away from him, or throw him into the fatal embrace of the usurer.

The discussion extended to recriminations about the rush buying that preceded the panic. Cash advocates considered it proof of the speculative nature of the credit system, while the system's defenders insisted that cultivators, not speculators, had done the purchasing. But despite their moral force, the dichotomous images of settler and speculator were essentially fallacious, and did more to obscure the real interests at stake than to explain them.[39]

The interests of settler and speculator actually joined at many points. Indeed, once the moral filters are removed, it is hard to tell the two types apart. Farmers as well as financiers bought land for resale, using the credit system to secure large tracts with the first payment instead of purchasing small farms outright for cash. And the characteristic speculator in the postwar boom was not an Eastern or foreign capitalist who cared nothing for the West beyond profits, but a Westerner himself, a resident of Kentucky or Tennessee, if not Illinois or Alabama. His interests, his attitudes, and his hopes for the future of the West matched those of the settler.

Nearly every prominent Westerner dabbled in speculation during the boom. Henry Clay, Andrew Jackson, Senator John Walker of Alabama, and House Public Lands Committee chairman Richard Anderson of Kentucky all purchased land for profit. All the leading Illinois politicians speculated, including Senators Edwards and Thomas and Representative Daniel Cook. Nor was trading in land confined to the wealthy and famous. At the height of the boom an Illinoisan observed that everyone, including the farmers, was speculating, for the good reason that it paid more than anything else. In remote frontier communities, lacking facilities for industry and commerce, producing little but crops and providing no transportation to market, land speculation was the lifeblood of the economy. It was, as one authority has noted, "the only outlet for any considerable amount of capital. But it was more than that—it was practically the only activity in which men could give free scope to their business ability." It was also perfectly honorable. For contrary to contemporary myth, the characteristic speculator was a doer, a booster. He stood to gain by promoting Western growth, not by thwarting it. Passivity was not in his nature. He wanted cities, farms, roads, canals; he dreamed of Western power and Western glory. As a beginning to all of this, he wanted population growth.[40]

No doubt the interests of settler and speculator could at times conflict. One need not entirely discount the squatter's plea for protection against the rich man who could buy his farm out from under him, leaving him homeless and penniless, though it is always well to remember that it was in the petitioner's interest to cast himself as an innocent victim of lurid schemes. But on the question of price, the interests of settler and speculator were essentially as one. Both wanted to buy cheap, and both hoped for population growth to bring rising values. The false dichotomy of settler and speculator centered attention on the seductive but fallacious idea that under a uniform system the prices and credit arrangements could somehow be juggled so as to encourage the one and discourage the other. Only a few contemporaries understood this; most notably Jeremiah Morrow, who after trying to show that cash sales would aid settlers against speculators, conceded that "the idea of providing equal facility to the poor and to the rich by any regulation is incompatible with that of disposing of the land for a valuable consideration. While the Government require a price, he who possesses the means of payment will have an advantage in making purchases over him who does not possess such means."[41]

The need to conform their arguments to a ritualized agrarian rhetoric put both credit and cash men in a false position. Speculating Western politicians piously denied any knowledge of speculation, while cash advocates from the Atlantic states voiced a concern for the welfare of Western "actual settlers" that they did not always feel. But though Westerners hid behind the rhetorical smokescreen, they were not themselves blinded by it. Behind the homilies of the reformers they detected a covert motive to inhibit the growth of the West.

Suspicions of Eastern jealousy troubled even those Westerners who approved the change in the land system on its merits. The Ohio and Mississippi congressmen, and some from Kentucky and Tennessee, voted to abolish the credit system in 1820. The land boom had barely touched Mississippi, and had largely passed over the other three states. Ohio, Kentucky, and Tennessee no longer stood on the cutting edge of the frontier; they were becoming suppliers, not recipients, of Western emigrants. Already frontier publicists lured their residents to the fresh lands of Illinois, Missouri, and Michigan Territory. Ohioans, Kentuckians, and Tennesseans therefore viewed the Land Act of 1820 from a different perspective than frontiersmen. In addition, Kentucky and Tennessee, not being themselves public land states, held the same pecuniary interest in the public domain as the Atlantic states. In Ohio, there was the influence of Jeremiah Morrow, and also the fact that

Rufus King and his Senate allies had bottled up an Ohio internal improvement bill in committee and held it hostage for the fate of the land bill.[42]

It is therefore significant that even the Ohioans who approved the change in the land system distrusted its motives. "I regret that the delegation from the Atlantic section of the Union are so much opposed to the present land laws," said John Sloane of Ohio on the House floor. "It is this opposition which induces me to consent to the change proposed in this bill. I consider it of importance that all jealousy against the Western country should be allayed." An Ohio representative who helped push a Cumberland Road appropriation through the House in 1819 found it "astonishing with what jealousy the Western interests are viewed by many. All the relief that purchasers of public lands need expect will be a suspension of forfeiture. No mercy, it seems, can be expected for future purchasers." Another Ohio congressman abandoned his quest for a federal land grant to the state university in 1819, for, as he confided to Governor Ethan Allen Brown, "the Public Lands are also beginning to be considered more valuable and I fear I might [arouse] a jealousy of the future greatness of the West." Governor Brown himself greeted the Land Act of 1820 with trepidation. "I hope and [no less] believe that it will beneficially affect the public interest," he wrote to Senator Benjamin Ruggles; "the debt incurred by purchasers certainly amounts already to a considerable an enormous sum" [*sic*]. Brown thought the change might hurt previous purchasers, but would

> enable the government to grant greater indulgence to those now indebted, and do away one pretext for the jealousy of our Eastern neighbors who for many years have pretended an alarm at the increasing debt of the purchasers of public lands. At all events, it became apparently necessary to make this experiment (of doubtful effect on the particular interests of the western Country) or rather it became almost impossible to avoid it, if I have been correctly informed of the temper of Congress in this respect.[43]

Western suspicions of Eastern animosity were in truth well founded. In private, Rufus King of New York, Senate leader against the credit system and slavery in Missouri, poured out his bitterness against the "Western country, that has been indulging in golden dreams, and fascinating our Northern People." Early in 1819 King lamented that "the demands and strength of the West are increasing daily, and the vigorous decision and union of the old States decrease in a fully equal degree." King applauded the separation of Maine from Massachusetts as contributing to hold "the balance of power in the Senate, which shifts rapidly towards the West." If the credit system with its attendant annual relief bills were allowed to continue, he complained, "the result will be to draw off our active population, to become purchasers of western lands, which are nominally sold, but which will in effect be acquired, without payment by the purchasers." King hoped that stopping credit at the land offices would do just what Westerners feared it was intended to do: it would apply a brake to emigration.[44]

King dared not avow such sentiments in public, but others were less reticent. There was "too great a disposition in the American people to diffuse themselves over a large space," New Jersey Representative Ephraim Bateman told his constituents. "The rapid course of emigration to the west, operates as a drain upon the capital, enterprize & industry of the east, paralyzing in no inconsiderable degree the improvement, especially in agriculture, of the Atlantic states." Bateman voted to abolish credit land sales, and thought it "would have been prudent and salutary . . . if our settlement could have been limited for many years to come to the east side of the Mississippi."[45]

Of course, Rufus King was hardly a fair representative of Atlantic opinion. He was a Federalist, the presidential nominee in 1816 of a declining party tied to a narrow Northeastern regionalism. King was as hostile to the South as to the West. Traditionally those two Republican regions had cooperated against the Federalist Northeast in national politics, and the doctrine of their natural affinity died hard. With the Missouri crisis threatening disunion early in 1820, Spencer Roane of Virginia advised his friend President Monroe to "cherish, also, the western people, they have an identity of interests with us, and they also hold the keys of the Mississippi. If driven to it, we can yet form with them a great nation."[46]

With his conspicuous support for slavery in Missouri and his fanatical resistance to a change in the land system, Ninian Edwards of Illinois had gone looking for this "identity of interests" in the Senate. He failed to find it, because it did not exist. Southeasterners as well as Northeasterners harbored jealousies of the new states and fears for the safety of the land revenue. Southerners who had not yet learned to trace all their economic woes to the tariff found in the competition of cheap, fertile, Western soils a plausible (and more accurate) explanation for falling property values and crop prices. Monroe and his predecessor Madison had always shown more interest in increasing the land revenue than in promoting Western settlement. Monroe once commented that Rufus King revealed his hostility to the West on every land bill that came before the Senate. With nearly equal accuracy Westerners might have said the same of Monroe himself, and some of them did.[47]

Antipathy to the West was traditionally strongest in the Northeast, but while political parochialism was withering there with the dying Federalist party, it was on the rise in the Old South. The Southern purist states' rights faction known as Old Republicans had always looked askance at the rise of the West. As extreme strict construction- ists, the Old Republicans opposed the growth of federal power through the Louisiana Purchase, the Cumberland Road, and the land system itself. The Old Republican congressional leaders, John Ran- dolph of Virginia and Nathaniel Macon of North Carolina, were patri- archs who, like King of New York, remembered and cherished the simpler Union of the Old Thirteen. The vigorous expansionist nation that emerged from the War of 1812 was to them an alien environment. It might truthfully have been said of them, as it actually was said of Rufus King (by Daniel Webster, a Yankee of a newer breed), that they "had no idea that the country west of the Alleghany formed any part of the United States." Randolph supported the Louisiana Purchase in 1803 and regretted it ever after; he bragged of never voting to admit a new state to the Union. On land questions, both he and Macon took a stubborn anti-Western line. In recent years they had defended the strict constructionist creed almost alone; but the Missouri crisis, awakening Southerners to the dangers of federal power, initiated a slow return to the abandoned principles of states' rights.[48]

The administration press offered little to allay Western suspicions. The *National Intelligencer* approved not only the Land Act of 1820 but also Monroe's suggested price increase in 1818; it even inquired whether lands "are not too industriously forced into market by acts of Congress." Descriptions of the Mississippi Valley as the future seat of empire drew acid comment from the *Intelligencer.* Late in 1818 the paper suggested eliminating private land entries after auctions in order to encourage bidding above the "low" minimum price. Hezekiah Niles of Baltimore was a staunch Republican, but his nationally- circulated *Register* proposed alterations in the land system that would "present a check to the greater spread of our population for some time to come." Both the *Intelligencer* and *Niles' Register* professed friendship for "actual settlers," a profession which, in the light of their specific proposals, Westerners could not have taken seriously.[49]

Frontiersmen accepted the verdict of 1820 with misgivings. Senator James Noble of Indiana hoped that "injury will not accrue to the western people or elsewhere; but I fear the consequences." An Illinois paper remarked that "sound policy may warrant the measure, but we fear its effects upon the future settlements of our state." But at least, as Representative William Hendricks of Indiana observed, the elimination of the credit system would quiet Atlantic apprehensions and so strengthen the case for generous relief to the thousands already in debt.[50]

The Relief Act of 1821

It remained to clear up the debris of the credit system. The Land Act of 1820 had done nothing to reduce the huge land debt, or to relieve the debtors of their distress. Credit buyers clamored for succor. The Sixteenth Congress, reconvening for its second session in November 1820, encountered an avalanche of petitions, accompanied by memorials from the legislatures of Alabama, Missouri, Kentucky, and Ohio. Debtors complained that the reduction of prices in the Land Act cut the resale market out from under them, leaving them stuck with lands they could neither sell nor pay for. To the *Cincinnati Gazette* it was an "unequivocal violation of the public faith," which if perpetrated by a private party "would receive no milder term than swindling." To enforce forfeiture upon the innocent victims of government price juggling "would carry features of oppression that might well enter into difinitions of despotism." Most petitioners sounded a less belligerent tone, but all said the shift in federal land policy entitled them to relief.[51]

Their pleas fell on receptive ears. With the credit system eliminated, the motive for refusing relief had largely disappeared. The sums owed were too large for another mere postponement of payment deadlines to do much good. "*The Debt cannot be paid,*" concluded Rufus King; better then to amputate it than to let it fester. President Monroe, Treasury secretary William Crawford, and the *National Intelligencer* joined in the call for relief. Crawford officially sanctioned a popular Western plan to let debtors relinquish subdivisions of their purchases to the United States, transferring payments made thereon to the portions retained. In this manner a buyer who had, for instance, made the first payment on four quarter-sections could get title to one of them by returning the other three to the government. For those who wished to retain all their lands, Crawford recommended extended credit for up to ten years, with substantial discounts for immediate payment in cash.[52]

A bill based on Crawford's recommendations passed Congress easily. In the Senate all was sweetness and light. Rufus King and Ninian Edwards together urged their colleagues to be generous. Edwards professed to see "in some recent measures a pledge of those liberal feelings towards them [Westerners], which has allayed all former fears, and forbids the belief that any motive of hostility or jealousy could, in the least degree, influence your decision." In this relaxed setting the rhetoric of the previous sessions could be safely abandoned, and Edwards and Walker of Alabama argued openly that relief was due to buyers who had engaged in "fair and authorized speculation" under the credit system. Some opponents of the credit system complained that Congress was rescuing speculators from the consequences of their own folly, but the need to liquidate the debt was generally acknowledged.[53]

Another motive for leniency toward the land debtors shortly appeared. Rufus King of New York hoped to obtain similar favors for "another portion of society," namely Eastern merchants. King calculated that his vocal support for the relief bill "ought to have its effect" in behalf of a bill to provide a uniform system of bankruptcy, then also before the Senate. In the House the same quid pro quo was offered. The bankruptcy bill eventually passed the Senate, but not the House.[54]

Not surprisingly, Easterners and Westerners differed over some details of the relief bill. On a motion to reduce the discount for prompt payment of land debts from 37½ percent to 25 percent, senators from Delaware northward voted in favor, 17 to 1, Westerners against, 15 to 0, while the Southeast split its votes. But in the prevailing air of sectional reconciliation nobody seemed to notice. The Senate engrossed the relief bill for its third reading on February 10, 1821, by 36 to 5, with only four Northeasterners and Nathaniel Macon of North Carolina in opposition. The House made some changes and passed the bill on February 28 by 97 to 40, with majority support from all sections.[55]

Ninian Edwards considered still further relief "both expedient and just," but on the whole the West was more than satisfied. William Hendricks of Indiana called the Relief Act "liberal, beyond the expectations and hopes of any portion of the Western country." Down in Huntsville, Alabama, where the flush sales of 1818 had created a state of "universal mortgage," Senator Walker urged a "proper feeling of gratitude" for the "paternal care and kindness of Congress." Daniel Cook of Illinois, who had opposed the cash bill the year before, considered the Relief Act "repulsive of the charge which has been made against the good feelings of the Atlantic states towards us—it shows, on the contrary, a most parental feeling."[56]

Taken together, said the *National Intelligencer*, the land laws of 1820 and 1821 "possess in themselves enough merit to redeem the character of the sixteenth Congress"—a Congress which, let it be remembered, also solved the Missouri crisis. The Relief Act immediately smoothed sectional tensions. It did not, however, eliminate the land debt, as many credit purchasers took the option for extended payment. It would require another eleven years and ten more relief laws to eradicate the debt, partly because Congress steadily widened the class of purchasers eligible for relief. But the Relief Act halved the debt in a single year, and silenced the fears of disunion to which it had given rise. As a subject of national importance and concern, the land debt ceased to exist when Monroe signed the act on March 2, 1821.[57]

Like a summer cloudburst, the storm over the land system cleared as quickly as it had come, leaving little visible trace of its passage. Westerners who greeted the new arrangements with suspicion quickly learned to live with them, so that within a few years hardly anyone regretted the loss of the credit system. The panic of 1819 and the Missouri slavery crisis had torn away the facade of prosperity and political harmony, exposing underlying hostilities and conspiring, for a brief moment, to infuse the land issue with an explosiveness that seemed to threaten the Union. The Missouri compromises settling the status of slavery in the West relaxed sectional tensions and smoothed the path for the reconciliation of 1821.

But larger questions connected with the public lands, as with slavery, remained unanswered. With the admission of five Western states in six years, the public land states were becoming a power in the Union. Though internally divided, they had dared in the crisis of 1819–1820 to challenge the dominion of the Atlantic states on the subject most vital to themselves. It was a false start. The credit system was the wrong issue, and Ninian Edwards was the wrong man. But the sense of sectional grievance still thrived on both sides of the mountains, while the contradictions imbedded in the Virginia Act of Cession and the Northwest Ordinance remained unresolved. Opposing slavery in Missouri in February 1820, William Hendricks of Indiana denied before the House of Representatives that new and old states were truly equal:

> Would to God they were. They would then have resources and wealth, almost inexhaustible, in the public lands. . . . The General Government can dispose of them or retain them as they please; can discourage emigration to the new States, prevent their population, and deprive them of taxing the lands within their jurisdiction.

Hendricks was not complaining. He was merely stating circumstances. But it was questionable how long the new states would be content to remain creatures of the federal government if they ever obtained power to control it.[58]

The animosities exhibited in the heat of the sectional crisis of 1819–1820 were transient, but they stemmed from a divergence of outlook that was fundamental. Fifteen years before, Albert Gallatin laid it down that the land system should "satisfy the demand for land created by the existing population" without "promoting migration beyond its natural and necessary progress." But none of the variables in that dictum were self-defining. The government could not escape defining them itself. Competition among the sections for capital and population would continue as long as those basic resources were in short supply. Saddled with the ownership of the public domain, Congress could not avoid taking sides, even if it wished to.[59]

The crisis of 1819–1820 presaged two sectional divisions: between North and South, and between East and West. In the end the former would predominate, but it was the latter that lingered after the emergency passed. For as events were soon to show, the catharsis of 1820 had not broken the sectional solidarity of the new West, of slave Alabama and Mississippi with free Illinois and Indiana. Rather, it had forged it.

CHAPTER 3
SECTIONALISM
1821–1825

Our swords are converted almost literally into plough-shares, and our spears, not into pruning-hooks, but into pick-axes and shovels. And why should it not be so?

National Intelligencer
June 10, 1826

The Great Migration was only one of many avenues for releasing the nation's pent-up energies after the War of 1812. While emigrants trudged westward, there were schools and factories to be built, canals to be dug, rivers to be bridged. The national imagination seethed with magnificent projects. Nothing was impossible. New Yorkers began work on the 364-mile Erie Canal, by far the longest in the world, while others planned to bring the waters of the Ohio over the Allegheny ridges to the nation's capital. Projects for school systems and colleges appeared everywhere. A Georgia governor caught the spirit of the age when he urged his colleagues to "legislate to the advancement of Public Education, Internal Improvement, good order and virtue"—though presumably not in that order. Even the strict constructionist "Richmond junto" of Virginia joined in the enthusiasm for internal improvements—but not at federal expense.[1]

The panic of 1819 and the subsequent depression could not still these energies, but they injected into them a new note of asperity. The urgency remained, but it was now an urgency born of competitiveness rather than of optimism. For it was suddenly apparent, as it had not been during the boom years, that the financial and human capital of the country was inadequate to the tasks at hand. There simply was not enough to go around. In the disparity between the nation's resources and its ambitions lay the seeds of conflict.

In politics that conflict emerged as economic sectionalism. Competing programs of recovery and development mobilized sectional constituencies and vied for supremacy in Washington. As they did so, sectional blocs coalesced around the three great national instruments for allocating wealth and population: the protective tariff, internal improvements, and the public land system.

Public lands for education: the Maryland proposition of 1821

The Relief Act of 1821 hardly had time to soothe sectional jealousies over the public lands before a new irritant appeared to inflame them. For several years the Maryland legislature had contemplated establishing a common school fund. Even in the prosperous postwar years inadequate revenues plagued the lawmakers' efforts, and the financial collapse of 1819 exhausted their resources. But in December 1819 Governor Charles Goldsborough suggested another source of funds. The public domain, "that great fund of national wealth," belonged to all the states in the Union, and if the United States were to donate lands for Western schools, as it had for years, the Atlantic states might also claim a share.[2]

That broad hint set the wheels in motion. Maryland state senator Virgil Maxcy drew up resolutions asserting the right of the Atlantic states to a share of federal school land donations. Nothing was done that session, but when the legislature reconvened a year later Maxcy was ready with new resolutions and some statistics to back them up. Reckoning the 16th-section donations at one thirty-sixth of each state's land area, and throwing in another fraction to balance the seminary townships granted to the new states, Maxcy calculated that it would take 9,370,760 acres to "do justice" to the fifteen Atlantic states and Kentucky. Maryland was due 298,665 acres; other allocations ranged from 33,705 acres for Rhode Island to 1,493,332 acres for Virginia. The Maryland legislature quickly adopted Maxcy's resolutions, with little opposition.[3]

Maryland's claim evoked echoes of its proud Revolutionary role, when its refusal to sign the Articles of Confederation prompted the state land cessions which created the national domain. But the Maryland resolutions also carried an ingenious and powerful appeal to sectional interests and jealousies.

The Maryland report spoke of friendship for the West, but complained that the school grants inured "to the exclusive benefit of those States and territories," in "violation of the spirit of our national compact, as well as the principles of justice and sound policy." Maxcy acknowledged that the 16th-section donations and seminary townships encouraged migration, thus raising the value and hastening the sale of the national domain. But this Western gain came at Eastern expense. The "inexhaustible supply" of Western lands kept Atlantic property values down, while the West siphoned off Eastern population. Hence Western settlement was no national object, but "exclusively advantageous to the new States, whose population, wealth, and power, are thereby increased at the expense of those States which the emigrants abandon." Had the Atlantic states consulted their own interests, "every impediment would have been thrown in the way of emigration, which has constantly and uniformly operated to prevent the growth of their numbers, wealth, and power; for which disadvantage the appreciation of their interest in the public lands, consequent upon emigration, can afford no adequate compensation."[4]

That the Western states might oppose the Maryland proposition Maxcy dismissed as "a supposition too discreditable to their character for justice to be admitted." But he also emphasized that the success of the scheme did not rest on Western acquiescence. For if the "favored" states should refuse justice to their Eastern brethren, the sixteen "excluded states" could still muster a majority of 169 to 17 in the House of Representatives. With this pointed reminder, and with the exact acreage due to the "excluded states" down on paper for each of them to see, the Maryland legislature sent off copies of the report and resolutions to all the other state legislatures. If enough of them backed Maryland's demands, Congress would have to act.[5]

Congress had already declined to move on its own initiative. Two years before, in 1819, a committee of the House of Representatives had rejected a proposal to give one hundred thousand acres to every state for higher education. While Maxcy's proposition was pending in the legislature, Senator Edward Lloyd of Maryland brought it before Congress, where it was referred to the Committee on Public Lands. In February 1821, committee chairman Jesse Thomas of Illinois reported against it. Thomas opposed entrusting Western lands to the old states, which could then dictate terms of sale and settlement. Moreover, referring to the compacts under which new states were admitted to the Union, Thomas claimed they had in effect paid for their school donations by agreeing not to tax federal lands until five years after they were sold. Hence the school grants, "though distinguished in common parlance by the name of *donations*, were in fact sales bottomed upon valuable considerations, in which the new States surrendered their *right* of sovereignty over the remaining public lands, and gave up the whole amount which might have been received in taxes before such lands were sold, and for five years thereafter." Here was a novel proposition baldly stated: that were it not for the admission compacts, the federal government would not own the public domain at all. Thomas proposed distributing a portion of the land revenue to the old states, but only if new states were allowed to tax federal lands immediately upon sale.[6]

Maxcy's scenario for state pressure began well. The legislatures of Connecticut and New Hampshire, meeting in the spring of 1821, endorsed the Maryland proposition. North Carolina had already done so the previous December. The Virginia House of Delegates greeted the Maryland report warmly, though without taking formal action. But in New York an assembly committee chaired by Gulian Verplanck rejected the Maryland scheme, decrying as "narrow and false" any "policy which looks with jealousy upon every appropriation, tending to promote the security and welfare of any portion of the country, as being a robbery of the rest." The Verplanck committee reaffirmed the national objects and benefits of the Western land-grant policy, and censured Maryland's appeal to sectional prejudices. Though not acted upon by the New York legislature (which received it just before the close of the session), Verplanck's report circulated widely in the press, undercutting the appearance of Atlantic unanimity Maxcy had hoped to create.[7]

In the fall of 1821 Maxcy and his allies launched an intensive campaign to influence the new Seventeenth Congress and the remaining state legislatures, most of which were to convene that winter. The *National Intelligencer, Niles' Register*, and the *North American Review* endorsed the Maryland project. Maxcy's many relations and friends (including John C. Calhoun, an enthusiast for the scheme) lobbied legislators and distributed pamphlet copies of the Maryland report all through the seaboard states.[8]

For a time it seemed these efforts would bring success. In October, Rhode Island sanctioned the Maryland proposition. Vermont and New Jersey followed in November, Georgia and Kentucky in December, Maine and Delaware in January of 1822. Altogether that made eleven of Maxcy's sixteen "excluded states." Governors of Massachusetts, New York, and Virginia endorsed the plan, while resolutions supporting it unanimously passed the upper house of the state legislature in both South Carolina and Pennsylvania.[9]

Despite the earlier setback in New York, the project by now had acquired a considerable momentum. But early in February of 1822 Massachusetts applied the brake. Lemuel Shaw of the state senate submitted a report attacking the legal foundations of the Maryland claim. Noting that "the form in which this claim is made, as well as the claim itself, appears calculated to awaken jealousy and discord," Shaw cautioned that its adoption "would be attended with consequences highly injurious to the harmony and best interests of the Union." The legislature adopted his resolutions against the Maryland plan.[10]

Maxcy rushed to plug the leak with a new pamphlet and a series of newspaper pieces, but the damage had been done. Meanwhile New York did nothing, while a Virginia committee reported adversely and the *Richmond Enquirer*, organ of the reigning clique in Virginia politics, decided that federal land subsidies to education violated states' rights and strict construction. No further encouragement from that quarter could be expected. Without support from Virginia, New York, or Massachusetts, the prospects of the Maryland proposition waned considerably.[11]

If the response from the East was not all Maxcy had hoped, the reaction of the West was all he could have expected. The Indiana house of representatives said that if the state had not "fairly purchased" its school grants by surrendering its right to tax other federal lands, then "words have no meaning." Governor Ethan Allen Brown of Ohio devoted half of his annual message to denouncing "a scheme founded on principles, believed to be mistaken and erroneous; and fraught with serious wrong to this, with the other new states, and the territories"—a scheme, moreover, "proposed to be triumphantly carried by a majority formed of 'ONE HUNDRED AND SIXTY NINE VOTES against SEVENTEEN!' "[12]

The Ohio legislature duly condemned the Maryland proposition and suggested that new states could just as legitimately claim a portion of the vacant lands within the old states! The committee report approved by the legislature followed the logic advanced by Jesse Thomas in the United States Senate a year earlier, but went much further. If, during the Revolution, the old states acquired the unowned domain within their boundaries as "an inherent right, a necessary appendage of their sovereign characters," then the same held true for the new states at the time of their creation. Hence the "unavoidable" conclusion that "the new states have an indisputable claim, to all the unappropriated lands, within their respective limits."[13]

Nor was this all. The Virginia Act of Cession guaranteed the states in the Northwest Territory "the same rights of sovereignty, freedom, and independence, as the other States"; the Northwest Ordinance promised admission to the Union "on an equal footing with the original States, in all respects whatever." Did not this include the ownership of the public domain, a right enjoyed by the old states themselves? True, the Virginia Act of Cession also reserved the public lands as a "common fund for the use and benefit of such of the United States as have become, or shall become, members of the Confederation . . . and for no other use or purpose whatsoever." But, said Ohio, this plainly applied only before, not after, statehood; any other interpretation contradicted the clause securing the sovereignty of the new states. The Northwest Ordinance injunction that "the legislatures of those districts, or new States, shall never interfere with the primary disposal of the soil by the United States in Congress assembled" could be simply ignored. For one thing, the ordinance proclaimed its own provisions as "articles of compact, between the original States and the people and States in the said territory." But in fact no such compact had ever been made. Ohio had never agreed to it. Ohio had indeed agreed, "by an ordinance irrevocable" upon admission to the Union, not to tax United States lands for five years after sale; but it never promised not to tax them *before* sale, while they were still in federal possession. Nor had Ohio ever abjured its natural sovereign right to all of its public domain.

The Ohio legislature stopped short of formally claiming ownership of or taxation rights over the public lands. But the mere elucidation of the logic behind such a claim, whether convincing or not, served its purpose. Maryland sought to exploit a perception of the new states as pampered children, lavishly endowed by a benevolent government at the expense of their elder brethren to the East. Easterners might think of the West this way, but Westerners did not. They saw the federal land system as an extra burden piled upon the already great travails of pioneering. The school grants and the road funds hardly made up for the sacrifice of sovereignty over the public domain, to say nothing of the cartloads of cash drained from the West through the land offices. Atlantic states sponsored handsome internal improvements with the income from land sales and land taxes; but to the West, which needed them most, the government denied those vital revenues. Developing the West was a national priority, and when it offered the school grants in order to encourage migration, the federal government had consulted not sentiments of philanthropy but calculations of its own interest, both as a nation and as a great landholder. It was a "*bargain and sale*," and in its compacts with the new states the federal government had done well for itself indeed. It had, in fact, taken advantage of their political powerlessness to extort concessions that came close to blackmail. Once the territories acquired enough population, they had a clear right to admission under the Virginia Act of Cession and the Northwest Ordinance. What right had the federal government to impose debilitating conditions upon them?[14]

To Westerners, the Maryland proposition confirmed the Eastern animosity whose existence they had suspected all along. "If the truth were known," confided a friend of Governor Brown's, "the rising grandeur and importance of the West were becoming the subjects of ill digestion and bad taste to the aristocratic pride of our Eastern Brethren." The *Illinois Gazette* charged that "the whole may be traced to motives unfriendly to the growth and prosperity of the west, which have been viewed with jealousy by certain politicians for a long time." The paper characterized Maxcy's resolutions as untenable, wicked, treasonable, unhallowed, unrighteous, preposterous, shameful, and unjust, and suggested that to their title "should be added the words '*to defraud the people of the Western States.*' "[15]

Opponents of Maxcy's scheme responded in kind to his hints of sectional coercion. "An Ohioan" writing to the *American Farmer* admitted that "as the Legislature of Maryland, says 2-3ds of the Union are against us—However, the day is probably not far distant when the tables will be turned, * * *." (The editor suppressed the rest of the letter as "too *sectional* for this journal.") The public lands are a "*national concern*," announced the *St. Louis Enquirer*; when states demand "*their share,* . . . we cannot but ask them, if they wish to *dissolve the co-partnership?*" The *Cincinnati Gazette* lamented that at Ohio's admission to the Union, the school lands "were purchased at an enormous sacrifice, which was suffered to be extorted from us by our foolish hastiness to form a state government." The paper warned that the Maryland proposition, "a deliberate act of iniquity," would "throw the shades of barbarism, of outrage and of violence, over the fair fame of our country."[16]

Under this barrage of intemperate rhetoric, enthusiasm for the Maryland project wilted. In mid-January of 1822 the *National Intelligencer*, while still hopeful, judged its prospects as "at present very doubtful"; the editors admitted glumly that "some among our best citizens, even in the Atlantic states," were opposed to it. In a show of impartiality, the *Intelligencer* even ran a series of anonymous communications attacking the plan. Maxcy answered them all, but he was visibly in retreat.[17]

Even those who approved the Maryland scheme in theory had to acknowledge certain practical problems. Should the land grants be apportioned according to state land area (as Maxcy had assumed), population, or Revolutionary War services? In any case, sixteen separate state land offices going into business simultaneously would upset the current uniformity of survey and sale procedures and undercut the federal land revenue. The obvious solution was for the federal government to retain the lands and distribute a portion of the sale proceeds. But that would constitute a direct federal subsidy to education, sure to raise hackles in the constitutional environs of Richmond, Virginia; and anyway, the land revenue was already pledged to the repayment of the national debt.[18]

Had there been agreement on the principle of the Maryland resolutions, a way might have been found around these difficulties (as it was forty years later), but by February 1822 even the most sanguine conceded that no consensus existed. None of the largest Atlantic states had sanctioned the project. Certainly little encouragement could be expected from the remaining public land states. In Missouri, where the scheme had some newspaper sympathy, the legislature discussed it but failed to adopt resolutions.[19] The Alabama and Mississippi legislatures, remote from the center of controversy, adjourned without acting at all. In Louisiana, Governor Thomas Robertson took the occasion to criticize the entire federal land system. Louisiana lands stood unsurveyed and unsold, private claims had yet to be settled, the promised school sections had not been delivered and would probably be worthless anyway—"and yet it seems to be supposed that we have been highly favored." Robertson accused the Atlantic states that controlled federal land policy of deliberately blocking Louisiana's growth. Legislative committees echoed his sentiments and his angry tone.[20]

The honor of delivering the final blow to the Maryland proposition fell to Senator Ninian Edwards of Illinois. Aside from some desultory discussion in the House of Representatives, Congress had held back while waiting to hear from the state legislatures. By the end of February 1822 there was no point in further delay, so Senator Lloyd of Maryland called up his resolutions. On March 1 Edwards delivered a carefully prepared speech against them. He said nothing that had not been said somewhere before, but his speech systematically summarized all the scheme's defects for the first time. Edwards had learned from his disastrous performance in the Senate three years earlier. This time he avoided histrionics and personal abuse, while stressing the Atlantic objections to the scheme: its dubious constitutionality and its impact on the federal land revenue.[21]

The speech was a tremendous success, and a redeeming triumph for Edwards. A South Carolina congressman told him that "this very *able* speech has probably saved him from giving an erroneous vote," and the governor of North Carolina also changed his mind upon perusing Edwards's "unanswerable" arguments. In the West the speech circulated in the newspapers and as a pamphlet. The *Cincinnati Gazette* hooted that the advocates of the Maryland proposition "have retired from the contest without either the laurels or the emoluments which they expected to gather from the supineness and imbecility of the new states. We congratulate our country on its escape, so far, from the disastrous revolution which the cupidity of a few designing politicians was hastening to consummate." Even the *National Intelligencer* had to admit that Edwards had shaken confidence in the Maryland scheme.[22]

In fact the campaign for the proposition had run its course. After Edwards's speech Congress simply dropped the matter. Gradually the remaining Western responses filtered in. The legislature of Mississippi and the governor of Alabama denounced the project later in the year, but by then it was already dead. With Illinois' resolutions against the plan in February 1823, the episode was closed.[23]

Despite its failure, the Maryland proposition occupied a key juncture in the evolution of the controversy over the public lands. The timing of Maxcy's campaign was not fortuitous. It came directly in the wake of the sectional crisis of 1820, and it traded nakedly on the antagonisms aroused by that crisis. The Maryland episode exposed the emergence of an internally unified New West, and revealed also that this new section could rely on no general friendship from either Northeast or Southeast. Eleven states from Maine to Georgia had approved a project justified mainly by sectional resentments. Feeding on sectional jealousies, the episode also exacerbated them.

Yet the Maryland project also spoke to a genuine and growing concern for public education in the several states. Its origins lay in Maryland's efforts to foster schools, efforts which were not unique. By 1820, eleven states had established permanent common school funds; others had made lesser provisions for school support. The panic of 1819 jeopardized those funds. The pinch was especially tight in the small states which, unlike Massachusetts or New York, had no state public domain from which to raise a revenue. Not surprisingly, those small states were the first to jump on the Maryland bandwagon. With federal land policy under debate in 1820 and 1821, Eastern legislators naturally saw the national domain as the solution to their problems.[24]

Westerners wanted schools for their children too. Their response to the Maryland proposition showed that Westerners were perfectly willing to devote the land revenue to education. It was the discriminatory nature of Maxcy's proposal, promising to the East what it claimed the West had already received, that aroused their anger. Ohio offered to "cheerfully concur" in any appropriation of land proceeds for education "conformable to principles of justice and equality"—that is, any that included the West as well as the East. In trying to float his project on sectional jealousies, Maxcy began by antagonizing some of its strongest potential supporters.[25]

The West opposed the Maryland proposition on nationalistic grounds. Emigration and the settlement of the frontier brought national benefits, and it was both futile and unfair to superimpose on them calculations of state loss or gain. The United States was a Union of people, not a confederation of states. It was the nation, not, as Maryland claimed, the old states, that had wrested the public domain from England and France. Just as all Americans had helped acquire the West, so its opportunities were open to everyone, Marylanders as well as Ohioans. The notion of parceling out the national assets in bits and pieces to individual states belied the very idea of American nationhood.

These Western arguments fell within the nationalistic tradition which had characterized the region from its beginnings—a tradition rooted in its status as a creation, not a creator, of the federal Union. But the Ohio legislature had also discovered an argument that rested on quite different foundations. As children of the Union, still absorbed in the arduous task of pioneering, the Western states looked to Washington to supply the facilities for education and internal improvement they could not afford themselves. They asked federal aid not as a favor but as simple justice, an obligation inseparable from federal control of the public domain. But if need be, Westerners could learn to talk the language of strict construction too. In 1822 Ohio served notice that if doctrines of strict construction and state particularism prevailing to the eastward should cause the paternal hand of government to be withdrawn, the West would proclaim its own maturity, and demand as its inheritance the public domain, the very symbol and substance of sovereignty, on those selfsame grounds of states' rights.

Internal improvements: the sectionalization of an issue

No domestic political question proved more intractable during the years of Republican party ascendancy than that of federal power over internal improvements. From the earliest days of the confederation, prominent Americans had identified the need to improve internal transportation. Roads and canals would do more than facilitate the movement of goods and people, important as that was. They could counteract the centrifugal tendencies inherent in America's sprawling size, scattered population, and formidable mountain barriers. Binding the Union with cords of commerce and communication, they might prove essential to the preservation of the nation itself. They could transform into living reality the aspiration of *E Pluribus Unum.*

Despite the interest of Presidents Washington and Jefferson, the federal government did little to aid construction of internal improvements before the War of 1812. Jefferson twice brought the subject before Congress, and in 1808 his Treasury secretary, Albert Gallatin, submitted a comprehensive internal improvement plan which in scope, clarity, and mastery of detail matched the famed productions of his predecessor, Alexander Hamilton. But Jefferson's plans rested upon Treasury surpluses and a constitutional amendment to give the federal government explicit authority over internal improvements. He never got his amendment, and the embargo and war with Britain put the Treasury deeply in debt.[26]

Aside from some road surveys in the territories, the only real internal improvement accomplishment of Jefferson's administration was the Cumberland Road, fruition of the Ohio Enabling Act of 1802. Beginning at Cumberland in western Maryland, with connections eastward to Washington and Baltimore, the road cut northwestward through the Allegheny ridges into southern Pennsylvania, thence westward to Wheeling, Virginia, on the Ohio border. Pursuant to the compact with Ohio, the road was to be financed by 2 percent of the proceeds from the sale of federal lands within the state. But roadmaking in the mountains was expensive, and the fund accumulated slowly. Cheerfully exploiting the constitutional loophole, Congress began with the very first survey appropriation in 1806 to advance funds from general revenue, to be repaid as the 2-percent fund accrued. Through this device $140,000 was spent on construction by 1812, far outdistancing the 2-percent fund.[27]

Though other federal internal improvement schemes were floated before the war, none were adopted. But the return of peace in 1815 brought internal improvements to the center of the political stage. The military disasters on the Northwestern frontier had exposed the perils of inadequate overland communication. A new generation of nationalist politicians, led by Henry Clay of Kentucky and John Caldwell Calhoun of South Carolina, studied the lessons of the war as well as the opportunities of the peace. Having challenged and mastered Great Britain, they looked for new giants to slay, and found them in the mountains and forests of the interior. The sudden onrush of postwar prosperity provided Treasury funds to feed their dreams, while the growing Western congressional delegation added echoes to their voices.

They reckoned without the opposition of Presidents Madison and Monroe. The nationalists' campaign opened in 1817 with Calhoun's bill to allocate the United States Bank bonus and annual dividends as a fund for internal improvements. The bill narrowly passed Congress, but President Madison, after recommending internal improvements in his two preceding annual messages, recalled his strict constructionist principles and vetoed it on his last day in office.[28]

The new president, James Monroe, promptly informed Congress of his "settled conviction" against the constitutionality of federal aid to transportation. Like Madison and Jefferson, he recommended a constitutional amendment. However, the failure of an amendment campaign might jeopardize whatever ambiguity currently existed on the subject and thus threaten the future of the Cumberland Road, a risk internal improvement men refused to run. But test votes in the House of Representatives in 1818 showed insufficient strength to override executive vetoes. A resolution offered by William Lowndes of South Carolina, declaring that "Congress has power, under the Constitution, to appropriate money for the construction" of roads and canals, passed by 90 to 75; but three other resolutions, respectively declaring Congress's power to construct post and military roads, roads and canals for interstate commerce, and canals for military purposes, all failed. With that, the campaign for federal sponsorship of roads and canals ground to a halt.[29]

The voting patterns on Calhoun's bonus bill of 1817 and on the Lowndes resolutions of 1818 reflected a complex of sectional, partisan, and constitutional concerns. New Englanders generally opposed federal improvements. They already had the best roads in the nation, and geography blocked them from trans-Appalachian connections. Moreover, much of New England's voting strength was still in the hands of Federalists, who had retreated into a petulant parochialism. At the other end of the political spectrum, Virginia's delegation, led by Old Republican paragons Philip Barbour, John Randolph, and John Tyler, also opposed internal improvements, viewing them as a dangerous departure from the original strict constructionist Jeffersonian creed. The other South Atlantic states were divided. Nearly half of the House votes for internal improvement came from New York and Pennsylvania, two sprawling states with port cities that hungered for overland trade with the West (see table 3.1).

The West itself was divided. It supported Calhoun's bonus bill in 1817, but by less decisive margins than the big mid-Atlantic states. Tennessee voted regularly against internal improvements. On the crucial third Lowndes resolution concerning roads and canals for interstate commerce, the West split down the middle.

The alignments on internal improvement in 1817 and 1818 thus defied a simple sectional analysis. There were no grounds for regarding it as a specifically Western issue. Except for an occasional burst of

venom from the West's archenemy, John Randolph, sectional considerations also rarely entered into the floor debate.[30]

Meanwhile the Cumberland Road proceeded apace. From 1812 to
1816 Congress had appropriated another $570,000 for construction,
all chargeable to the 2 percent fund. The precedent was also extended.
Like Ohio, Indiana in 1816 and Mississippi in 1817 came into the
Union under compacts obligating Congress to spend 2 percent of their
net land proceeds upon roads "leading to" them. Madison signed the
Mississippi Enabling Act two days before vetoing Calhoun's bonus
bill.[31]

Advocates of federal internal improvements could, and did, invoke
these measures to support their constitutional claims. A committee of
the House of Representatives answered Monroe's "settled conviction"
by observing that legislation signed by both Jefferson and Madison
"clearly admitted that there are *some cases, at least*, in which the General
Government possesses the constitutional privilege of constructing and
improving roads through the several States." Monroe himself was
troubled by the argument, and appealed to his predecessor Madison
for enlightenment.[32]

Faced with the unfortunate task of repairing a constitutional breach
which he, as president, had done much to widen, Madison groped
painfully for the source of this undermining flaw in the bulwark of
strict construction. He suspected, without proof (and probably incorrectly), that on the original Cumberland Road appropriation "the
Executive assent was doubtingly or hastily given," thus exonerating
Jefferson. Beyond that he bewailed

> the use made of precedents which cannot be supposed to have had in
> the view of their Authors, the bearing contended for, and even where
> they may have crept, thro' inadvertence, into acts of Congs. & been
> signed by the Executive at a midnight hour, in the midst of a group
> scarcely admitting perusal, & under a weariness of mind as little
> admitting a vigilant attention.

This, perhaps, was by way of explaining his own presidential signature
on seven Cumberland Road bills. But one distinction could still halt the
flood of internal improvement projects through the opened crack, and
this the ex-president drew as follows:

> 1. that the road was undertaken essentially for the accomodation of a
> portion of the Country with respect to which Congs. have a general
> power not applicable to other portions. 2. that the funds appropri-
> ated, & which alone have been applied, were also under a general
> power of Congs. not applicable to other funds.[33]

TABLE 3.1
INTERNAL IMPROVEMENTS, 1817–1818

	Bonus Bill Senate[a] (1817)		Bonus Bill House (1817)		First Lowndes Resolution House[b] (1818)		Third Lowndes Resolution House[b] (1818)	
	For	*Against*	*For*	*Against*	*For*	*Against*	*For*	*Against*
Vermont		2		5	1	5	1	5
New Hampshire	1	1	1	5	3	3	3	3
Massachusetts		2	4	16	6	12	3	15
Connecticut		2		6		7		7
Rhode Island		2		2		1		2
New England	1	9	5	34	10	28	7	32
New York	2		25	2	20	6	19	6
New Jersey	1	1	3	3	5	1	3	1
Pennsylvania	2		17	4	17	2	14	6
Delaware	2		2		2		2	
Maryland	2		2	6	5	3	4	4
Mid-Atlantic	9	1	47	17	49	12	42	17
Virginia	2		6	14	5	13	3	16
North Carolina	1	1	6	6	2	11	1	12
South Carolina		2	6	3	4	3	3	3
Georgia	1	1	5	1	4	2	3	3
South Atlantic	4	4	23	24	15	29	10	34
Kentucky	2		4	5	5	3	5	4
Tennessee		2	1	3	2	3	1	5
Ohio	2		5		6		5	1
Indiana	2		1		1		1	
Mississippi					1		1	
Louisiana	2			1	1		1	
West	8	2	11	9	16	6	12	12
Total	22	16	86	84	90	75	71	95

Sources: For the bonus bill, *Senate Journal*, 14th Cong., 2d sess., pp. 327, 341; House Journal, 14th Cong., 2d sess., p. 369. For the Lowndes resolutions, *House Journal*, 15th Cong., 1st sess., pp. 334–341.

[a]The first column shows the Senate vote on engrossing the bonus bill for third reading, with a 100% cohesion with the vote on its passage the next day. (see note to table 2.1)

[b]The two Lowndes resolutions not shown failed by 82 to 84 and 81 to 83, falling midway on a scale pattern between the resolutions in the table. The third and fourth columns of the table thus show the maximum and minimum strengths of the internal improvement forces.

In other words, what justified the Cumberland Road was the public domain. Federal ownership of the Western lands entailed a unique relationship with the new states. It created special obligations and supplied special powers to discharge them. Land revenue was not like other revenue; it came under a "general power" that overrode constitutional limits on federal spending. At the same time, of course, the land proceeds were committed, by a pledge that preceded the Constitution, to the payment of the national debt. Therefore the United States, like any trustee, should manage its common fund to yield the maximum return. No one doubted that roads to the West would hasten the sale of public lands and bring better prices for them too. One last consideration might be cited. As Madison himself had recently hinted to Treasury secretary William Crawford, spending land proceeds on internal improvements "would enlist all parts of the Union in watching over the security and sale of the lands," thus protecting the national property from land-hungry Westerners.[34]

Apparently these explanations satisfied President Monroe. The campaign for a federal system of internal improvements lapsed after the defeat of 1818, and road and canal men went back to the Cumberland Road. Despite his "settled conviction," Monroe proved as willing as his predecessor to sign these appropriations and to extend the precedent in the admission compacts with Illinois, Alabama, and Missouri, all of which contained the 2-percent clause. In 1818 and 1819 Congress spent more than $800,000 to complete the Cumberland Road to Wheeling; like all previous appropriations, this was to come from the 2-percent fund of Ohio, Indiana, and Illinois, amounting by September 30, 1819, to precisely $179,641.29. In 1820 Congress appropriated another $141,000 (this time without mentioning the fund), and, using the justification that "the lands of the United States may become more valuable" thereby, authorized a survey of the road from Wheeling westward to the Mississippi.[35]

Meanwhile projects of improvement were afoot in the states. Despairing of federal aid, New York began its great canal to link the Hudson and the Great Lakes in 1817. Long before it was finished in 1825, the Erie Canal captured the enthusiasm of Northwesterners who craved an alternative to the New Orleans outlet for their produce. But they also understood that New York's enterprise required a corresponding effort on their own part: construction of a network of canals to bridge the Mississippi and Great Lakes watersheds, connecting farmers throughout the Northwest to the burgeoning markets of the East.

In Ohio, by now the most populous of the transmontane states, the need for better transportation was particularly pressing. Ohio had passed the stage where it could thrive on land speculation and the cash of arriving immigrants. Access to markets was a necessity if farmers were not to drown in their own abundance. But the state's resources were inadequate to the task. Compared to its Eastern neighbors, Ohio was still a poor state. Ohioans paid dearly for manufactured goods hauled up the Mississippi or over the Appalachians. In addition, they sent up to a million dollars a year over the mountains in land payments. The prohibition on taxing federal lands for five years after their sale narrowed the tax base. Governor Ethan Allen Brown estimated the cost of a canal from Lake Erie to the Ohio River at less than $3 million, but recent annual tax revenues averaged only $200,000. The 3-percent fund on land sales, insufficient in any case, had been frittered away on local roads.[36]

The panic of 1819 both dramatized the need for transportation and shook the precarious finances of the Western states. In 1820 Ohio requested federal aid for its canal. The state asked for a donation of federal lands or the right to purchase them on credit at $1.00 per acre. Ohio could then borrow on landed collateral to build the canal and sell the lands at advanced prices upon its completion, paying off the United States and the construction loans.[37]

Governor Brown, author of the plan, felt that Ohio was asking no favor of the United States. The nation would benefit immensely from increased commerce and from the rise in value of adjoining federal lands. Ohio's offer of $1.00 per acre Brown considered generous in the currently depressed market, where few lands were selling at all.[38]

But the proposition was singularly ill-timed. It reached Congress early in 1820, when sectional jealousies had reached their highest pitch. In the Senate, William Trimble of Ohio secured the appointment of a committee "favourable to the principle," including himself and chaired by Rufus King of New York, hitherto a strong internal improvement man. But the committee stalled, and finally ruled, with Trimble the only dissenter, that it was "unsound policy for a State to contract obligations to the United States" and "inexpedient for the United States to sell any part of the public lands to a State on credit for any purpose or on any account." Clearly the government's experience with land debtors had influenced the committee. When Trimble gave up the original proposition and asked for a mere survey of the canal route, he was told bluntly that the committee would do nothing until the pending bill to abolish the credit system passed Congress. Internal improvement would be held hostage for land reform. Eventually the committee did report Trimble's weakened bill; it passed the Senate by 20 to 13, but failed in the House of Representatives.[39]

Both Trimble and Governor Brown traced the defeat to sectional motives. Trimble warned that "from the south & even from the east there is a strong jealousy of the rising prosperity of the north west." Brown was furious. "This state has deserved better treatment. The proposition required no sacrifice from Congress—asked nothing of their bounty." If Congress would help build the canal, then Ohio "would go on, as before, cheerfully to contribute to the defense of the Seaboard, tho' our own frontier be neglected—to the support of the navy, on which our Atlantic brethren doat," and to the construction of lighthouses and buoys, all perfectly useless to Ohio. Ohio had done much for the Union, but received little in return:

> I regret, extremely, this disposition, in the East and South, to impede our improvements; it will tend, to weaken the affections, of the people N.W. of the River Ohio; whose strength is growing too mighty to be treated with contempt; as the next caucus will demonstrate; and whose prosperity is, in most cases, intimately connected with their own.[40]

In reality, the lines of sectional cleavage on Trimble's canal bill did not run along the peaks of the Appalachians. Under the malignant influence of the Missouri question, familiar issues assumed strange and fanciful shapes—in this case, the shape of a division between North and South. Senators from Maryland northward favored the bill by 19 to 2; those from Virginia southward opposed it by 11 to 1. (The alignment was as ephemeral as it was unnatural; given a chance to reconsider when the same bill came up a year later, five New England senators reverted to form and voted nay. The bill was indefinitely postponed.) But Brown's remarks perfectly reflected Western opinion. Throughout the West the internal improvement issue was growing in importance, and increasingly it was viewed in sectional terms.[41]

In 1821 Illinois tried its chances before Congress. The short portage from Lake Michigan to the Illinois River seemed the easiest canal route between the Mississippi system and the Great Lakes. Illinois requested cash from the 2 percent fund and a donation of land one mile wide along the canal route. Congress responded, in March of 1822, by granting a right-of-way through the public lands and permission to gather construction materials from the adjacent property, on condition that the state never lay tolls or charges on federal traffic along the canal. But what Illinois wanted was not mere permission to build, but hard cash, or land that could be sold for cash. It was even questionable whether the grant was worth the condition. Illinoisans differed on whether to praise the government for at least doing something, or to condemn it for its stinginess in endowing a project which would, after all, presumably increase the value of its own public domain.[42]

Congressional recalcitrance both bewildered and infuriated Westerners, who considered public-works spending essential to right the sectional financial balance. As they saw it, Westerners paid their fair share of the tariff revenue, only to see it all expended at the seaboard on navies, lighthouses, harbor improvements, customshouses, and fortifications. On top of this was the cash lost through the land offices, a burden borne by the West alone. "The lands it is true are part of the common stock," sputtered the *St. Louis Enquirer, "but we pay for them!"*[43]

Westerners argued that if sectional justice did not require federal aid for roads and canals, national interest did, for doubtless public lands would gain in value thereby, and the cost of the grants would be returned manyfold into the Treasury. In fact, as the governor of Illinois put it, a canal land grant was "not, strictly speaking, an appropriation of public property to internal improvements, but only such a disposition of it, as is best calculated to advance its value." If the argument for financial aid to Western roads and canals was strong, the case for land grants seemed nearly tautological. Such grants cost the government nothing but a minute portion of its inexhaustible public domain.[44]

Deeply persuaded by this logic, Westerners puzzled over the motives for Eastern opposition. In the aftermath of the sectional crisis of 1820 and the Maryland proposition of 1821, many attributed congressional rebuffs to sectional animosity. "Every thing here among certain men of certain views look with a very jealous eye upon any proposition which touches the Public Lands or the completion of our great Western national road; more so than I could have believed before I witnessed it," observed an Indiana congressman. An Ohioan ascribed the failure of the Ohio Canal to the same cause. "For years past, a jealousy of our rising importance has plainly betrayed itself in Congress"; even the Cumberland Road bills had to be "literally, fought through Congress, by the zeal, the eloquence, and activity of Mr. Clay" and a few other friends of internal improvements.[45]

In 1822 a bill to repair and erect tollgates on the Cumberland Road reopened the internal improvement debate in Congress. The measure represented a significant step toward an outright system of federal improvements. So far Congress had funded only construction, not repair. But as tollgates meant permanent federal responsibility for the road, they raised the whole constitutional question and prompted the first general airing of the internal improvement issue since the Lowndes resolutions of 1818.

But now sectionalism dominated the debate, as Easterners and Westerners disputed which had received the largest share of federal favors. And the tollgate vote revealed the coalescence of a Western internal improvement bloc in the four years since 1818. In the House of Representatives, only Tennessee of the nine Western states cast any votes against the bill. With other Westerners voting 21 to 0, the tollgate bill passed the House by 87 to 68. The Senate passed it with only seven dissenting votes, five of them Southeastern. Monroe vetoed it the next day.[46]

Monroe objected that tollgates entailed "a complete right of jurisdiction and sovereignty for all the purposes of internal improvement, and not merely the right of applying money." Even that lesser right Monroe had denied in his first message to Congress, though he had signed some Cumberland Road appropriations since. But now he reconsidered his position, conceding that if roads and canals served "very important national purposes" (among them to "enhance the value of our vacant lands, a treasure of vast resource to the nation"), then he could "not see any well-founded constitutional objection" to appropriations for them. Monroe still denied federal authority "to adopt and execute a system of internal improvement"—that is, to usurp the states' sovereign powers of eminent domain, police, and revenue by building and maintaining roads within their boundaries and without their permission. But no matter. Monroe's new constitutional interpretation left Congress free to subsidize state and private projects and to continue the Cumberland Road, for which it had received explicit permission from the states concerned. The president's retreat from strict construction opened the way to a vigorous improvements policy.[47]

When Congress reconvened in the fall of 1822, Monroe followed through with a recommendation to repair the Cumberland Road, without erecting tollgates. "Surely if they had a right to appropriate money to make the road they have a right to appropriate it to preserve the road from ruin." In floor debate, Virginia strict constructionists objected that the Cumberland Road rested solely on the admission compacts, which helped secure the public domain and thus fell under the constitutional power to "make all needful Rules and Regulations respecting the Territory or other Property belonging to the United States." The compacts authorized construction, not repair. This was Madison's line, but Monroe had irretrievably abandoned it, and Congress duly approved a $25,000 repair appropriation which mentioned neither the lands, the compact, nor the 2-percent fund. The House vote was 89 to 66. Western representatives voted 19 to 3, the nays coming from Kentucky and Tennessee. The Senate passed the appropriation by 26 to 9, all the nays coming from east of the mountains. Monroe signed it without qualm.[48]

The increasingly sectional cast of the debate and the voting in the Seventeenth Congress revealed the influence of the crises of 1819–1820 upon the internal improvement issue. And just as internal improvement emerged as a specifically Western concern, Congress and the president threw the door open to a federally-financed network of roads and canals.

Internal improvements and the election of 1824

Many years later, Thomas Hart Benton of Missouri recalled how "the candidates for the Presidency spread their sails upon the ocean of internal improvements" as the election of 1824 approached. The jockeying for position had commenced even before Monroe's uncontested re-election in 1820. By the summer of 1823 the campaign was in full swing, with four political veterans—John Quincy Adams of Massachusetts, John C. Calhoun of South Carolina, William Crawford of Georgia, and Henry Clay of Kentucky—and an outsider, Andrew Jackson of Tennessee, battling for the succession. Though the long campaign centered largely on personalities, sectionalism ran just beneath the surface. Every candidate but Calhoun was clearly identified with a section and hence, implicitly though vaguely, with sectional interests: Adams with the maritime Northeast, Crawford with Virginia-style strict constructionism, and Jackson and Clay with the developing West.[49]

As the election neared, sectional conflict focused on two issues, internal improvements and the protective tariff. On both, sectional positions had crystallized in the aftermath of the panic of 1819. Discriminatory duties on imports to protect American industry appealed to those who saw hope for economic recovery in the development of manufacturing and to farmers looking for an expanded home market. The bastions of protective sentiment were the mid-Atlantic states and the Northwest, including Kentucky and Missouri. The tariff threatened New England's import trade, but the core of the opposition was Southern. Staggered by the decline in staple crop prices, fearful for the safety of their overseas markets, and haunted by the spectre of a powerful federal government controlled by a Northern antislavery majority, planters from the Chesapeake to the Mississippi delta denounced the tariff as a mere redistributive device, a Northern subsidy at Southern expense. Southerners took refuge in strict construction, which in the Southeast—but not the Southwest—also meant stiffening opposition to federal internal improvements.

The tariff intruded only distantly on the election, for tax policy was a congressional prerogative over which presidents exerted little influence. But for internal improvements the executive sanction was essential, and had often been refused. Accordingly internal improvement men carefully scrutinized the positions of the candidates.

Shielded in Monroe's cabinet, Secretary of State Adams and Treasury secretary Crawford said little on internal improvement, though their home constituencies were hostile to it. Jackson's views were a mystery, but he was a Westerner. Calhoun used his War Department post in the cabinet to argue the military advantages of roads and canals, just as he had earlier expounded their domestic benefits in Congress. And in the House of Representatives, Henry Clay summoned his vaunted eloquence to urge a coordinated program of internal improvements and domestic manufactures—a program which he would soon name the American System.[50]

Calhoun's internal improvement posture rested on a high-minded nationalism; South Carolina had little direct interest in the program. Clay too was a nationalist of panoramic vision, but at the same time the spokesman (if not, as his nickname "Harry of the West" suggested, the personification) of the West. From his first appearance in Washington in 1806, Clay had yoked his fortunes to the rise of the West and to internal improvements. In 1807 he had sought federal aid for a canal around the falls of the Ohio; he had championed the Cumberland Road, the Lowndes resolutions, and the bonus bill.[51]

Clay was absent from the Seventeenth Congress. But his return to Washington, coupled with Monroe's constitutional concessions, portended a renewal of the internal improvements campaign abandoned in 1818. The West could now speak with a louder voice, having gained nineteen of twenty-six new House seats under the recent reapportionment. "Daily we hear in conversation that it is time for the western world to be *felt* at the *seat of the national government*," remarked Representative John C. Wright of Ohio, "& yet all is unsettled as to what mode we shall resort to to effect the object. Every thing is crude & undigested." For many Western politicians, the answer lay in internal improvements and in Henry Clay's presidential candidacy.[52]

In Congress in 1824, the internal improvement issue arose on a bill appropriating thirty thousand dollars for surveys "of such roads and canals as he [the president] may deem of national importance, in a commercial or military point of view." The bill was carefully modeled to suit Monroe's constitutional scruples, and its appropriation was modest. But its significance was apparent. Surveying roads and canals was the prelude to building them. The survey bill was the opening wedge for federal financing of internal improvements.

In the House of Representatives debate turned mainly on the constitutional question. But Clay, Speaker of the House, interjected a stirring plea for justice to "the West, the poor West." John Randolph of Virginia, dean of the Old Republicans, responded with a frankness calculated to smother any sympathy for strict construction that might linger west of the mountains:

> What have we done for the West? Sir, let *me* reverse the question. What have we *not* done for the West? Do gentlemen want monuments? . . . They may find them in Indian treaties for the extinguishment of title to lands—in grants of land, the effects of which begin now to be felt in Ohio, Kentucky, and Tennessee, as they have long been severely felt in Maryland, Carolina, and Virginia; they will find them in laws granting every facility for the nominal payment—and, he might also say, for the spunging, of the debts due this Government, by purchasers of the public lands—in the grants, which cannot be found in the older States, for the establishment of schools, and for other great objects of public concernment, for which nothing has been given to the States of the East.

To which Clay rejoined:

> Sir, the Western States have never yet received any thing from this Government for which they have not given an equivalent. They have paid a *quid* for every *quo*.[53]

Clay and Randolph were old adversaries, but more than personal antagonisms were at work. The survey bill passed Congress on a vote which completed the Westernization of the internal improvement issue. The House tally paired a solid Western phalanx with the mid-Atlantic bloc—except for New York, which had nearly completed the Erie Canal without federal help and was disinclined to aid its rivals for the trans-Appalachian trade. The House vote also marked the growing opposition to internal improvement in the Southeast, balanced by a surprising show of support from Massachusetts. A similar alignment appeared in the Senate (see table 3.2).

Monroe signed the measure without comment. Despite the fulminations of Old Republicans, the constitutional question by this time was as settled as it was ever likely to be. With the principle secured and with a

TABLE 3.2
GENERAL SURVEY BILL, 1824

	House		Senate[a]	
	For	*Against*	*For*	*Against*
Maine	1	5		2
Vermont	1	4		2
New Hampshire		6		1
Massachusetts	8	5	1	1
Connecticut		6	1	1
Rhode Island	2			2
New England	12	26	2	9
New York	7	24		2
New Jersey	6		2	
Pennsylvania	23	2	2	
Delaware	1			2
Maryland	8		2	
Mid-Atlantic	45	26	6	4
Virginia	6	15		2
North Carolina	1	12		2
South Carolina	5	4	1	1
Georgia	3	3		2
South Atlantic	15	34	1	7
Kentucky	10		2	
Tennessee	8		2	
Ohio	13		2	
Indiana	3		2	
Illinois	1		1	
Missouri	1		2	
Mississippi	1		2	
Alabama	3		1	1
Louisiana	3		2	
West	43	0	16	1
Total	115	86	25	21

Sources: *House Journal*, 18th Cong., 1st sess., pp. 224–226; *Senate Journal*, 18th Cong., 1st sess., pp. 318, 321.

[a]The Senate column combines the roll calls on third reading and passage, with a cohesion of 100% (see note to table 2.1).

working majority in Congress guaranteed by their own unanimity, it
was time for Westerners to turn to specific projects.

These now began to multiply. Mississippi asked for aid to improve
navigation on the Pearl River, and Indiana, emulating Ohio and Illinois, bid for help in cutting a canal from the Wabash to the Maumee,
hoping the time was "not far distant, when this parsimony on the
subject of public lands will disappear." Congress granted Indiana the
same right-of-way privilege as Illinois—an offer which, according to an
Indiana legislative committee, "bears upon its face such a character of
closeness and penury, that no politician, having a just regard to the
interest of the state, ought to be willing to accept it."⁵⁴

In contrast to Ohio's earlier proposal, no Westerners now offered to
buy government lands for waterway projects. They demanded donations pure and simple. There was even precedent, for in 1823 Congress actually deeded Ohio a swath of land two miles wide through the
Black Swamp to aid in building a road. True, this was a special case.
The road secured communications with the isolated Michigan Territory settlements, for whose welfare and defense Congress was solely
responsible. Some far-sighted negotiator had even written a stipulation
for the road into an Indian treaty back in 1808. That provision enabled
an Ohio congressman to argue, with a more or less straight face, that
the nation was morally obligated to build the road—though the Indians
were now long gone, and the road was clearly a concession from them
to the United States, not the other way around. If Congress could
swallow such logic, surely it could not refuse other reasonable re-
quests.⁵⁵

But before the Western states could press their demands, the presidential election intervened. Clay and Calhoun rode the internal improvement issue hard, but the effect upon the canvass of what New
Yorker Martin Van Buren derisively called "splendid schemes of Internal Improvement at the expense of the Federal Treasury" proved, to
his relief, to be problematical. The returns spelled a major rebuff for
Clay and something of a shock to politicians everywhere. Adams, as
expected, carried New England. Calhoun, who lacked a regional base
and was almost everybody's second choice, had withdrawn, settling for
the vice-presidency. Jackson, the outsider, divided the West with Clay,
the Southeast with Crawford, and the mid-Atlantic states with Adams,
gathering a plurality of the popular and electoral votes. In a brief
Senate term just before the election, Jackson had supported internal
improvements and a "judicious" protective tariff. But the popularity of
a candidate who could carry New Jersey and Pennsylvania along with

the Carolinas and the Southwest clearly transcended issues as it transcended sections.[56]

The choice between Adams, Jackson, and Crawford, the top three candidates, now devolved on the House of Representatives. What happened next is still uncertain, though after it was over the *Indiana Journal* assured its readers that Adams's pledges on internal improvements convinced Western congressmen to deliver the votes he needed to win. At least one Western delegation, that of Ohio, did systematically canvass the candidates on internal improvements. In a private meeting with Adams, Clay himself, whose influence on Western congressmen was strong, requested and received assurances on "some principles of great public importance." The upshot was that on the first ballot in the House, Adams garnered the votes of six states—Louisiana, Kentucky, Missouri, Ohio, Illinois, and Maryland—that went against him in the electoral college. They were just enough to make him president. Three of those states had been Clay's in the general election, five of them were Western, and all six were enthusiastic for internal improvement.[57]

It would have been easy for Clay and Adams to reach agreement on internal improvement, and it would have cost Adams none of the guilt pangs he suffered over his other campaign maneuvers. Adams had long nurtured an enthusiasm for internal improvement, though he had discreetly not emphasized it during the campaign. In fact, he considered Clay's internal improvement stance the redeeming feature in his otherwise suspect character.[58]

But for Clay, an internal improvement alliance with Adams courted political danger. For natural and even inevitable as such an alliance might seem to the two principals, it was sure to strike outsiders as most unnatural indeed. During the campaign, rumor had arranged the candidates in various pairings. An Adams–Clay permutation was not among them, and for good reason. Clay's campaign strategy was frankly sectional, designed to secure enough Western votes to get him into the House, where he could wield influence as Speaker. To that end Clay's supporters had touted his peculiarly Western virtues, including his championship of internal improvements. But they had also attacked the opposition. Since Calhoun and Crawford had no real Western following and Clay did not take Jackson seriously until it was too late, Adams bore the brunt of his assault. Thomas Hart Benton of Missouri and other Clay partisans charged the New Englander with an unremitting hostility to the West. They began with his Federalist past, dredging up evidence from his early Senate career to allege his opposition to the Louisiana Purchase and to internal improvements. Since then, he had betrayed the West at the peace negotiations with Britain at Ghent in 1814, and had given away Texas to Spain in the Florida treaty of 1819. He was even, they whispered, the secret instigator of the Missouri antislavery campaign.[59]

In the East, Clay's attack misfired. When Representative Jonathan Russell, acting for Clay, challenged Adams's conduct at Ghent, the secretary annihilated him in a pamphlet war. But in the West the accusations circulated more widely than the denials, and were remembered long after. There Clay's campaign of vituperation was largely successful—too successful, in fact. For if Clay himself could instantly forget the charges, his followers could not. To them the idea of a Clay–Adams alliance was so preposterous that when word of it first leaked out many refused to believe it. Schooled by Clay himself to consider Adams the archenemy of the West, they could only attribute their leader's strange reversal to some dark and insidious motive. Adams's subsequent offer—and Clay's acceptance—of the State Department revealed that motive. The "corrupt bargain" explained the unexplainable: the man Andrew Jackson called the "*Judas* of the West" had sacrificed his section to personal ambition.[60]

Meanwhile, as would-be president-makers stalked the back stairs of Washington boardinghouses, Congress again tackled the internal improvements question, this time on a $150,000 appropriation to extend the Cumberland Road into Ohio.

In past years Virginians had supplied the principled core of Southern opposition to internal improvements, while the South Carolina nationalists had favored them. But the 1824 session of Congress had produced, along with the general survey bill, a protective tariff, passed with the unanimous votes of Ohio, Indiana, Illinois, Kentucky, and Missouri, and over the strident opposition of South Carolina. South Carolina nationalists George McDuffie and James Hamilton, both friends of the survey bill, had then warned the Northwesterners that the tariff might cost them Southern support on internal improvements. The truth was that the combination of the tariff, fears over slavery, and competition from a states' rights political faction headed by erstwhile senator William Smith was fast eroding the altruistic nationalism of the Calhoun school. Resolutions declaring both tariff and internal improvements unconstitutional passed one house of the South Carolina legislature in 1824 and both houses a year later.[61]

So on January 18, 1825, with the presidential election still pending in the House, George McDuffie of South Carolina, long an internal improvement man, rose to oppose the extension of the Cumberland Road. McDuffie attacked the bill as inexpedient: funds were lacking, and it was wrong to proceed until a general plan of internal improvement had been digested. Besides, the government had done enough for the West already.

Quickly Representative Daniel Webster of Massachusetts seized the mantle of nationalism discarded by the South Carolinian. Webster waved aside McDuffie's quibbles: "This road was wanted—it was wanted now—it was wanted more now than it would be to-morrow; and the expense of making it to-day would be no more than of making it to-morrow." Surely the road would enhance the value of the public lands, said Webster,

> yet he could never think that the National domain was to be regarded as any great source of revenue. The great object of the Government, in respect to those lands, was not so much the money derived from their sale, as it was the getting of them settled.

McDuffie responded:

> I think that the public lands are settling quite fast enough. . . . The gentleman says, that the great object of Government, with respect to those lands, is not to make them a source of revenue, but to get them settled. . . . It amounts to this, that those [original thirteen] states are to offer a bonus for their own impoverishment—. . . Sir, I say if there is any object worthy the attention of this Government, it is a plan which shall limit the sale of the public lands. . . . At this moment we are selling to the people of the West lands at one dollar and twenty-five cents an acre, which are fairly worth fifteen, and which would sell at that price if the markets were not glutted.[62]

The import of the exchange was unmistakable. McDuffie had taken John Randolph's part; and Webster, Henry Clay's. Just as the West's last ally in the Old South turned its back, uttering sentiments that were anathema to every Westerner, New England in the person of Daniel Webster offered the hand of friendship. Webster, to be sure, had always been for internal improvement. He supported the survey bill the previous session, and years before as a New Hampshire member he had cast its lone vote for Calhoun's bonus bill. But never before in congressional debate had a New Englander—and an ex-Federalist at that—risen to repel views so closely associated with New England itself. And Webster was no ordinary congressman. He was the voice of Massachusetts and, implicitly, of the Massachusetts candidate, John Quincy Adams.[63]

The House vote on the Cumberland Road bill resembled that on the survey bill a year before, but the deviations, though slight, were of interest. Among members present on both occasions, New England delivered four more votes for the Cumberland Road than for the survey bill. But no Southerners switched to internal improvement, while six, including four South Carolinians (Hamilton and McDuffie among them) deserted to the opposition. In the Senate the shift was even more striking. New England contributed eight votes for the bill, the mid-Atlantic states four, the Old South none (see table 3.3). Monroe signed it on March 3, 1825, his last day in office. Along with it he approved the purchase of 1,500 shares of stock in the Chesapeake and Delaware Canal Company, the fruit of his new constitutional latitudinarianism.[64]

Internal improvement would figure prominently in the policy of the incoming administration. Now that the Ohio River was crossed, Cumberland Road advocates pressed for its completion to the Mississippi, while plans were afoot for another great national road from the capital to New Orleans. In the outgoing Congress, Illinois and Indiana secured reports favoring land grants for their canals, while Ohio demanded similar assistance in language which almost dared Congress to refuse. The *Illinois Intelligencer* castigated Congress for behaving "with a parsimony becoming a stingy stepmother." But as the West achieved internal unity and found new friends in hitherto hostile New England, it faced rising sectional opposition in the Old South.[65]

Public lands: relief and graduation

While Congress grappled with the tariff and internal improvements, the seeds of a new controversy over the land system appeared in the West.

Land debtors under the credit system had rushed to take advantage of the Relief Act of 1821, with its three options of relinquishment, cash payment at a discount, or extended credit. Relinquishment liquidated more than $3 million in debt at the Huntsville, Alabama, land office alone. Nationally, the Relief Act slashed the land debt in half, to $11,957,430. But Westerners complained that administrative delays and poor communications prevented some debtors from filing for relief before the law expired on September 30, 1821. In 1822 and again in 1823 Congress obligingly extended the deadlines, but the extensions worked only small further reductions in the debt.[66]

The extensions drew caustic comment from the national press, which had approved the act of 1821 on the assumption it would put an end to the relief business. The *National Intelligencer* remarked that if extensions became routine, "the debtors will laugh at the government." *Niles' Register* snapped that "the statute book is disgraced by such acts,"

TABLE 3.3
CUMBERLAND ROAD EXTENSION, 1825

	House[a]		Senate	
	For	*Against*	*For*	*Against*
Maine	2	4	1	1
Vermont	2	3	1	
New Hampshire	1	4	1	1
Massachusetts	7	5	1	1
Connecticut	1	5	2	
Rhode Island	1	1	2	
New England	14	22	8	3
New York	9	19		2
New Jersey	3	3	1	1
Pennsylvania	17	6	1	1
Delaware	1		1	1
Maryland	7		1	
Mid-Atlantic	37	28	4	5
Virginia	6	13		2
North Carolina		12		2
South Carolina	1	8		1
Georgia	2	4		1
South Atlantic	9	37		6
Kentucky	10		2	
Tennessee	8	1	2	
Ohio	14		2	
Indiana	3		2	
Illinois	1		2	
Missouri			2	
Mississippi		1		2
Alabama	3		2	
Louisiana	3		2	
West	42	2	16	2
Total	102	89	28	16

Sources: *House Journal*, 18th Cong., 2d sess., pp. 143–144, 155–157; *Senate Journal*, 18th Cong., 2d sess., pp. 192–193.

[a]The House column combines the roll calls on third reading and passage, with a cohesion of 100% (see note to table 2.1).

and suggested that Congress settle the matter forever by "directing that the debtors for lands should satisfy their debts 'sixty days after it is convenient,' *if* convenient then." To Hezekiah Niles the demand for new relief measures proved that "the march west has been more rapid than the public good has justified."[67]

Aside from these grumblings, the extensions attracted little attention; they sailed through Congress without debate or division and almost without notice. With the threat of sectional crisis removed, the land debt was no longer of much interest to Easterners. That was not true, however, in the West. There the Relief Act of 1821 was so popular that congressional and presidential candidates were still disputing the credit for it years later. Yet grateful as they were, Westerners hoped for further indulgence. In 1823 the Alabama legislature and some Illinoisans petitioned Congress to allow the 37½ percent discount for cash payment to those who had completed their purchases after the Land Act of 1820 but before the passage of the Relief Act; they were asking, in effect, for a refund of the difference between the former $2.00 minimum per acre and the current price of $1.25. And in 1824 Indiana requested that those who had already forfeited their lands for nonpayment before the Relief Act went into effect be credited at the land offices for their losses. While ignoring these proposals, which would have created whole new categories of beneficiaries, Congress acted again to reduce the existing debt. A law of 1824 offered those who had taken a further credit in 1821 another opportunity to wrap up their debts through relinquishment or discounted cash payment. This measure liquidated almost $4 million in debt, reducing the total to $6,322,765 by June 30, 1825.[68]

Yet while the debt dwindled, the Western states still contained millions of acres of federal land, unsold and unlikely to sell even at $1.25 per acre in the depressed market of the early 1820s. Hoping to re-stimulate the migration which had sustained their vanished prosperity, Westerners began to beg for a reduction of federal land prices. Following requests from Indiana and Louisiana, in April 1824 Missouri senator Thomas Hart Benton introduced a bill to re-auction lands unpurchased after five years in market, at a new minimum price of 50¢ per acre. He also proposed to donate eighty acres free to anyone who fulfilled a three-year residency requirement.[69]

Benton and his bill would dominate the land debate for the next thirty years. Benton had served in the Senate since Missouri's admission in 1821; there his loud voice and overbearing manner had earned him from his homestate enemies the sobriquets of "Senator Pomposo" and "The political LUNGS of Missouri." A former editor of the *St. Louis*

Enquirer, and at this time a strong proslavery man, Benton had busied himself in the Senate mainly with Missouri's special interests in the fur trade, the settlement of Spanish land claims, and the occupation of Oregon. As a newspaperman he had also advocated a more liberal land policy, and he had recently begun a campaign to force the government to sell, instead of lease, its Western ore-bearing lands.[70]

Benton later credited his ideas on land policy to his childhood meditations on the Bible. Critics found his inspiration closer at hand, in his desire to embarrass the 1824 reelection bid of fellow Missouri senator David Barton. The origin of the feud between Benton and Barton is obscure, but like much of the ill feeling in the Era of Good Feelings, it fed on political factionalism and personal rancor, spiced by frontier violence. A friend of Benton's had recently killed Barton's brother Joshua in a duel.[71]

Benton's land bill went to the Senate Committee on Public Lands, chaired by Barton. For a unanimous committee, Barton reported against it, saying it would jeopardize the land revenue and halt sales for five years while purchasers awaited the price reductions. The Senate tabled the bill.[72]

Considering the scope of his proposal and the fact that he introduced it very late in the session, Benton could hardly have expected any other result, which led his enemies to dismiss the bill as a mere "electioneering project." Benton did indeed enlist the issue against Barton; he stumped the state, distributing handbills which included opposition to his land bill in a lurid catalogue of Barton's personal and political sins.[73]

The outcome embarrassed Benton. The legislature returned Barton to the Senate by a large majority. But it was already becoming evident that Benton could not have chosen a better issue on which to stake his political fortunes in the West. The Missouri legislature that reelected Barton also memorialized Congress in behalf of Benton's bill. Illinois did the same, while the *Illinois Intelligencer* said the bill was "of deep interest to the Western people." Only "jealousy of the gigantic march of the west to influence and strength," thought the editor, could explain opposition to Benton's proposition.[74]

When Congress reconvened, Benton again submitted his bill; again it was tabled. In the interim Benton had modified his plan. He now proposed to reduce the price of lands not taken at the initial auction in a series of annual steps. To this plan he gave a name it would bear for the next thirty years: graduation.

Meanwhile the House was electing a president. The choice of Missouri fell upon its sole representative, John Scott, a friend of Benton's and, like both Benton and Barton, a partisan of Henry Clay. Clay had swept Missouri's popular vote, with Jackson second and Adams a distant third. But with Clay eliminated in the House, Barton declared for Adams. Scott hesitated, then followed him. But Benton had never had any use for Adams (the feeling was mutual), and he had recently made up with an old personal enemy, Andrew Jackson. Benton tested the Western political winds, and found them blowing strong for Old Hickory. With the election of Adams, Benton broke his ties with Scott and moved deliberately into the camp of the opposition. He took his graduation bill with him.[75]

Between 1820 and 1825 the sectional antagonisms unleashed by the Missouri crisis and the financial panic had fastened upon the competition for scarce resources of capital and population. As Americans redefined their interests and hopes for the future in geographic terms, sectional positions appeared in Congress on the tariff, internal improvements, and public lands. Sectionalism also underpinned the presidential campaign of 1824. But the elevation of a New England president by the aid of Western votes, and the convergence of the opposition behind the defeated Andrew Jackson, began the metamorphosis by which sectional feelings were enlisted and eventually subsumed in the national contest for the presidency. The next four years were to carry it far forward.

CHAPTER 4
ELECTIONEERING
1825–1829

The great effort of my administration was to mature into a permanent and regular system the application of all the superfluous revenue of the Union to internal improvement—improvement which at this day would have afforded high wages and constant employment to hundreds of thousands of labourers, and in which every dollar expended would have repaid itself fourfold in the enhanced value of the Public Lands.

John Quincy Adams to Charles W. Upham, February 2, 1837

The American System and its enemies

John Quincy Adams entered the White House on March 4, 1825, by the grace of a handful of Western congressmen. In the House of Representatives he carried five Western states; in the preceding general election he had carried none. Single representatives cast the votes of Illinois and Missouri. The Kentucky delegation's vote for Adams defied explicit instructions from the state legislature. Western congressmen had risked their political necks to make Adams president; he owed it to them, to Henry Clay, and to his own political future to redeem their trust.

Adams understood the odds against him. His administration was secure only in New England. Jackson had outpolled him nationally in 1824, and, as a slaveholder, would inherit most of Crawford's Southern strength in a rematch. Lacking a Southern base, Adams could sustain his measures in Congress and defeat Jackson in 1828 only with substantial Western support. The appointment of Clay as Secretary of State (and thus chief counsellor and heir apparent) was a beginning, but Westerners were still wary of the new president. The alliance with Clay, instead of teaching them to trust Adams, only taught many of them to distrust Henry Clay. Adams would have to prove himself with measures as well as men.[1]

71

Ohio congressman Joseph Vance begged Adams to say something for the West in his first message to Congress, "as you know that their has been much complaint hertofore of wilful neglect from that quarter." Vance thought Westerners cared most for the Cumberland Road and the proposed New Orleans road, along with more aid for land debtors—"you have no Idea what intrest the People feel on the subject of a further relief." Ninian Edwards of Illinois, now an ex-senator, also touted internal improvements, especially the Illinois River–Lake Michigan canal, "a favorite object, and indeed a political hobby" in Illinois and Missouri. "Nothing could sustain the administration or its friends in these two states, so effectually as its countenancing this measure."[2]

Then there was graduation. Nine-tenths of the West was "exceedingly anxious" for it, wrote a Clay informant. Should Adams commend it to Congress, "it would fasten him in the affections of tens of thousands of the citizens of the West—& who of the East or else where could reasonably object?"[3]

For Adams the choice was easy to make. He harbored a grand vision of a united American nation striding toward economic, intellectual, and moral achievement under the fostering care of a benevolent central government. To consummate this vision and dissolve sectional barriers required federal internal improvements, which would also woo Western majorities and satisfy the friends of Henry Clay. Knowing that his plans would offend strict constructionists, Adams cast aside caution and set before Congress an ambitious program of public works: roads and canals, scientific explorations, a national university and astronomical observatory. About graduation he said nothing.[4]

For the first time internal improvement had an active ally in the White House. Financial conditions were also favorable. Treasury secretary Richard Rush projected a federal revenue surplus for 1826 of nearly five million dollars. Furthermore, at the current rate of repayment the national debt of eighty million, already down a third from its wartime peak, could be cut to forty million by 1830. Its extinction, which would free the Treasury of a charge that consumed nearly half its annual income, drew closer day by day.[5]

But while abundant funds and a compliant executive fired internal improvement men with energy and enthusiasm, from opponents they evoked only dread and fear. John Randolph's warning, delivered in the survey bill debate of 1824, still rang in the ears of Southerners: "If Congress possesses the power to do what is proposed by this bill, . . . they may emancipate every slave in the United States." Strict constructionists braced themselves for the nationalists' assault on the Constitution.[6]

Several weapons of defense appeared early in Adams's first Congress. The first was New Jersey senator Mahlon Dickerson's proposal to distribute part of the national revenue to the states for education and internal improvement. Dickerson had supported federal internal improvements for seven years in the Senate, culminating with the survey bill of 1824. But during the next year he apparently underwent a change of heart (perhaps connected to the demise of William Crawford's presidential prospects), for beginning with the Cumberland Road extension in 1825 he opposed them at nearly every opportunity. Dickerson's idea of distributing surplus funds to the states was not new. Internal improvement men had promoted it from time to time to ensure an equitable distribution of federal favors. But Dickerson showed less interest in the improvements themselves than in removing funds for them from federal control. Treasury surpluses, he argued, "will impair the most important principles of our constitution." Direct federal spending "will, in time, so far decrease the powers of the State Governments, and increase those of the United States Government, as to destroy the federative principle of our Union, and convert our system of confederated republics into a consolidated government." Distribution would siphon off the dangerous surplus into harmless channels.[7]

Dickerson touted his plan through the Adams years, and though it never came to a vote, it acquired an uncertain following among foes of direct federal road and canal subsidies. In Congress, distribution mainly attracted opponents of the administration, including Dickerson himself, while Adams men attacked it as unconstitutional. By 1828 it had secured endorsements from several state legislatures and, privately, from Andrew Jackson.[8]

But Dickerson's plausible scheme concealed a double motive. A more direct way to avoid what he called "the serious inconvenience of an overflowing Treasury" was to reduce the revenue by lowering the tariff. Dickerson's plan would actually postpone tariff reduction by diverting funds from debt service to distribution, delaying the retirement of the public debt. Further, the states might well demand that the subsidies, and the tariff to fund them, continue even after the debt was paid. This was fine with Dickerson, who was a militant protectionist. But others, friends of neither the tariff nor internal improvement, wanted to cut the flow of dollars at the fount. Foremost among them were the Old Republicans.

The Old Republicans combined philosophical and constitutional objections to a strong central government with a growing sectional emphasis on strict construction as a shield for slavery and the plantation system. For years they had fought every engine of federal "consolidation," including internal improvements. They also guarded the revenue, including the land proceeds, with a jealous eye—not because they favored liberal spending, which they did not, but because they abhorred a national debt. They remembered how Alexander Hamilton had once made the public debt a potent instrument of centralization. To prevent a recurrence the Old Republicans wanted the debt paid off expeditiously and in full; that done, they would cut revenue to the bone and usher in the Jeffersonian utopia of frugality, simplicity, and states' rights.

Alert to the perils of an empty federal treasury, the Old Republicans recognized in Adams's message the dangers of a full one. Through public works and benevolent enterprises, a nationalizing president and Congress could undermine the Constitution by bribing the states out of their principles with their own taxpayers' money.

The Old Republicans were no friends to the West. They feared its nationalizing politics and the competition of its fertile soils. Concern for the land revenue led John Randolph and Nathaniel Macon to oppose cheaper public lands and leniency for land debtors. But the legislation of recent years revealed the land system's efficacy as an agent of consolidation. It showed how the public domain could cover federal intrusions into the state preserves of education and internal improvement, to say nothing of the patronage network it spread throughout the West. And the enhancement of the value of the public lands served as a ritual justification for every Western public works appropriation.

Therefore, in the middle of a Cumberland Road speech proclaiming his eternal hostility to the West, John Randolph as "the friend of state rights" suddenly ventured to "wish that every new State had all the lands within the State, that, in the shape of Receiverships and other ways, these States might not be brought under the influence of this ten miles square." Randolph's rhetoric often descended into hyperbole. But later Martin Van Buren of New York, as cautious a speaker as Randolph was profligate, echoed his sentiments, and Virginia's other senator, Littleton Tazewell, submitted a resolution to "cede and surrender" the federal lands to the states "upon such terms and conditions as may be consistent with the due observance of the public faith, and with the general interest of the United States."[9]

This was welcome news to Senator Thomas Hart Benton of Misouri. Benton was back with a new version of his graduation bill, which would reduce the price of lands unpurchased at the auction to 25¢ an acre within four years, and donate free tracts to actual settlers. Although Benton's bill had no chance to pass during that session, he rose on May 16, 1826, to speak formally in its behalf for the first time.

Benton's speech betrayed signs of exhaustive study in musty archives. It bulged with facts and figures, interspersed with quotations from authorities ranging from Alexander Hamilton and Edmund Burke to Abbys Mirza, King of Persia. Weaving through this scholarly graveyard ran Benton's argument, impressive in its own right. Benton played brilliantly on the agrarian strain in Jeffersonian Republican ideology. The government locked up millions of idle acres, he cried, while thousands of landless poor suffered miserable lives as tenants and wage slaves. Was not something radically wrong? Should a government created to serve the people act the cruel landlord toward its own citizens? Fairly distributed, the public domain could guarantee a farm to every willing settler. And as every good Jeffersonian knew, the security of republican government lay in its freehold farmers:

> I speak to statesmen, and not to compting clerks; to Senators, and not to *Quaestors* of provinces; to an assembly of legislators, and not to a keeper of the King's forests. I speak to Senators who know this to be a Republic, not a Monarchy; who know that the public lands belong to the People, and not to the Federal Government.[10]

Benton also appealed to plain common sense. Why sell all the lands at the same "odious and arbitrary *minimum*" of $1.25 an acre? Why not sell them for what they were worth? Adams talked of a "swelling tide of wealth" from the public domain, yet the lands brought only a paltry revenue—a result, said Benton, of the government's perversity in pricing them out of the market. Better to realize an immediate return "by letting the land go for what it is worth—by selling for the present value—instead of waiting for a future, distant, and uncertain rise." Current policy was extortionate as well as foolish. The improvements of settlers, unaided by government, raised the value of nearby federal land and made it saleable, so by idly waiting for the rise the government was actually speculating on the labor of its own citizens.

Though he thought his own graduation plan had the best chance of passage, Benton also endorsed the more drastic remedy of ceding the public lands to the Western states. Either way, he invited "all the friends to State rights" to help pull down the federal land system. The government's refusal to relinquish its Western domain was a policy "fraught with injustice" and "destructive to the sovereignty and independence of the new States," reducing them to *"tenants* of the Federal Government."

The graduation bill lay on the table. Benton paraded his agrarian rhetoric and ostentatious scholarship more for the eyes of Western voters than for his fellow senators. But Benton's speech was more than a consummate summary of all the arguments for graduation. It was also a declaration of war against President Adams. Benton castigated the administration's mineral land policy so severely that one critic thought his arguments "about as well calculated to prove that Jackson ought to have been elected president instead of Adams, as they are to show the utility of reducing the price of public lands." The speech unveiled Benton's strategy for the 1828 presidential campaign. Either the West would get cheap lands, or John Quincy Adams would bear the blame.[11]

Adams had said nothing yet against either graduation or cession. By recommending either, as some Westerners urged him to do, he could silence Benton's attack. But Adams would have none of it. Personally he despised Benton, but beyond that Benton's proposals fatally undermined his own cherished policy of nationalization. Adams was no agrarian. His hopes for America's future, like Henry Clay's, encompassed a diversified economy balancing agriculture with industry and commerce. To foster their growth required an active federal role. But ceding the domain to the states would sever the hand of federal benevolence in the West at a stroke, removing responsibility for internal improvements from Washington to the state capitals. The land system bound the Western states tightly to the Union, forcing them to turn to it for essential services and thus making them friends of federal power. Returning the lands to the states would render the centripetal force of the public domain centrifugal.

Graduation threatened to produce the same result by other means. It would entice population from the settled East to the frontier, crippling commerce and industry to favor a subsistence agriculture. It would also undercut the revenue Adams needed to fund his internal improvement program. Adams dismissed Benton's argument that graduation would actually raise receipts by stimulating sales through lower prices. Left alone, the lands would someday bring the current minimum. There was no hurry abut selling them. Adams looked for a steady income rather than a quick one, for a national system of roads and canals would take years to complete. So seriously did Benton's schemes jeopardize the administration's plans that Adams and Clay privately considered them "treasonable in their character."[12]

The lands belong to the people

"The lands belong to the people!" Benton's magnificent phrase focused all the resentments that had been gathering in the West for nearly a decade. Benton offered a simple, comprehensive explanation for Western embarrassments: an oppressive, unconstitutional, irrational land system, based upon greed and Eastern hostility to Western growth. Benton's speech was soon in print. The Missouri legislature distributed five thousand copies, while Benton himself franked bundles through the mail and strewed others along his route home at the end of the session. Within months his arguments spread throughout the public land states.[13]

The effect was startling. Between 1826 and 1828 a veritable mania for cheap lands swept through the frontier regions. Within a year, governors of five of the seven public land states pronounced for graduation or cession. The legislatures of Missouri, Illinois, Indiana, Louisiana, Alabama, and of the Arkansas and Florida territories all memorialized Congress for graduation, also variously requesting cession, free lands or pre-emption privileges for "actual settlers," abolition of the auction system, more relief for land debtors, and sales of land in forty-acre parcels.[14]

Local politics in the West soon felt the impact of the craze. Westerners in Washington produced a flood of letters and circulars, reciting their efforts for land reform and promising its imminent success. Newspapers demanded graduation, while candidates for state and even local office vied to outdo each other in enthusiasm for it. Support for cheaper lands quickly became a test of political orthodoxy in the public land states.[15]

Cession competed with graduation for Western favor. Politicians cried that the federal land system made a mockery of state sovereignty and equality. They revived the Ohio argument against the Maryland proposition of 1821 and made it the staple of a demand for outright cession of the public lands to the states. Curious exercises in constitutional logic and batteries of quotations from digests of international law embellished the argument. For instance, some Westerners discovered that the admission compacts by which the states pledged noninterference with the federal domain were in fact treaties, prohibited under Article I of the Constitution and hence null and void. But the core of the case remained that federal landownership violated the intrinsic rights of the states and the true meaning of the Virginia Act of Cession, the Northwest Ordinance, and the Constitution. Expert critics like James Madison and Albert Gallatin dismissed the argument as nonsense, and indeed it was difficult to overlook the phrases in those same documents which explicitly vested the title to the public domain in the federal government. But sound or not, the idea that the federal land system was illegal and unconstitutional was a Western commonplace by 1828.[16]

In the White House, President Adams observed dismally that Benton had "stimulated all the people of the Western country to madness for the public lands," and "made himself amazingly popular" by doing so. Adams attributed the graduation furor to Benton's ambition to supplant Clay as leader of the West. But in truth it was not all Benton's doing. Western impatience was already there, building in intensity and waiting to be tapped. In 1826 Benton smote the rock, and the waters of resentment gushed forth. Adams could read the results. "The best days of our land-sales are past. We shall have trouble from that quarter."[17]

Here and there in the West appeared islands of resistance. Ninety-five members of the "moral population" in Michigan Territory complained that Benton's bill would entice "the dregs of community from the Old States" to invade their "respectable neighborhood." In Missouri, graduation was already entangled in the feud between the Benton and Barton factions. In the United States Senate it was Barton who leaped to denounce Benton's "studied, popularity-hunting, Senate-distressing harangue." The Barton press in Missouri inveighed bitterly against graduation, "the most shallow and shabby *scheme of speculation in lands*, that has ever been proposed." It pilloried Benton's speech as "the rant and quibble of a demagogue," with its "quibbling, shuffling, awkward attempt at logical deduction" and truisms strung together "like ropes of onions." A Missouri legislative committee even produced a report against graduation, sparking an animated local controversy. But though Barton led the congressional opposition to graduation, he felt the issue hanging "like an impending guillotine over my neck." In self-defense, he too advocated free lands for actual settlers.[18]

Ohio stood high and dry. No demand for graduation issued from its governor, legislature, or congressmen. Their silence is instructive, for in Ohio far more than anywhere else there was real cause to regard the unsold lands as worthless "refuse" that should be sold for whatever they could bring. Some of them had been in market for decades. Ohio's silence cannot be attributed to partisanship, though the Adams party was strong there. In other Western states politicians of all persuasions

rode the graduation bandwagon. But in Ohio, economic metamorphosis was rearranging political priorities. The state passed a milestone
in 1825, when it began building a mammoth canal system without
waiting longer for federal aid. As its economy matured, Ohio looked to
manufacturing and commercial agriculture, not to migration and land
sales, as the keys to future prosperity, and the American System of
protective tariffs and internal improvements assumed first importance
for its citizens.

Ohio had come so far from the frontier outlook that two of its
congressmen opposed additional frontier land surveys in 1826,
arguing that a glutted market depressed property values and retarded
the sale of Ohio's remaining public domain. Easterners had been
voicing the same complaint for years. Like the Atlantic states, Ohio was
feeling the competition for population, and beginning to look westward as well as eastward for its source. In 1826 Ohio's political transformation was not yet complete. Ohioans were still Westerners, and
two years hence both Ohio senators would vote for graduation. But in
Ohio cheap land could never be the panacea it became out on the
frontier. In December 1826 Henry Clay assured the president that
Ohio was "perfectly sound" on the land question, and so it was—sound
for the American System, if not for John Quincy Adams.[19]

The merits of Benton's graduation plan are difficult to evaluate even
with a century of hindsight. By 1828 many Americans on both sides of
the mountains had concluded with Benton that the federal land system
was malfunctioning. After the Land Act of 1820, sales stabilized at
about 800,000 acres a year, yielding a gross revenue slightly more than
a million dollars. But all sales from the beginning of the system down to
1827 totaled only 19 million acres (deducting forfeitures and relin-
quishments), while in that year 82 million acres were still in market in
the seven public land states and three organized territories. Another
128 million acres had been acquired from the Indians but not yet
offered at auction. At this rate it would indeed, as Benton cried, be
"ages and centuries" before the entire public domain passed into
private hands.[20]

Even in Ohio, where all the public lands had been in market at least
four years and some for upwards of twenty-five, nearly half of the
acreage remained unsold in 1827. In Illinois, nine years a state, only 8
percent of the offered land had found buyers; in Missouri, 7 percent.
Counting in Indian holdings and lands not yet offered for sale, only 3
percent of the land in Missouri was privately owned by 1826.[21]

The system had also failed to meet revenue expectations. Graduation men pointed out that the annual receipts equalled 6 percent interest on a capital of only sixteen million dollars. Adams himself observed that the costs of acquisition, survey, and sale had thus far outweighed revenues. The auction system too had largely broken down. The average price for all lands sold from 1821 through 1828 was $1.34 per acre, only 9¢ above the minimum. Auction sales assumed a competition based on scarcity. Presumably all land was worth $1.25 per acre, and the best land was worth much more. But land values were not fixed entities. They fluctuated with supply, and in the 1820s the supply was huge. Hence instead of bad land selling for $1.25 and good land selling for more, the best land sold for around $1.25 and the rest did not sell at all. The minimum price had become the maximum.[22]

The dilemma went all the way back to Albert Gallatin's dictum of 1804: the system should "satisfy the demand for land created by the existing population" without "promoting migration beyond its natural and necessary progress." But what was natural and necessary progress? According to Benton, thousands of farm tenants and millhands in the old states were poised to move West and begin life anew as soon as the government allowed them into the market. Squatters would rush to purchase the farms they could not now afford. A great demand for land already existed; greed and Eastern malevolence alone blocked the rapid sale and settlement of the Western domain.

Easterners and Benton's Missouri foes, on the other hand, attributed the problems of the land system to a veritable excess of federal benevolence. The government's rush to survey and sell Western lands had glutted the market. Between 1823 and 1828 five new acres were thrown on the market for every one sold. The fault was not an arbitrarily high price, but a supply that outran demand at any price. Easterners generally regarded the $1.25 minimum not as an impediment to settlement, but as an artificial lure. They denied that price reductions would stimulate migration; instead, only speculators would profit from graduation, by snapping up lands at 25¢ an acre and waiting for population growth to bring high resale values.

Benton's adversaries offered a solution as simple as his own: stop surveying and offering new land. Eventually the balance of supply and demand must right itself; as it did, values would rise and the untaken lands would become a good buy, first in Ohio, then later in Illinois and Missouri and the territories. Only time was needed to solve the problem of unsold lands, and nothing but time could solve it. Benton's critics pointed out that in Ohio, where the best lands had long ago been taken, land sold twice as fast during the 1820s as it did in Illinois, where first pickings on millions of acres were available. It was not in the old gleaned-over districts where sales lagged, but on the frontier, where supply exceeded demand.

Even a dispassionate observer might have had difficulty choosing between the analyses of Benton and his critics, for the variables in Gallatin's equation defied solution. When abstracted from specific circumstances and deliberate policy choices, Gallatin's "natural and necessary progress" of migration was a phantom quantity. But there were few dispassionate observers in any case, for the land issue touched sensitive sectional chords. The new states were naturally enthralled at the prospect of attracting new settlers with cheap lands. Lower land prices would also reduce the cash flow eastward, while faster sales put more land on the state tax rolls. And everyone—squatters, farmowners, businessmen—could acquire ample tracts for both personal use and investment. As before, the oft-made distinction between the interests of "speculators" and "actual settlers" was largely rhetorical. There was plenty of land for everyone.

But in the East graduation found no friends. Benton spoke of liberating the surplus population of the East, but no one there could see any surplus. Rather, they saw deserted farms, declining property values, glutted crop markets, and stunted manufactures, all attributable to the lure of fertile Western soils. A Pennsylvanian inquired "what farther bounties the government can be reasonably asked to offer for the DISPERSION of the American people? . . . Is it the policy of the Union, or does justice to the West require, that the government should continue to add temptations to the strong ones already existing" to entice migrants from their homes? According to Westerners, justice to the West required exactly that. They saw the present land system as a hindrance to migrants, not an inducement. The discrepancy between Eastern and Western viewpoints was fundamental and unbridgeable, for each thought present policy unfairly favored the other. To Easterners, the Western demand for what amounted to an immediate equality in population and political power, attained through the artificial stimulus of a giveaway land policy, smacked of youthful arrogance. Let the new states wait, as Ohio had waited, and their turn would come in time. Already their growth was phenomenal. But Westerners measured their progress less by how far they had come than by how far they had still to go to match their Atlantic neighbors. They had been admitted to the Union as equals, but they were not equal. By that standard, growth was frustratingly slow. Westerners blamed the land system, and demanded immediate reform. They wanted their future now.[23]

Internal improvement in the Nineteenth Congress

The first session of the Nineteenth Congress sketched the outlines of the contest between Benton and the administration for Western favor. While Benton demanded changes in land policy, internal improvement advanced on several fronts. A bid to erect tollgates on the Cumberland Road failed, but an appropriation for new construction on the road passed, along with stock purchases in two canal companies and funding to continue surveys under the act of 1824. But when a land grant for the Illinois River–Lake Michigan canal came before the Senate, the internal improvement majority mysteriously vanished. Key absences, perhaps prearranged, produced a 17–17 tie, thrusting responsibility for the bill's fate on the vice-president. Calhoun, an internal improvement man, a Southerner, and a Jacksonian convert at the crossroads, cast his deciding vote in the negative.[24]

That setback scarcely dampened the enthusiasm of canal men in Indiana and Illinois, who expected victory at the next session. Internal improvement projects of all sorts had begun to proliferate in the states, and the encouragement of Congress and the executive prompted their sponsors to seek aid from Washington. The Nineteenth Congress, reassembling for its second session in December 1826, encountered a deluge of petitions, memorials, and bills, begging assistance in cash or land for roads, canals, and river improvements. The House Committee on Roads and Canals, trying to fix some criteria for disposing of the mass of proposals, agreed with the Western supplicants that providing access to federal lands was a national object, and that internal improvements for that purpose came within Congress's clear constitutional authority over the public domain.[25]

Western internal improvement agitation bore fruit in the closing hours of the Nineteenth Congress. The short session again yielded appropriations for the Cumberland Road and for surveys under the act of 1824. It also produced four land grants for Western roads and canals.

Two of the grants went to Illinois and Indiana for the Illinois River–Lake Michigan and Wabash River–Lake Erie canals. Each state received alternate sections five miles deep on each side of the canal route, or 3,200 acres per linear miles of construction. (The alternate-section device secured the federal government a share in the anticipated rise in land values along the canals.) Ohio also received one section per mile for a road from Columbus to Sandusky. Lastly, Congress confirmed a grant to Indiana for a road from Lake Michigan to the Ohio River. Copying Ohio's maneuver with the Black Swamp road, Indiana negotiators had inserted the grant into a recent Potawatomi Indian treaty.[26]

The debate on these measures aired sectional grievances, and sectional loyalties prevailed in the voting. In the House of Representatives, a unanimous Northwest joined with large mid-Atlantic majorities for Western roads and canals. Led by Massachusetts, New England strengthened its support. But the Southwest wavered, while the Southeast hardened in opposition. In the Senate, the contrast between New England and the Old South was even more striking. The eight South Atlantic senators delivered not a single vote for any Western internal improvement measure in the Nineteenth Congress. (See tables 4.1 and 4.2.)[27]

In the Senate, twenty of the twenty-eight steady friends of internal improvement were Adams men, while fourteen of the sixteen opponents were Jacksonian.[28] It was much the same in the House of Representatives, though there voting patterns were more diffuse and party lines less firmly drawn.[29] However, the partisan division was less a consequence of partisanship itself than an artifact of political imbalance within sections. Administration men predominated in the Northwestern delegations, where support for internal improvements was strongest, while almost all the Southeastern members were Jacksonian. Divisions within regions did not follow strict party lines. The mid-Atlantic and Northwestern internal improvement majorities were bipartisan. Some Southwestern Jacksonians were thoroughgoing internal improvement men, while others were consistent opponents. New England Jackson men opposed roads and canals, but so did some Adams men. The meager South Atlantic support for Adams and internal improvements came from the mountain and upper Potomac districts of Virginia, geographically oriented toward the adjacent mid-Atlantic and Western regions rather than toward the tidewater.[30]

In short, the voting alignments on internal improvement in John Quincy Adams's first Congress did not spring from partisanship, but continued the trend seen in votes on the survey and Cumberland Road bills in 1824 and 1825. The direction of change matched regional presidential proclivities (New England for Adams and internal improvement, the South against both), but also reflected sectional concerns. In the mid-Atlantic and Northwestern states, voting showed almost no trace of party influence. But though the divisions on internal improvement did not follow party lines, they could still be put to partisan purposes.

TABLE 4.1

INTERNAL IMPROVEMENTS, HOUSE, 1827

	Cumberland Road (construction)		Surveys		Cumberland Road (repair)		Illinois Canal Grant	
	For	Against	For	Against	For	Against	For	Against
Maine	2	4	3	2	2	3	1	4
Vermont	1		3	1	1	3	3	
New Hampshire	1	4	2	2	2	4	1	4
Massachusetts	11		10	2	11	1	7	4
Connecticut	2	3	3	1	4	1	3	3
Rhode Island	2		1		1			
New England	19	11	22	8	21	12	15	15
New York	11	12	14	13	12	14	16	9
New Jersey	5	1	4		4	2	4	
Pennsylvania	20	3	14	6	18	4	10	13
Delaware	1							
Maryland	5		6		7		6	
Mid-Atlantic	42	16	38	19	41	20	36	22
Virginia	7	10	7	12	6	11	4	9
North Carolina		9		10	2	9		8
South Carolina		4		6	3	4		5
Georgia	1	3		5	1	4		4
South Atlantic	8	26	7	33	12	28	4	26
Ohio	14		12		14		11	
Indiana	3		3		3		3	
Illinois	1		1					
Missouri			1		1		1	
Kentucky	12		11		11		12	
Northwest	30		28		29		27	
Tennessee	4	1	4	4	6	1	5	3
Alabama	1	1		3		1	1	
Louisiana	2		2		3		2	1
Mississippi	1							
Southwest	8	2	6	7	9	2	8	4
Total	107	55	101	67	112	62	90	67

Source: House Journal, 19th Cong. 2d sess, pp. 314–315, 320–321, 335–336, 375–376.

Note: Tables 4.1 (House) and 4.2 (Senate) show the major internal improvement roll calls in 1827. Each house passed some of the bills without a division. Though most members

TABLE 4.2
INTERNAL IMPROVEMENTS, SENATE, 1827

	Indiana Canal Grant		Cumberland Road (construction)		Surveys	
	For	*Against*	*For*	*Against*	*For*	*Against*
Maine	1	1	1	1	1	1
Vermont	2		2		2	
New Hampshire	1	1		1		1
Massachusetts	1		2		2	
Connecticut	1	1	1		1	
Rhode Island	2		2		2	
New England	8	3	8	2	8	2
New York		1		2		2
New Jersey	1	1	1		1	1
Pennsylvania	1	1	1	1	1	1
Delaware	1	1	1	1		2
Maryland	2		2		2	
Mid-Atlantic	5	4	5	4	4	6
Virginia		2		2		2
North Carolina		2		1		2
South Carolina		2		2		2
Georgia		1		2		2
South Atlantic		7		7		8
Ohio	2		2		2	
Indiana	2		2		2	
Illinois	2		2		2	
Missouri	2		2		2	
Kentucky	1		1		1	1
Northwest	9		9		9	1
Tennessee	1		1	1		2
Alabama	2		1	1	2	
Louisiana	2		2		2	
Mississippi	1		1		1	
Southwest	6		5	2	5	2
Total	28	14	27	15	26	19

Source: *Senate Journal*, 19th Cong., 2d sess., pp. 179, 233–234.

voted consistently either for or against internal improvement, individual variations on particular measures preclude scaling or combining roll calls.

The campaign begins

While Congress deliberated, partisans of Andrew Jackson and John Quincy Adams began laying plans for the approaching presidential campaign of 1828. In the West, the emerging question was whether Adams's internal improvement policy could overcome Jackson's personal popularity and the odium of the "corrupt bargain." The 1826 congressional elections offered a preliminary test of strength, especially in Illinois and Missouri, where the congressmen who had delivered their states for Adams in 1825 sought vindication at the polls.

In Missouri, three-term incumbent John Scott faced challenger Edward Bates, a nonpartisan who received Bentonian and Jacksonian backing. Both candidates favored ceding the public lands to the Western states. Scott also advocated graduation, distribution of the land revenue to the states to support schools, and internal improvements. Scott justified his presidential choice in terms that Adams men throughout the Northwest would reiterate endlessly for the next two years:

> The union of interest and intercourse between the east and the west, is much stronger and more apparent, than that between the south and west. . . . The southern states, always have been, and still are, opposed to all our leading interests, such as the tariff, relief to purchasers of lands, manufactures, and all internal improvements whatever. . . . every appropriation we have had on those subjects, and more particularly roads and canals are due to the east.

The congressional voting record of Jackson's home state exposed the danger of his candidacy, Scott warned, for Tennessee was Southern as well as Western, and "as such she has always been divided . . . on all those great questions on which the west proper depends for prosperity."[31]

The outcome boded ill for Adams in 1828, and testified to the growth of Benton's power since his abortive attempt to unseat David Barton two years earlier. Bates beat Scott decisively in the August election; four months later, Benton himself was returned to the Senate, partly on the strength of the graduation issue.[32]

In Illinois, an unknown Jacksonian named Joseph Duncan challenged four-term incumbent Daniel Cook, while Cook's father-in-law, Ninian Edwards, ran for governor. Duncan declared for graduation. Cook stressed his record on internal improvements, while his press ridiculed graduation as an electioneering scheme.

Cook's opponents in three previous campaigns had accused him of opposing the reduction of land prices in the Land Act of 1820. Thrice Cook fought the charges down, showing that he had favored price reductions but opposed abolishing the credit system, in company with Edwards and Henry Clay. But in 1826 an "ingeniously contrived" election handbill repeated the slanders against both Edwards and Cook. Edwards won the governorship anyway, but Duncan scored a stunning upset over Cook. Edwards thought the land issue "had far more influence than all other considerations united" upon Cook's defeat. Cook agreed, ruefully informing Adams that on the subject of the public lands, the minds of the Western people were "all debauched." Apparently the land issue could unseat an entrenched and popular congressman; perhaps it could also help to unseat a president.[33]

Northwesterners hurrahed for the internal improvement legislation of the Nineteenth Congress. "Appropriations for Canals Indian Treaties Roads & Everything ask^d. for have been obtain^d Huza for Indiana her fortune is made," exulted one breathless Hoosier. Both Jackson and Adams men hastened to exploit the issue. The latter credited the actions of Congress to the president's benign influence. He had made internal improvement the centerpiece of his policy; he was the patron of the West. "No President could have been more favorable to western interests than Mr. Adams," insisted the *Illinois Gazette*; "the West cannot, consistently with their own interests, desert him." He had done more for the new states in two years than any other president in four.[34]

In the Northwest the tariff also provided grist for the Adams campaign mill. Administration men pointed to the woolens bill of 1827, a protectionist measure which, like the Illinois canal a year earlier, was killed in the Senate by Calhoun's tie-breaking vote. From this vote and the preponderance of Jacksonians among internal improvement's congressional foes, Adams men drew the moral that Jacksonism was incompatible with the American System.[35]

According to Adams partisans, the votes of Southern Jacksonians offered the surest guide to the policy of a Jackson administration. "It cannot be disguised," warned the *Indiana Journal*, "that the opposers of the present administration, as a party, are also opposed to internal improvements—to encouraging domestic industry by imposing duties on foreign fabrics—to every thing which is demanded by the interests of the west." The abandonment of internal improvement by the South Carolinians just as they joined the Jackson coalition exposed the plan to sacrifice the West to Southern unity. "If it be on these grounds that General Jackson and Mr. Calhoun's friends are desirous to raise an opposition to the present administration, deserting their old grounds of friendship for the West and Western interests, we can state to them distinctly and confidently, that Illinois is not with them," said the *Illinois Gazette*. Recalling the Webster–McDuffie debate of 1825, a *Missouri Republican* writer warned that Jackson represented "the narrow, selfish paralyzing policy, which Mr. McDuffiie so unequivocally advocates, and which the South generally support him in."[36]

Western Adams men argued that Jackson's support for internal improvement in his brief 1824 Senate tenure did not constitute a commitment. Regardless of his personal views, Jackson's policy as president must be governed by the wishes of the Virginians and Carolinians who promoted him for office, and who were hostile to Western interests. Besides, Jackson himself was unreliable. His Western friends touted him as a Westerner, but was he? Some Adams men saw in the General's candidacy a plot to smuggle in a Southerner under a Western guise. "Let not the friends of the American System deceive themselves," enjoined an administration meeting in Indiana. "General Jackson is a southern man, in every sense of the word, and as such he was brought forward by southern politicians, who believed, with no other man could the western people be so easily deceived; and they knew very well, that without western aid, he could not be made President." Had Jackson been a true Westerner, the South would have rejected him, as it did Henry Clay, for that very reason.[37]

Such arguments were tailored more for Northwestern than for Southwestern ears. Internal improvement did still command a strong following in the Southwest, as evidenced by its prominence in local campaigns. In 1826 Thomas B. Reed, Mississippi candidate for United States senator, denounced Virginia strict constructionism and demanded internal improvements as a matter of "justice—*sheer justice!*—to the *new* States." His opponent, Powhatan Ellis, was "looked upon as a monster of political sin" for favoring a federal power of appropriation only, without right of jurisdiction. In Alabama, Mississippi, and Louisiana, governors and legislatures continued to press for federal aid to state road and canal projects.[38]

But two factors were working to undermine the Southwest's natural enthusiasm for federal internal improvements. The first was a growing suspicion that the region was being deliberately shortchanged. Congress showered the Northwest with Cumberland Road appropriations (more than two million dollars by 1827) and land grants; it subsidized canal companies in the mid-Atlantic and even South Atlantic states, and dotted the North Atlantic coast with harbor improvements. But Southwesterners had only trifling rewards to show for their efforts. While some saw that as all the more reason to push on, others were having second thoughts. "Our Citizens are very impatient to *feel* in their State the benefical effects of internal improvement," Louisiana representative Henry Gurley warned Henry Clay in 1826. "They are in favor of the system, but they want something here."[39]

More effective in corroding Southwestern support for internal improvement was its association with the protective tariff. Outside Louisiana, where powerful sugar interests required protection, the tariff was as roundly hated in the New South as in Virginia, the Carolinas, and Georgia. On this subject Mississippians and Alabamians agreed with their fellow planters to the east, not with their fellow pioneers to the north. And when joined to the tariff through the American System, an otherwise benign and necessary internal improvement policy acquired sinister and dangerous connotations. For, as Virginians had long complained, road and canal subsidies absorbed surplus revenues and thus perpetuated a tax burden borne mainly by the South. Following the lead of states' rights politicians in the Old South, a few Southwesterners began to construe the American System as a monstrous Northern plot to plunder Southern wealth. Their complaints, however, sounded a distinctively Western note. A *Louisiana Courier* correspondent warned that the American System, "stripped of its glittering mask, is in fact the most perfidious attack ever meditated against the prosperity of the new States," its real object "to stop the tide of emigration, in order to retard the population and the civilization of the Western regions." In January of 1827 the Alabama legislature, following Virginia and South Carolina, declared both the tariff and "a general system of internal improvements in the states as a national measure" unconstitutional. Even so, the state continued to solicit aid for its own projects. Alabama's resolutions stemmed at least partly from partisan motives (they also attacked Adams's controversial Panama mission), and did not pass without objection. But such a declaration from a Northwestern state would have been unthinkable under any circumstances.[40]

So the American System was likely to do Adams more harm than good in the Southwest, except perhaps in Louisiana. It did not much matter, as he had scant hope of carrying Alabama, Mississippi, or Tennessee anyway. But in Ohio, Indiana, Illinois, Missouri, and Kentucky, "American System" was a magic phrase. There no misgivings on the tariff compromised the universal enthusiasm for internal improvement, because Northwestern devotion to the protective policy was firm and longstanding. It was not the product of an ephemeral political coalition, least of all a coalition with New England. Every House and Senate member from the five Northwestern states had voted to raise the tariff in 1824; they would do so again (the Missouri representative alone excepted) in 1828. Apart from their future as manufacturers (held back according to Ohio's governor only by the efforts of "panic struck" Atlantic politicians "to impede our progress") and as food suppliers to urban centers, Northwesterners required immediate protection for existing industries—hemp in Kentucky, lead in Missouri and Illinois, and whiskey, flax, and wool. No part of the country gave the tariff and internal improvements, taken together, more wholehearted backing throughout the 1820s than the Northwest—not even Pennsylvania, the Eastern bastion of the American System. Adams needed some Northwestern states to carry the election, and if he could make the American System his own he might get them.[41]

Western Jacksonians dared not concede the issue. Led by Washington editor Duff Green, a Westerner and like Thomas Hart Benton an alumnus of the *St. Louis Enquirer*, they charged the president himself with hostility to the West. They denied that internal improvement was a party issue, pointing to the General's voting record in 1824 and the support of Western Jacksonians for the canal land grants. They even defended Jackson's running mate, Calhoun, assuring Westerners that he had not abandoned his internal improvement principles. The real difference between the candidates, according to Green's *United States Telegraph*, was that Adams would loose a sycophantic horde of tollkeepers and policemen to trample on the rights of the states, while Jackson, like Monroe, would provide aid without seeking jurisdiction. James Polk of Tennessee and other Jackson lieutenants also attacked the administration for holding out as "lures to the people in different sections of the Union, many projects of Internal Improvement, never seriously intended to be performed."[42]

Jacksonians scoffed at the very idea of Western votes for Adams. "John Q. Adams, the old opponent of the improvement of the west, now its pretended advocate!" a Natchez paper sneered. The president's record exhibited a "spirit of systematic hostility" to the new states. "He *has* been their enemy, he *is* their enemy, and no doubt forever *will* be." Jacksonians hauled out Henry Clay's indictment of Adams from the last campaign and gleefully paraded it to show the administration's true colors. The Louisiana Purchase, the Ghent negotiations, the Texas treaty, and the Missouri crisis were all exhumed and

offered in evidence (however inaccurately) to convict Adams of im-
placable hatred toward the West. "By the authority of Mr. Clay himself,
I had been taught that Mr. Adams was an enemy to the West," explained Kentucky congressman Thomas Moore. For good measure,
Moore accused Adams of opposing the tariff and internal improvements.[43]

Western Jacksonians also hinted at the administration's opposition
to graduation. They could do no more, for Adams kept his opinions to
himself and no bill had yet come to a vote in Congress. In the Senate
David Barton railed against graduation, but Adams senators Josiah
Johnston of Louisiana and William Hendricks of Indiana spoke for
ceding the public domain to the states. The administration's position
was so unclear that as late as December 1827 an Indiana politician
hoped to receive the gift of the public domain "at the hand of *Either* of
the Grate Political parties—or both as I believe it is possible, to unite
thim on this object; from the rivalship that exists between them and
their disposition, to secure the support of the states concerned; to their
respective parties." Benton's graduation weapon was primed and
ready to fire, but he lacked ammunition.[44]

The Twentieth Congress

To many, the fate of the Adams administration appeared to rest in the
hands of the new Twentieth Congress, which convened in December of
1827. "Whether the present Administration was to stand or fall . . . we
do not hesitate to say, is to be decided during the ensuing session," said
the Huntsville, Alabama, *Southern Advocate*. A Pennsylvania Adams
man, frustrated at his neighbors' simultaneous enthusiasm for Jackson
and the American System, hoped the session would "open their eyes."
Planners in both camps surveyed the agenda with an eye to advantage
at the polls.[45]

Administration strategists Henry Clay and Daniel Webster planned
to press again for a higher tariff, defeated by Vice-President Calhoun's
casting vote in the Senate the previous year. As for internal improvements, Clay told Webster he was "most anxious . . . that they should be
supported in New England, and that the West and Pennsa. should be
made sensible of that support. . . . You have your equivalents in other
forms. . . . We must keep the two interests of D[omestic] M[anufac-
tures] & I[nternal] I[mprovements] allied."[46]

Since his daring first annual message, Adams had avoided controversial recommendations on domestic issues. But the Western
clamor for cheap land alarmed him, and this might be his last chance to

address Congress except as a lame duck. He decided to say something in defense of the current land system:

> The acquisition of them [the lands], made at the expense of the whole Union, not only in treasure but in blood, marks a right of property in them equally extensive. . . . The system upon which this great national interest has been managed was the result of long, anxious, and persevering deliberation. Matured and modified by the progress of our population and the lessons of experience, it has been hitherto eminently successful. More than nine-tenths of the lands still remain the common property of the Union, the appropriation and disposal of which are sacred trusts in the hands of Congress.[47]

A few years before, Adams's remarks would have been considered innocuous truisms, the like of which appeared regularly in the messages of Presidents Madison and Monroe. But that was before Benton's discovery that the public lands belonged to the people, not to the federal government. In cabinet discussion Clay approved the passage, though he anticipated Western displeasure. At his suggestion Adams softened the impact by recommending that forfeiters under the credit system be allowed land office credit to compensate their losses. This and other relief measures were still universally popular in the West.[48]

The president's language implied rather than stated his opposition to graduation or cession. The real bombshell came four days later, in the annual report of Secretary of the Treasury Richard Rush. Adams had not mentioned the tariff, but with his approval Rush recommended an increase in protective duties. He recited several standard arguments, but the one that caught the eye of Thomas Hart Benton was this:

> The creation of capital is retarded rather than accelerated by the diffusion of a thin population over a great surface of soil. Any thing that may serve to hold back this tendency to diffusion from running too far, and too long, into an extreme, can scarcely prove otherwise than salutary. . . . It cannot be overlooked, that the prices at which fertile bodies of land may be bought of the government, under this system, operate as a perpetual allurement to their purchase. . . . It has served, and still serves, to draw, in an annual stream, the inhabitants of a majority of the States . . . into the settlement of fresh lands, lying still farther and farther off. If the population of these States, not yet redundant in fact, though appearing to be so under this legislative incitement to emigrate, remained fixed in more instances, as it probably would, by extending the motives to manufacturing labor, it is believed that the nation at large would gain.[49]

Probably neither Adams nor Rush saw anything controversial in the passage. Like the president's homily on the public lands, Rush's argument contained nothing novel, and, by pre-Bentonian standards, nothing exceptionable. Former president Madison, certainly no American System man, found nothing wrong in it—and he noted that the competition of cheap Western lands also thwarted agricultural rejuvenation in Virginia. In 1824 Andrew Jackson himself had invoked identical logic and used much franker language in endorsing a "judicious" but definitely protective tariff. Jackson thought there was "too much labor employed in agriculture"; he suggested dragooning six hundred thousand people off the farm and into workshops. But all this was now forgotten.[50]

Administration presses hailed Rush's vindication of the American System. "The Secretary of the Treasury's warm recommendations of INTERNAL IMPROVEMENTS and the encouragement of DOMESTIC MANUFACTURES, have confounded the opposition Editors, and left them scarcely a single thing to carp at," crowed the St. Louis *Missouri Republican*. But in fact Rush's report, coupled with Adams's message, gave Thomas Hart Benton exactly what he wanted: proof that the administration opposed graduation.[51]

For three years Benton had directed all his energies to politically reuniting the West and South. While in the East his ally Martin Van Buren labored to attach Pennsylvania and New York to Jackson's cause by reviving the old Jeffersonian coalition of "planters of the South and the plain Republicans of the North," Benton worked to combine West and South under the banner of states' rights, strict construction, and Andrew Jackson.[52]

The chief barrier to Benton's alliance was the American System. Unifying the South posed little problem: Southeast and Southwest were as one in their defense of slavery, and their mutual opposition to the tariff was working to erase, or at least obscure, their differences on internal improvements. But Northwesterners hailed both the tariff and internal improvements as Western policies, and branded opponents of either as enemies of the West. As long as this attitude prevailed, there existed no basis for cooperation between Northwest and Old South.

But just as the South hated the tariff, the West craved cheap land. Rush's report provided the essential link between the two in the form of a common Northeastern enemy, allowing Western Jacksonians to denounce the Adams–Rush version of the American System as not really Western at all, but rooted in hostility to Western growth. The tariff, charged Benton, now appeared "under new and revolting auspices, as the antagonist to my Graduation bill, and as having the foundations of its success laid in a diminution of emigration to the West." An alliance of Northeast and West was "*an unnatural connection,*" cried Duff Green's *United States Telegraph*; the Northeast had never lost its desire "*to check the growth of the West!*" Rush's report, said Green, meant simply this: "Any thing that will stop the emigration to the *West*, will be good for the *East*."[53]

In the Senate Benton repeatedly held out the hand of friendship to the states' rights men of the Old South. He emphasized the increased revenue his graduation bill would produce, thus hastening the extinction of the national debt and the reduction of the tariff. He even introduced resolutions denying federal powers of jurisdiction and repair over the Cumberland Road. Given his Missouri constituency, that was as far as he could go. He continued to vote for internal improvements and, reluctantly, for the protective tariff of 1828. Even so, his overtures prompted his Missouri enemies to charge that he had "abandoned his former principles, or rather professions, on the Tariff and Improvements, and has bound himself, body and soul, to the South."[54]

Benton expected his payoff on graduation. In the two years since Virginians Randolph and Tazewell first offered to give up the public lands to preserve strict construction, a constitutional confrontation between Georgia and the Adams administration over Indian lands had further assimilated the frontier and the Old South to a common states' rights viewpoint. Georgia answered the president's efforts to protect the Creeks and Cherokees with an assertion of sovereignty and jurisdiction that exactly paralleled the Western claim to ownership of the public domain. Here was an excellent opportunity for sectional cooperation, for frontiersmen from Alabama to Indiana were eager to drive out Indians and grab Indian lands. Seizing his chance, Benton wrote the Senate committee report sustaining Georgia's position against Adams. Alabama and Mississippi promptly prepared to follow Georgia's lead.[55]

For four years Benton had merely placed his graduation bill before Congress, sometimes at the tail end of a session. In 1828 he brought it in early, and pressed it to a vote. An amendment substituting cession for graduation allowed William Hendricks of Indiana and John McKinley of Alabama to deliver lengthy harangues on state sovereignty, which circulated widely in the Western press. But cession was too drastic a remedy to draw any Atlantic support. The amendment was shelved, and the issue joined on graduation.[56]

The ensuing debate followed familiar sectional lines, with Easterners and Westerners disputing which had received the greater share of federal largesse. But with an eye on the Old South, Western Jacksonians also harped on Rush's tariff recommendations. Benton, summing up, paid court to the Southerners, promising to cheerfully accept amendments at their "friendly hands."[57]

Benton's foes unwittingly strengthened his hand on the very first graduation roll call. David Barton proposed an amendment to lengthen the intervals between land price reductions from one year to five, and to measure the intervals in each case from the date of auction. Benton's bill, by contrast, would reduce prices on all untaken lands simultaneously, no matter when they had come into market. Barton's substitute would abruptly lower prices in the old districts, while postponing reductions on lands recently put up for sale. The amendment patently favored the old West over the new. But, Benton exclaimed, it also favored the North over the South, Ohio and Indiana (where land offices had long been open) over Mississippi and Louisiana, and Michigan Territory over Arkansas and Florida, all in order to shift political power to the North and sneak in a new free state before its slave counterpart.

Benton's bold seizure of the slavery issue produced a startling sectional division on Barton's amendment:[58]

	For	Against
New England	8	2
Mid-Atlantic	6	2
South Atlantic		7
West	1	17
	15	28

The graduation bill went through seven subsequent amendment roll calls, four of a sectional character. On each the West was unanimous, except for Barton and a stray vote in Kentucky. Most of the South Atlantic senators aligned with the West against the Northeast. Webster of Massachusetts, Van Buren of New York, and Dickerson of New Jersey all spoke against the bill. On the amendments the coalition of West and South held the majority, but on the bill's third reading John

Tyler of Virginia and the four Carolinians faltered, and graduation failed by a narrow margin:[59]

	For	Against
New England		12
Mid-Atlantic	1	7
South Atlantic	3	5
West	17	1
	21	25

Benton could take some satisfaction at the outcome. Graduation had very nearly passed the Senate, and had clearly received more Southern than Northern support. That in itself was phenomenal, for recently no region of the country had more implacably opposed Western sectional measures than the Old South. On the other hand, the Southern failure to deliver a majority spelled defeat for the bill, and this after it was extensively modified to suit Southern specifications. Westerners still had reason to doubt professions of friendship from Virginia, the Carolinas, and Georgia. They were reminded only three weeks after graduation's defeat, when a bill to compensate land forfeiters in accordance with Adams's recommendation—an extremely popular measure in the West—provoked the following Senate division:[60]

	For	Against
New England	5	6
Mid-Atlantic	7	2
South Atlantic		6
West	17	
	29	14

Clearly there still existed something less than a perfect community of interest between the Old South and the West on matters pertaining to the public domain.

Meanwhile the friends of the American System had been active. As usual a Cumberland Road appropriation prompted the first division on internal improvements, and as usual Virginians and Carolinians squared off against Westerners in debate. The vote leagued nearly all the Adams men with Jacksonians from the mid-Atlantic and Northwestern states. The Jackson camp split sharply, Northwesterners voting for the road and Southeasterners against it. Southwestern Jacksonians divided evenly. Louisianians supported the road; Tennesseans opposed it (see table 4.3).[61]

TABLE 4.3
CUMBERLAND ROAD, 1828

SENATE[a]

	Adams		Jackson		Total	
	For	*Against*	*For*	*Against*	*For*	*Against*
New England	7	1		2	7	4[b]
Mid-Atlantic	3	1	4	2	7	3
South Atlantic				8		8
Northwest	6		4		10	
Southwest	2		3	3	5	3
Total	18	2	11	15	29	18

HOUSE

	Adams		Jackson		Total	
	For	*Against*	*For*	*Against*	*For*	*Against*
New England	25	3		2	25	5
Mid-Atlantic	26	1	29	6	55	7
South Atlantic	6	4	4	31	10	35
Northwest	17	1[c]	13		30	1
Southwest	2		6	6	8	6
Total	76	9	52	45	128	54

Sources: *Senate Journal*, 20th Cong., 1st sess., pp. 116, 291; *House Journal*, 20th Cong., 1st sess., pp. 352–354. Presidential affiliations are from George R. Nielsen, "The Indispensable Institution: The Congressional Party During The Era of Good Feelings" (Ph.D. diss., University of Iowa, 1968), pp. 269–271, 303–307, 314–316. Nielsen's House affiliations are identical to those listed in *Niles' Weekly Register* 35 (September 20, 1828): 55–57, except in two instances.

[a]Senate data combine two roll calls, with a cohesion of 98% (see note to table 2.1). The single senator who voted inconsistently, Samuel Bell of New Hampshire (an Adams man), has been omitted from the table. Another roll call, on Benton's resolutions against federal powers of jurisdiction over the road, yielded a partisan division (*Senate Journal*, 20th Cong., 1st sess., pp. 321–322, 346).

[b]The party columns omit Albion K. Parris, an obscure Maine senator whom Nielsen does not classify, and who served only a single session. He voted against internal improvement.

[c]The lone Northwestern vote against the bill came from Jonathan Jennings of Indiana, who wanted to strike the "unfair and illegitimate condition" that the appropriation must be repaid out of the 2 percent fund. Jennings feared that the huge overdrafts on the fund would be invoked as an excuse to shut off further appropriations (Jennings to his constituents, April 7, 1828, in *Governors Messages and Letters*, vol. 12 of the Indiana Historical Collections [Indianapolis: Indiana Historical Commission, 1924], 3: 258–262).

The same mix of sectionalism and partisanship appeared on roll calls on a million-dollar purchase of Chesapeake and Ohio Canal stock and an omnibus internal improvement bill, both of which passed. But partisanship prevailed on an appropriation to continue internal improvement surveys under the Survey Act of 1824. Opponents attempted to restrict the expenditure to surveys already begun, charging that Adams was distributing them for electioneering purposes. The restriction failed in the House, but passed in the Senate as Calhoun again cast his deciding vote against the American System.[62]

Eventually a compromise was arranged limiting the appropriation to works "deemed of national importance"—really a victory for the administration and the American System, since the wording merely repeated the language of the Survey Act of 1824. But the interjection of presidential politics produced a partisan voting pattern, as Jackson men from the mid-Atlantic and Southwestern states defected from the internal improvement coalition. (In New England and the Old South, there were no Jackson internal improvement men to defect.) But in the Northwest the loss was minimal. Only three Kentuckians deserted the fold, leaving Adams and Jackson men on the same side of the question in that region alone. Others might play party politics with internal improvement, but Northwesterners would not (see table 4.4).

The previous Congress had produced no land grants for the Southwest and only a small one for Ohio, though that state had borrowed heavily to build canals and held sixteen electoral votes in the coming election. The Twentieth Congress undertook to correct the oversights, beginning with a grant of 400,000 acres to Alabama to improve the Tennessee River (see table 4.5).

The Alabama bill offered Southwesterners an internal improvement bequest financially and constitutionally disentangled from the hated tariff. It required no federal spending, and, as it was explained by James Polk, the most thoroughgoing Western foe of internal improvements in Congress, it set no precedent for loose construction, since land grants derived from Congress's explicit authority over the public domain. All the Southwesterners, including Polk, voted for the bill.[63]

Now it was the turn of the Adams men to flee the fold. As Adams could not hope to carry Alabama, his followers gave the bill only tepid support in comparison to other internal improvement measures. Yet even in New England they delivered a majority for it, while neither sectional nor partisan considerations could shake the inflexible opposition of the Jacksonian intransigents of the Old South.

Land grants to Ohio occasioned frantic maneuvering in the closing days of the session, as party lieutenants bid for the vote of the state. In

1825 Ohio had authorized two canals from Lake Erie to the Ohio River: the Ohio Canal via the Cuyahoga, Muskingum, and Scioto valleys, and the Miami Canal from Cincinnati to Dayton, with a planned northward extension via the Maumee. Early in the congressional session Representative John Woods of Ohio, an Adams man, produced from the Committee on Roads and Canals a land grant for the Miami Canal extension (five sections per mile on the alternate-

TABLE 4.4
INTERNAL IMPROVEMENT SURVEYS, 1828

SENATE[a]

	Adams		Jackson		Total	
	For	*Against*	*For*	*Against*	*For*	*Against*
New England	8	2		2	8	4
Mid-Atlantic	3	1	2	4	5	5
South Atlantic				8		8
Northwest	6		3	1	9	1
Southwest	2			6	2	6
Total	19	3	5	21	24	24

HOUSE[b]

	Adams		Jackson		Total	
	For	*Against*	*For*	*Against*	*For*	*Against*
New England	29	4		4	29	8
Mid-Atlantic	29	2	15	25	44	27
South Atlantic	7	3	2	35	9	38
Northwest	18		11	2	29	2
Southwest	2		1	12	3	12
Total	85	9	29	78	114	87

Sources: *Senate Journal*, 20th Cong., 1st sess., pp. 288, 290, 350–351; *House Journal*, 20th Cong., 1st sess., pp. 388–390, 625–627, 692–694.

Note: "For" indicates a vote against restricting expenditure to surveys already begun.

[a]The Senate tabulation combines three roll calls with cohesion of 100% (see note to table 2.1).

[b]The House tabulation combines three roll calls with paired cohesions of 94%, 95%, and 94% (see note to table 2.1). Fifteen House members did not vote consistently. Eleven who voted the same way two out of three times are included on that side in the table; four who voted on each side once and were absent once are omitted.

section plan, with the federal sections to sell at double minimum, or $2.50 per acre). Thereupon the Public Lands Committee reported a grant of 500,000 acres for the Ohio Canal, sponsored by Ohio Jacksonian William Stanbery. Stanbery's efforts to reverse their order on the calendar having failed, the House passed Woods's bill, then narrowly rejected Stanbery's as administration men dove for the exits. The Senate also passed Woods's bill, but appended Stanbery's entire bill as an amendment. With only one day left before adjournment, Ohio was either going to get two land grants or none at all. In the House enough foes of Stanbery's bill relented to allow the Senate's amendment to stand, and Ohio emerged twice endowed.[64]

Both sides played politics with the Ohio land grants. Twenty-eight of the thirty-one representatives who favored Woods's bill but opposed Stanbery's were Adams men. On the other side, thirteen members, all

TABLE 4.5
ALABAMA LAND GRANT, 1828

SENATE

	Adams		Jackson		Total	
	For	*Against*	*For*	*Against*	*For*	*Against*
New England	4	3		2	4	5
Mid-Atlantic	2		1	1	3	1
South Atlantic				7		7
Northwest	2		4		6	
Southwest	2		5		7	
Total	10	3	10	10	20	13

HOUSE

	Adams		Jackson		Total	
	For	*Against*	*For*	*Against*	*For*	*Against*
New England	12	10	1	2	13	12
Mid-Atlantic	17	4	15	13	32	17
South Atlantic	5	5	5	23	10	28
Northwest	13	3	13		26	3
Southwest	2		12		14	
Total	49	22	46	38	95	60

Sources: Senate Journal, 20th Cong., 1st sess., pp. 238–239; *House Journal*, 20th Cong., 1st sess., pp. 788–790.

Jacksonian, voted for Stanbery's bill and against Woods's. But again party concerns were strongly crossed by sectionalism. Three-quarters of the House voted either for or against both bills. While Eastern representatives bandied the grants back and forth, the Ohioans cheerfully voted for both of them, as did every other member from the public land states and most of the Kentuckians and Tennesseans. On the other side, Virginia, the Carolinas, and Georgia contributed more than half of the fifty-nine votes against both grants.[65]

Meanwhile Congress also took up a bill to raise the tariff. Partisan manipulation of the individual schedules caused the end product to be dubbed the "tariff of abominations," but in the final voting party lines broke down altogether. Mid-Atlantic and Northwestern members were nearly unanimous for protection, Southerners united against it. Only New England failed to take a clear sectional stand (see table 4.6).[66]

The congressional divisions on the tariff, internal improvements, and land policy produced a precise picture of political alignments on the eve of the 1828 presidential election. It was an instructive demonstration for those who thought in terms of sectional alliances. On the American System issues the Northwest and the Old South stood at opposite poles. The Southwest fluctuated between them, joining with the Northwest on land grants but with the Old South on the tariff. On internal improvement subsidies, contradictory impulses pulled Southwesterners both ways. Northwesterners, undisturbed by qualms about the tariff, voted for internal improvements of all kinds. The mid-Atlantic and New England members also generally favored Western road and canal projects, but theirs was a fluctuating support, a support bottomed partly on partisanship—a support that could be bought. Daniel Webster made no bones about it. "It may be said, with entire truth, and it ought to be said, and it ought to be known, that no one measure of internal improvement has been carried through congress, or could have been carried, but by the aid of New England votes. It is for those most deeply interested in subjects of that sort to consider in season, how far the same aid is necessary for the further prosecution of the same objects." On the other side, the Old South held forth the promise of lower land prices. But it was only a promise and, judging by the Senate vote on the relief question, one of questionable sincerity.[67]

The campaign in the West: graduation versus the American System

Adams men invoked the record of the Twentieth Congress as a text for their favorite theme: "The real question, the only question of policy and principle, that is at issue between the supporters of Mr. Adams and those of Gen. Jackson, is this: 'Shall the American System be adopted as a great leading national measure or not?' " The administration press followed the internal improvement roll calls closely all through the session, highlighting the votes of Jackson's Southern friends. Adams men also ascribed the land debtor relief legislation to the president's influence, proving again his benevolence to the West.[68]

The Jacksonians responded in kind. The Indiana Jackson convention proclaimed him "the sincere and zealous but consistent friend" of the American System. According to party conventions in Illinois, Jack-

TABLE 4.6
PROTECTIVE TARIFF, 1828

SENATE[a]

	Adams		Jackson		Total	
	For	*Against*	*For*	*Against*	*For*	*Against*
New England	6	3		2	6	5
Mid-Atlantic	3	1	5	1	8	2
South Atlantic				8		8
Northwest	6		4		10	
Southwest	1	1	1	5	2	6
Total	16	5	10	16	26	21

HOUSE[b]

	Adams		Jackson		Total	
	For	*Against*	*For*	*Against*	*For*	*Against*
New England	15	20	1	3	16	23
Mid-Atlantic	27	5	33	6	60	11
South Atlantic	3	7		39	3	46
Northwest	17	1	13		30	1
Southwest		2		14		16
Total	62	35	47	62	109	97

Sources: *Senate Journal*, 20th Cong., 1st sess., pp. 406, 410; *House Journal*, 20th Cong., 1st sess., pp. 577–580, 607–609.

[a]Senate divisions on third reading and passage were identical.

[b]The House tabulation combines the roll calls on third reading and passage, with a cohesion of 99 + % (see note to table 2.1). The sole representative who changed his vote is omitted from the table.

son was also "friendly to the reduction of the present price of public lands," an assertion based rather on faith than on evidence. Jacksonians claimed the credit for the Ohio canals and other internal improvements, pointing out that Jacksonian majorities controlled both houses of Congress. Thomas Moore explained that "Gen. Jackson himself is a *Western man*, and those who support him, naturally have a friendly feeling for the Western country." The Indiana Jackson central committee declared that "Jackson is not, nor ever was, southern in his locality, or southern in his policy." Even Calhoun was defended as "the FRIEND and ZEALOUS ADVOCATE of *Internal Improvements*."[69]

Jackson himself followed Thomas Hart Benton's advice and said nothing. At last the Indiana state senate, tiring of this peculiar campaign by proxy in which just about anything could be asserted about a candidate and demonstrated by reference to the opinions of his friends, decided to smoke the General out. At its direction Governor James B. Ray brought the discrepant views of his Western and Southern followers to Jackson's attention and demanded to know just where the candidate really stood. Jackson answered Ray's request for "your *present* opinions of Tariff laws" and internal improvements with a copy of his 1824 endorsement of a "judicious" protective revision of the tariff of 1816. What this meant now he did not explain.[70]

Western Jacksonians preferred to discuss another subject altogether—graduation. In a widely broadcast pamphlet edition of his speeches, Benton laid the blame for graduation's defeat at the administration's door. Graduation "has been defeated in the Senate by the New England votes," said Mississippi representative William Haile, proving them "enemies of the West, and of the South." Benton's Missouri paper shouted "that the Administration party in the Senate, with *David Barton* at their head, VOTED AGAINST THE GRADUATION BILL.—Can there now be any doubt of the hostility of Messrs. Adams & Rush, *and their whole party in Congress*, to the adoption of any measure calculated to promote the prosperity or grandeur of the West?" A Missourian explained to Jackson:

> I am a *Western* man. I have my sectional feelings as well as other men. I know, of which you Sir, are aware, the difficulties of settling a *new* Country. I know the services you have rendered to the Nation & particularly to the West. . . . Our mutual and distinguished friend Col. Benton has contributed much to the good cause in this state by exposing the unfriendly disposition of M. Adams & Rush to the growth and prosperity of the *West*, by interposing their influence against his favorite graduation bill—A measure that all most every one feel the deepest interest in, who live in the New States. I have

taken the liberty, General, to state to my acquaintances, on the authority of Col. Benton, that you are friendly to that measure. I hope he has
not misled me. Indeed, it appears, to me, such a commonsense measure, that I cannot see how any honest politician can seriously oppose
it, unless indeed, it be to keep *down* the West![71]

A Louisiana Jackson meeting declared the contest to be "between
those who desire the settlement of the western lands, and those who
wish them to remain a howling wilderness." The *Louisiana Advertiser*
said the president's mind was "warped by the desire of retaining our
population in the Atlantic and Eastern States and by hostility to the
West." While Adams men attacked Calhoun as an enemy of the American System, Western Jacksonians villified Adams's vice-presidential
nominee, Richard Rush, for torpedoing graduation with his tariff
recommendations.[72]

Senator William King of Alabama cried that "every feature" of the
American System was "marked with injustice and oppression." Jacksonians to the northward dared not attack the system itself. But they
denounced the administration's version as a travesty of the original.
The true American System, they said, protected Western products and
promoted Western growth through internal improvements, but
Adams's policy, though masquerading under the name, did nothing of
the sort. Rather, it aimed at subordinating the West to the Northeast.
The tariff drew wealth from Western consumers to Northeastern
manufacturers. Internal improvements wasted the excess tariff revenue on improving the rivers and harbors of New England. The third
and crucial element, revealed by Rush, was a land policy designed to
prevent emigration, impede Western political growth, and immobilize
the Eastern population as a cheap labor force for manufacturers.[73]

"The party which supports Gen. Jackson is the same which supports
the bill for Graduating the price of public lands," announced the *St.
Louis Advertiser*. In Missouri this was true. David Barton's press stood by
Adams and attacked "Benton's Land Hoax" all through the 1828
campaign. Representative Edward Bates, who had turned out to be an
Adams man after all, advocated Barton's alternative of free lands for
actual settlers, while the new Jacksonian challenger, Spencer Pettis,
stuck "to the *precise* letter" of Benton's graduation. But elsewhere in the
West Adams men went for graduation as enthusiastically as the Jacksonians. The *Illinois Intelligencer*, an administration paper, tirelessly repeated what was in fact true: the Senate vote on graduation was not a
partisan one, either in the West (Missouri excepted) or anywhere else.
Thirteen Adams senators and twelve Jacksonians had voted against the

bill. "Both parties in the western states agree as to the principle," said the *Intelligencer*; further, the charge that Adams himself had declared against graduation was "absolutely and positively false," a "barefaced attempt to deceive and delude the people."[74]

Most Western Adams men preferred to skirt the president's opinions on the public lands. But in their local campaigns they cried for cheap land as loudly as the Jacksonians. In Illinois, George Forquer, administration candidate for Congress against Joseph Duncan (who had unseated Daniel Cook two years earlier) mounted a clumsy agitation for an immediate reduction in land prices. In Indiana, Adams congressman Jonathan Jennings urged "a well timed, a regular and prudent perseverance" for graduation, and begged to be returned to his seat "on account of the pending and unsettled question in relation to the public lands." The tendency of the Western presidential campaign to set off the American System against graduation did not reach down to local politics, where men of both camps toed the same line on sectional issues.[75]

Denouement

In the autumn of 1828 voters went to the polls. Adams carried New England, the small mid-Atlantic states, and part of New York. Jackson swept everywhere else. Thomas Hart Benton congratulated Martin Van Buren on Jackson's success in New York: "I also was right about the West, not one vote there!" A Missouri Adams paper despairingly surveyed the wreckage of the administration's hopes. Graduation had returned Benton to the Senate, "aided, most materially, in giving the vote of the State to Gen. Jackson," and "prostrated" Representative Bates's bid for reelection. Barton was marked as its next victim. Then what? "We cannot believe that the President elect will venture to recommend this policy in his first message, or even to countenance it. Why, then, is this popular delusion to be kept up . . . ?"[76]

What part did the land issue play in the election? Was graduation really, as the *Missouri Republican* said, a "political guillotine" in the Western states? Many politicians thought so. In July 1828 Daniel Webster had reported fading hopes for Adams in Indiana, because "Govr. Ray has been playing double; & the people in that State are also mightily taken with the project of graduating the price of the public lands." In Ohio, according to one informant, tenant farmers and new immigrants voted for Jackson believing that "Col. Benton's plan would succeed and each get a quarter section of land." In August of 1829

Benton himself advised Sam Houston, then between careers, that the public lands and the Texas boundary were "the two *levers* to move public sentiment in the West. If you have ulterior views your *tongue* and *pen* should dwell incessantly upon these two great topics." The eagerness with which Western politicians extolled graduation and cession showed their conviction of the issue's importance to voters.[77]

At the same time, for every newspaper column and campaign speech on the great national issues, there were three or four on Adams's White House furnishings, Jackson's premarital relations, and other such stuff. The role of specific issues in presidential elections, by nature unmeasurable, is always problematic and was never more so than in the 1828 campaign, which dealt largely in personalities and which ranks among the dirtiest in American history. The returns displayed a clear sectional pattern, but one not always explainable by reference to issues. In the West Adams nearly won Ohio, where graduation was weak and the American System strong; and he ran well in the protectionist sugar parishes of Louisiana. But in Pennsylvania, tariff to the core, Jackson beat him two to one.[78]

In retrospect, Jackson's election seems all but inevitable. Adams was not a popular man, and his administration never threw off the taint of illegitimacy that attached to its birth. His only real chance to win was to engraft the national majority for internal improvements and domestic manufactures onto his own candidacy. That this majority existed was made plain by the record of the last three Congresses. But the Jacksonians deflected the administration's efforts to make the campaign a referendum on the American System. They outmanaged the Adams forces at all levels, and capitalized superbly on their candidate's personal attributes. Given Jackson's unchallenged supremacy in the slave states, Pennsylvania alone was enough to seal the result.

The land issue cost Adams some votes in the West. That by itself it cost him any state is doubtful. Benton's exertions in the West, like Martin Van Buren's in the East, helped turn what might have been a close Jackson victory into a rout. Their real impact appeared after the election was over. The manipulation of issues for campaign purposes produced unforeseen consequences. As the electioneering "tariff of abominations" was father to the nullification crisis, so the electioneering crusade for graduation and cession threatened to produce a crisis in the public land system.

Spurred on by Benton in Jackson's behalf, the agitation for cheap land had intensified as the campaign drew to a close. The Western states bombarded Washington with memorials couched in language the president found "little short of frantic—a blustering, bullying style, which many of the State Governors and Governments adopt towards the General Administration, as if they considered insolence as their only means of demonstrating their sovereignty." Graduation's Senate defeat in 1828 only whetted expectations; the *United States Telegraph* promised success next year when Adams and Rush "will have no *official* influence . . . to oppose to the prayers, and wishes, and interests, of the western people!"[79]

The excitement crested just after the election. Emotions raised to fever pitch by the campaign now threatened to rage out of control. The governors of Mississippi and Louisiana again demanded graduation or cession. In December Ninian Edwards, now governor of Illinois, devoted nearly his whole biennial message to a tirade against federal landownership in the states. Edwards declared the system "absolutely null and void" and suggested forcing a judicial test of the federal title.[80]

Not everyone took Edwards seriously. Somehow his rhetoric always seemed too strident to carry conviction. An Illinois politician later recalled that Edwards put forth his "humbug" argument, "without having any confidence in its validity," to redeem his failing political fortunes in Illinois. Henry Clay, among others, suspected that Edwards was trying to follow Thomas Hart Benton on the land crusade to fame and popularity.[81]

The skeptics may have been right. The defeat of his son-in-law Daniel Cook in 1826 had surely taught Edwards the explosiveness of the land issue. And deep schemes were afoot in Washington, where Vice-President Calhoun's entourage was already girding for the succession struggle against Martin Van Buren. Edwards was a Calhounite from way back. In Calhoun's interest he had written the notorious "A. B." letters in 1823, impugning the integrity of Treasury secretary William Crawford. Backfiring, Edwards's accusations had wrecked his own promising national career and rendered his name an eternal curse in the mouths of Crawfordites. Now Duff Green, editor of the *United States Telegraph*, confidant to Calhoun, and brother-in-law to Edwards, advised the governor

> to press your land question, get up and continue the discussion in the newspapers of your own and the other Western states. Make yourself the head of that measure, and you will be forced into the Senate; . . . *Your* position in relation to the public lands brings you into company with the South and West and in direct conflict with the East. The consequences are easily seen, but the results will be the work of time, four years may not be enough.

Like Benton, Green contemplated a sectional alliance of South and West, but for the purpose of elevating Calhoun to the presidency.[82]

Leaving its motives aside (Green's letter was, in truth, after the fact), Edwards's message was well received in Illinois. The state press and Green's *Telegraph* in Washington greeted it warmly, the only uncertainty being whether the state should assert its rights with "a temperate manifesto" or another "whining memorial." After weighing both alternatives, the legislature chose the latter, though the memorial adopted in January 1829 read more like an ultimatum than a plea.[83]

Indiana went further. The legislature rejected a memorial to Congress, resolving instead "That this State, being a sovereign, free, and independent State, has the exclusive right to the soil and eminent domain of all the unappropriated lands within her acknowledged boundaries." In form this was neither a request nor an argument, but a bald statement of fact. But since the fact as stated by Indiana was of little import unless acknowledged by Congress, further resolutions required the governor to communicate with the other six public land states, and urged the state's congressmen "to use every exertion in their power, by reason and argument, to induce the United States to acknowledge this vested right."[84]

Some Westerners thought this was going too far. Critics like Senator James Noble and Representative Jonathan Jennings pointed out the inconsistency of Indiana's claim with its many requests for graduation, internal improvement land grants, and debtor relief, all of which tacitly acknowledged the federal right to the land. But their voices were drowned in an outpouring of sectional rhetoric unmatched since the debate over the Maryland proposition. Talk of state rights and state sovereignty filled the air. Alabama and Louisiana solicited Congress for cession the same winter, while Missouri demanded graduation in words that admitted no possibility of refusal. Senator John McKinley of Alabama thanked Congress for its recent river improvement land grant, but also reiterated the state's claim to all of the public domain. Extremists demanded that Alabama refuse the grant rather than acknowledge Congress's right to make it.[85]

Cession now bid fair to eclipse graduation as the leading object of Western land reformers. But the reaction of Congress in the lame duck session of 1828–1829 dampened the enthusiasm. The House of Representatives, openly hostile to the Indiana resolutions, at first rejected even the routine motion to print them. Congress did not debate cession directly, no bill having been offered, but a measure to cede the government's scattered holdings in Tennessee came under fire as "an entering wedge to the plan of getting rid of the whole of the public domain" and was quashed on a sectional vote.[86]

The reaction against cession even prompted a brief revival of the Maryland proposition. More significantly, it also produced a plan, drafted by Representative James Stevenson of Pennsylvania, to distribute the net land revenue among the states in proportion to their population. Distributing the land revenue had been much discussed in connection with the Maryland proposition of 1821, and since then several specific plans had been laid before Congress. In those earlier days distribution was not regarded as a sectional measure. Many Westerners favored it, as it would return part of the money they spent on land purchases. But that was before graduation dramatically raised Western expectations. Land revenue distribution now appeared as a device to thwart Western desires, not satisfy them. For as James Madison and Rufus King had both realized, vesting the Atlantic states with a direct pecuniary interest in the land revenue was the surest way to foil Western giveaway schemes.[87]

Preventing graduation or cession was Stevenson's avowed purpose. His report pounded home "the indisputable *right of soil*" belonging to the United States, and proposed "to give the States a direct interest in the income arising from the sales of the public lands" in the hope that it would "effectually check in the future the *giving away* this most invaluable national property."[88]

Stevenson's report lay on the table. But public reaction against cession in the old states matched the vehemence of the Western demands. The Eastern press, Green's *Telegraph* alone excepted, ridiculed the Western pretensions. (A few months later Russell Jarvis, Green's former partner, listed Green's approval of Ninian Edwards's "most startling doctrines" among the "political blunders" leading to the breakup of the partnership.) Northerners and Southerners, Adams and Jackson men, all spurned the Western claims. A North Carolina Jacksonian promised his constituents "to meet, promptly, such unjust pretensions, and, with measures suited to the emergency, resist the grasping usurpations" of the West.[89]

The land controversy merged into a general political uneasiness as Jackson's inauguration drew near. In the South as in the West, a clamor was rising. The great forward strides of the American System under Adams made Southerners feel they were being systematically plundered to feed the rest of the nation. *"We alone pay without indemnity,"* cried John C. Calhoun in 1827. In the cotton states of the Southwest, Southern and Western grievances merged, though some Southeast-

erners accused the whole West of complicity in the plot to reduce the
Old South to "a complete state of vassalage." The tariff of 1828
brought Southern outrage near the breaking point.[90]

To Calhoun in July of 1828, it seemed that "the goverment is rapidly
degenerating into a struggle among the parts to squeeze as much out of
one another as they possibly can." Calhoun held his newly fashioned
constitutional remedy in reserve and looked to Jackson to calm the
waters. Yet Jackson had promised nothing. His following included
American System men in the mid-Atlantic and Northwestern states,
Southern free traders and states' righters, and Western land reformers. Which of these would prevail in the new administration? No one
knew, certainly not Calhoun. Writing in January 1829, the vice-
president figured the protective system could be dismantled within two
or three years if Jackson would but pay the public debt "and prevent
the *distribution of the surplus revenue*, the point in my opinion of the
greatest danger." While Calhoun wrote, Jackson labored on a draft of
his inaugural address. It endorsed the distribution of the surplus.[91]

As the nation awaited the unveiling of the Hero's policy, uncertainty
surrounded all of the great internal questions—the tariff, internal
improvements, and the public lands. Confrontation between North
and South threatened over the tariff, while the lame-duck session of
the Twentieth Congress showed that victory at the polls had done
nothing to reconcile Western and Southern Jacksonians over internal
improvements. Lastly there was the growing Western threat to seize
the public domain, so ominous that Henry Clay, speaking "with great
concern of the prospects of the country" to President Adams, mentioned it in the same breath with Southern disunionism. All in all,
observed the *National Journal* in January of 1829, the land question
"begins to become a very tender one; and the time is not remote when it
will lead to a discussion involving more time and temper than any other
topic now or recently before congress."[92]

CHAPTER 5
SECTIONAL ALLIANCES
1830–1831

But the public lands—the public lands—this is the exciting theme, which brings every man to his seat, and every other question—tariff, roads, revenue, education—all slide insensibly into this.

New York Evening Post
January 26, 1830

Mr. Foot's resolution

Westerners greeted the new administration with high expectations. During the campaign they had been promised cheap land, and now under a Western president they expected to get it. Benton stoked the fires of sectional animosity all through the summer of 1829. Newspaper pieces poured from his pen, castigating the "cruel and inexorable spirit indulged by the North East against the West," and blaming the late administration for thwarting graduation. The tariff he attacked as an Eastern device *"for the purpose of preventing migration to the west—for the purpose of preserving the population to the old states."* And to his stock of Southern and Western issues—graduation, tariff reduction, Indian removal—Benton now added another, the annexation, or rather "re-annexation," of Texas. Benton improved the issue with the accusation that Secretary of State John Quincy Adams had intentionally surrendered the province to Spain in the Florida treaty of 1819 in order to block Southwestern expansion.[1]

But when Congress met in the fall of 1829 the East, not the West, took the offensive. In the House of Representatives Jonathan Hunt of Vermont revived the project to distribute the land revenue among the states. Hunt's resolutions sparked a sectional debate that fulfilled the *National Journal*'s prediction of "a long, arduous, and animated discussion" on distribution.[2]

Since the abolition of the credit system a decade earlier, most people in the Atlantic states had taken little notice of the land issue. However,

Benton's graduation campaign, the apparent Western preparations for state seizure of the public domain, and now the House distribution debate alerted many Easterners to the threat of an imminent sectional collision over land policy. The *American Quarterly Review* observed that in the West "the time is fast approaching"—it had already arrived— "when political aspirants, whatever may be their principles in other respects, will be required to be orthodox upon this all-absorbing question." A correspondent of the Philadelphia *United States Gazette* wrote that on the "momentous question" of the public lands "we may expect to have discussions which will shake the halls of Congress." The *Richmond Enquirer* saw the land system "beginning to present some of the most serious questions, which have ever been agitated in our public counsels," while a correspondent of the Fayetteville *North Carolina Journal* labelled land policy "a subject of much interest, great intricacy, growing importance, and one which will occupy much of the time and attention of Congress; indeed, it seems to pervade and have its influence over almost every other subject." The Milledgeville (Georgia) *Southern Recorder* thought "the time is approaching and perhaps near at hand, when the public lands . . . will become the cause of jealousy, if not a bone of contention, between the *old* and *new* States."[3]

All these forecasts of political foul weather appeared around the new year, so it surprised no one when the storm broke in the Senate in mid-January of 1830, while the House was still debating distribution. Only the source of the tempest was unexpected. For instead of graduation or distribution, the Senate was to spend much of the next four months discussing a resolution offered by Samuel A. Foot, an undistinguished Connecticut senator and an old foe of the West:

> That the Committee on Public Lands be instructed to inquire into the expediency of limiting for a certain period the sales of the public lands to such lands only as have heretofore been offered for sale, and are subject to entry at the minimum price. And also, whether the office of Surveyor General may not be abolished without detriment to the public interest.[4]

Foot offered his resolution on December 29, and there followed three weeks of preliminary rhetorical sparring. Benton's first major speech on January 18 opened the main event. Although Foot had seized the initiative, his resolution, like the messages of Adams and Rush two years before, yielded Benton the advantage. The revival of the old alliance of South and West hinged on transferring their mutual resentments on the tariff and the public lands to some third party. New England was the obvious choice. Its hostility to westward expansion in the Republic's early years was legendary (if perhaps exaggerated), and though New England was not responsible for the tariffs of 1824 and 1828, it could easily be made to appear so; for Daniel Webster and the Boston textile interests he represented were becoming the most visible advocates of protection. There were also the sins of John Quincy Adams, as delineated in the 1828 campaign, and the fact that he and Webster were both ex-Federalists. The cry of "Hartford Convention!" was always on Jacksonian lips, and the party devoted much of its rhetoric to attaching to Adams and his followers the odium of the Essex Junto and the Sedition Act. Foot, the mover of the resolution (and an Adams man), was no Federalist, but he was a known enemy of the West who had long opposed cheaper lands and had not, like Webster, balanced that stance by supporting internal improvements.[5]

Such were Benton's materials, and his speech on Foot's resolution made the most of them. The resolution's real purpose, he cried, was "to deliver up large portions of new States and Territories to the dominion of wild beasts"; it and distribution continued a long series of "measures of the same class, all tending to check the growth, and to injure the prosperity of the West, and all flowing from the same geographical quarter"—New England. Harkening back to Rush's report, Benton decried the tariff and Foot's resolution as twin instruments of a manufacturers' plot to close the Western safety valve and reduce Eastern workers to wage slavery. "A most complex scheme of injustice, which taxes the South to injure the West, to pauperize the poor of the North!" Benton begged the "solid phalanx of the South" and the "scattering reinforcements" of Northeastern Republicanism to rescue the beleaguered West.[6]

The very next day Senator Robert Hayne of South Carolina accepted Benton's alliance of South and West. Hayne was one of those Southern senators who had voted against the graduation bill in 1828. Though he had stood with its friends on preliminary questions, he had never then or since said a word for cheaper lands. But now, comparing the sufferings of the West to those of the South under the tariff, Hayne said the new states should "be invested in due season with the control of all the lands within their respective limits." He dismissed revenue as a consideration, praising the old colonial governments that wisely charged only " 'a penny,' or 'a pepper-corn' " for their lands.[7]

As he had defended the West from George McDuffie's reproaches in 1825, Daniel Webster now repelled the attacks upon New England. He began with a standard defense of the current land system, then took up the imputations of Northeastern hostility to Western growth: "I deny that the East has, at any time, shown an illiberal policy towards the

West. . . . I deny it in the general, and I deny each and all its particulars.
I deny the sum total, and I deny the detail." It was Benton, not Hayne,
who had indulged in sectional recriminations, but it was to Hayne that
Webster responded. And Hayne was vulnerable; for as Webster reminded the Senate, Hayne spoke for a section and a strict-
constructionist constitutional doctrine which sought to deny the West
every benefit it asked from the Union—protection for its industry,
appropriations and land grants for internal improvements and education, even the sanctity of the Union itself. "Consolidation!" taunted
Webster, "that perpetual cry, both of terror and delusion—consolidation!" Against Benton's examples of early New England hostility Webster cited the Northwest Ordinance, attributing its benign prohibition
of slavery to Massachusetts influence. Then he moved on to more
recent history:

> Will you take the Cumberland Road? Who has made that? Will you
> take the Portland Canal? Whose support carried that bill? Sir, at what
> period beyond the Greek kalends could these measures, or measures
> like these, have been accomplished, had they depended on the votes
> of Southern gentlemen?

Webster finished by quoting, with great relish, his 1825 exchange with
George McDuffie in the House of Representatives.[8]

The question was now clearly framed: would the West, or rather the
Northwest, continue to cooperate in Congress with the Northeast as it
had during the Adams administration, or would it cap the victory of
the Jacksonian electoral coalition of West and South by trading the
American System for a change in the land system? Consolidation or
states' rights? Internal improvements or graduation? The alternatives
appeared, sharp and distinct, in the first speeches of Webster and
Hayne, only to be obscured by issues even more pressing. Webster's
assault stung Hayne to defend both slavery and John C. Calhoun's new
doctrine of a state's right to nullify unconstitutional federal laws,
including protective tariffs. From there the public lands and even the
tariff were thrust aside as the two combatants grappled over the nature
of the Union itself, an exchange culminating in Webster's hosanna to
"Liberty *and* Union, now and forever, one and inseparable!"[9]

The Webster–Hayne debate quickly entered into patriotic legend,
for it struck to the heart of Americans' feelings about their country:
was the United States a great indissoluble nation, or a federation of
sovereign states? The debate also rose to the level of high drama, and
had it been shaped by a dramatist the curtain would have rung down
on Webster's peroration. But history, though often as interesting as

theatre, is rarely as compact; and by the time Webster sat down, he, Benton, and Hayne had let loose too many issues to be contained. Benton, spurning the American System, followed Webster with a four-day running indictment of New England, and from there the speakers blended into one another as the debate dragged on through February and March, taking in the lands, the tariff, internal improvements, slavery, nullification, the Supreme Court, presidential patronage, and a rehashing of the political history of the past fifty years. "The Tapeworm debate," observed John Quincy Adams in April, "is voiding all the sense and nonsense, all the wit and dulness, all the Patriotism and Scoundrelism of that body, with its commingled fragrance and fetidity to salute the nostrils of the Nation."[10]

In February Hayne's South Carolina colleague William Smith, a strict constructionist but no nullifier and no Calhounite, had denounced the American System and cheap lands alike. David Barton delivered a scathing (and, according to Jacksonians, drunken) personal attack on Benton, and was feted back to Missouri at the end of the session as the favorite guest speaker on the National Republican dinner circuit. (It was Barton's last hurrah. The guillotine hanging over his neck finally fell in November, when the Missouri legislature chose Alexander Buckner to replace him in the Senate. A comeback bid for Congress failed miserably the next year, and Barton's career in national politics was over. In 1837 he died, insane.) Benton, as usual, insisted on the last word. On May 21, following his final remarks and after nearly five months of discussion, the Senate laid Foot's resolution on the table.[11]

The Webster–Hayne debate was sectionalism personified, with Benton, Hayne, and Webster representing West, Southeast and Northeast. Yet partisanship pervaded the discussion, and in its later stages, when the great combatants retired and their auxiliaries took the field, dominated it. For the symbolism of the debate was a dual one. Out of the confusion of the 1828 campaign three great political combinations were emerging: the followers of Andrew Jackson's personal star, the Adams–Clay men calling themselves National Republicans, and the radical Southern states' rights, anti-tariff faction of Vice-President John C. Calhoun. Benton, co-architect with Martin Van Buren of the Jackson electoral coalition, now reigned as the administration's chief exponent in the Senate. Webster, in Clay's absence, guided the National Republicans; while rumor tabbed Hayne as the mouthpiece of Calhoun, who watched the debate, silent and attentive, from the presiding officer's chair.

Outside of Congress the response to the debate was strictly partisan.

Duff Green's *Telegraph* hailed the triumph of Benton and Hayne over "the Hartford Convention Federalists of the East." The same theme echoed in Jacksonian and Calhounite presses not only in the West and South, but in New York, in Maine, and even in Boston. "The good old party lines have been drawn," declared a correspondent of the *New Hampshire Patriot.* The New York *Courier and Enquirer* summoned Republicans to defeat the aristocracy's plot "to fill the coffers of the federal monopolists of the East—to increase the hoards of the wealthy capitalist." And the *Boston Statesman*, organ of Massachusetts Jacksonism, said the graduation bill would enable the "slaves" of the East to escape their bondage "and raise up Democratic States to counterbalance every aristocratic influence and sustain our republican institutions."[12]

In the debate, Hayne had carefully distinguished the Federalists from "the democracy of New England," who "have been, in times past, as they are now, the friends and allies of the South." Benton elaborated: there were two parties in New England, the "rich and well born above, the poor and ill-born below." The former, "the trainbands of New England federalism—the *elite* of the Hartford Convention," aspired not only to dominate the West and South, but to subjugate the New England democracy through Richard Rush's policy of tariff and high-priced public lands. With these declamations Benton aimed beyond mere sectional alliances. He envisioned nothing less than a revival of the old Republican party, of the part-sectional, part-class alignment of planters and plain folk that had vanquished the Federalists and elected Jefferson in 1800. And the cornerstone of its policy, the magnet to draw together the West and the farmers and laborers of the East, was to be the reduction of the price of public lands.[13]

Meanwhile, the National Republicans were scrutinizing the motives of Robert Hayne. The capital was alive with rumors of a succession struggle between Calhoun and Secretary of State Martin Van Buren. The *National Journal* spied a scheme to recruit Westerners to Calhoun's banner behind Hayne's sudden espousal of a land policy "utterly at variance with the true interests of his own State." Ohio representative Joseph Vance recalled earlier offers from Calhoun's agents to cede the public lands to the states if the West would support his candidacy. To John Quincy Adams, "the mutual surrender of the Public Lands to the West, and of the American System to the South, both at the expense of all the rest of the Union, of which this debate has revealed the project," exposed a "nefarious conspiracy" to elevate nullification along with Calhoun:

> This is the Key to the creed that Robbery is an attribute of Sovereignty, and that a State may declare itself the owner of all the Lands within its borders. Georgia by virtue of this doctrine, nullifies the Laws of Congress and the Treaties that promise protection to Indian tribes; South-Carolina nullifies the Tariff. Missouri nullifies all the Land Laws—and takes the Lands into her own keeping.[14]

Certainly some Calhounites were hoping to ride the land issue into the White House. Even before the congressional session began, one prophetic (and probably planted) rumor predicted that the "wealthy capitalists of New England" would oppose ceding the domain to the states, but that Calhoun and the South would stand with the West. Duff Green, an inveterate schemer and eternal optimist, spread the word that Jackson would not run again, and that Calhoun would "rally the South upon the subject of the tariff and the Western lands."[15]

Everyone claimed victory in the Webster–Hayne debate. The *St. Louis Beacon* rejoiced that Foot's aggression met "a signal and an irretrievable defeat," while Duff Green's *Telegraph* hailed Benton's refusal of the "new alliance" of North and West. On the other hand, a National Republican paper in Alabama congratulated Webster, "the Giant of the East," for overturning "the stupendous and unrighteous plan" to rob the old states of their interest in the public domain. Henry Clay thought that Benton's effort to detach the West from the Northeast and the American System had "entirely failed."[16]

Actually there were three distinct issues at stake—the constitutional, the presidential, and the legislative—and in none of them were the trophies of victory to be carried off by forensic display. The upshot of the constitutional controversy appeared in April at a Jefferson Day dinner gotten up by Benton and Hayne, when Jackson stamped his disapproval on nullification with the toast, "Our Union: It must be preserved." A bitter private quarrel soon alienated Jackson from Calhoun and cleared Martin Van Buren's path to the presidential succession.

How the debate would affect sectional alignments in Congress remained to be seen. Today the debate on Foot's resolution is remembered mainly for its drama and its exposition of constitutional principle. But hard choices on the tariff, internal improvements, and public lands lurked just off stage, and the speakers, while often straying, returned to them again and again. "You will of course understand that the adoption or rejection of that resolution is the least important object of the debate," said one Washington correspondent. "It is the indications of the future policy of the government on the engrossing subjects of the public lands, and the movements and views of parties in relation to that subject, connected with ulterior views of partizans which makes the discussion so interesting and important." Late in January John Quincy Adams listed the public lands first among the domestic "combustibles" likely to produce a new division of parties.[17]

Nullification was a practical remedy as well as a theoretical doctrine, and one that in 1830 appeared as likely to be tried in the West as in the South. In February the legislature of Mississippi, following Indiana, declared the admission compact by which the state abjured its claim to the public domain "invalid, null and void," and resolved that "this state, being a sovereign free and independent state, has the exclusive right to the soil and domain of all the unappropriated lands within her acknowledged boundaries." In Illinois, retiring governor Ninian Edwards devoted his entire valedictory to another denunciation of the federal land system.[18]

Which way would the West turn? Benton had rejected Webster's overtures on internal improvement. But Benton's undisputed command of the land reform movement hardly entitled him to speak for the West on all the collateral issues raised by the debate. His Jacksonism separated him from Western National Republicans, and partisanship had run just beneath the surface of the ostensibly sectional debate. Benton's and Hayne's impassioned defenses of slavery must also have inspired uneasy readers in Ohio, Indiana, and Illinois to wonder whether Benton was representing the West or the South. But most unsettling of all was his renunciation of trans-Appalachian internal improvements:

> The canal across the Alleghanies is mentioned. I utterly disclaim and repudiate that canal as a Western object.... My idea is this: That the great and bulky productions of the West will follow the course of the waters, and float down the rivers to New Orleans; that our export trade must, and will, go there. ... As to the idea of sending the products of the West across the Alleghanies, it is the conception of insanity itself! No rail roads or canals will ever carry them, not even if they do it gratis!

While Benton spoke, the Ohio Canal, first link between the Ohio River and the Great Lakes, was nearing completion. Within a decade Cleveland would ship a million bushels of wheat and half a million barrels of flour annually to the East via the Erie Canal, transforming central Ohio into a flourishing agricultural hinterland of the New York market. The astonishment of Ohioans at Benton's willingness to turn back the clock on Northwestern progress can well be imagined.[19]

So the debate on Foot's resolution did not answer the question of Western allegiance; it merely raised it. The answer awaited congressional action on land policy, the tariff, and internal improvements. And one other prize was still to be won—the support of President Andrew Jackson. His first message, advocating distribution of the surplus revenue among the states, pointed vaguely against internal improvements; but his tariff policy was unclear, and despite the promises of his Western promoters in 1828, he had yet to say a single word, in public or private, in favor of graduation.[20]

South and West: the alliance considered

The alliance of South and West was once enshrined in American historiography. In the writings of Frederick Jackson Turner's students, the coalition of the two great agricultural regions against the industrial Northeast shaped the politics of the antebellum era; the eventual realignment of Northwest with Northeast led the way to civil war. That view is no longer tenable. Recent investigations show that at the zenith of the party system in the 1840s sectional blocs simply did not operate in politics.[21] But for 1830, the year of the Webster–Hayne debate, accounts still divide between those seconding Raynor Wellington's judgment that "nothing was more natural" than an alliance of South and West "against their common enemy, the Northeast," and others which, denying the logic of the alliance, attribute its failure to the West's preference for Webster and nationalism over Hayne and nullification.[22]

The congressional alliance of South and West did, in 1830, briefly come into being. It collapsed from its own intrinsic weaknesses, not from rhetorical assaults. For although the affinity of South and West has echoed from the speeches of Thomas Hart Benton and the letters of Duff Green down into the history books, in reality nothing was less natural or less logical in 1830 than an alliance of the Northwest with the Old South; and an alliance which failed to embrace both of those regions was no alliance at all.

In Wellington's (and Benton's) analysis, the basis for the alliance was simplicity itself. The Northwest wanted cheap lands, while the Old South craved relief from the tariff. Each could satisfy its primary desire by sacrificing a subsidiary interest in the tariff and high-priced lands, respectively. For the Southwest, whose participation in the alliance could be presumed, no sacrifice was necessary. The real losers in this exchange would be the manufacturing North Atlantic states, chief beneficiaries of both the tariff and high land prices.

The reality was more complex. To begin with, Hayne's terms for the alliance involved more than a simple exchange on the public lands and the tariff. Hayne and the Southern extremists wanted the tariff set at a "revenue standard"—that is, a level just sufficient to meet essential federal expenses. They even contemplated repealing the tariff altogether and replacing it with direct taxes, whose unpopularity would insure against unnecessary spending. Their purpose was not only to provide tax relief for the South, but to prevent any public works that might strengthen federal power and thus indirectly threaten slavery. An alliance on Hayne's terms therefore not only meant the end of protection; it also meant abandoning internal improvements. Hayne made this quite clear in his speeches on Foot's resolution.

In return Hayne promised cheap land. But when studied closely his offer contained far less than the West was asking, or than his own rhetoric suggested. Though himself a nullifier, Hayne brusquely dismissed the Western claim to state ownership of the public domain as "untenable." Before reform could even begin, said Hayne, "the public debt must be first paid." But final retirement of the debt was not due until 1834, still four years away. At that time, said Hayne, the lands might be ceded or sold cheaply to the states, but perhaps "ought not to be entirely relinquished to any State until she shall have made considerable advances in population and settlement," as Ohio had already done. That criterion, applied to the frontier states, might postpone the cession for decades. While Hayne offered to relinquish the lands when the states reached maturity, Westerners considered the land system itself the chief impediment to achieving maturity, and demanded that it be changed forthwith. Where Benton and the West called for strong remedies, Hayne offered watery panaceas.[23]

The cords binding the Northwest to the Northeast were really much stronger than either Benton or Hayne would admit. The American System coalition is often accounted a simple tradeoff between Western internal improvement men and Northeastern manufacturers. But for the original parties to the axis, the Northwest and the mid-Atlantic states, no such bargain was necessary. Each supported the system for its own reasons. The mid-Atlantic states (except New York after completing the Erie Canal) wanted federal aid for internal improvements, and Northwesterners favored a protective tariff. Northwestern farmers and merchants hoped to foster an industrial home market, while the stake of hemp growers, fur traders, lead miners, and sheep raisers in the tariff was immediate and direct.

To extricate the West from the clutches of the American System, Benton linked the protective policy to high land prices, and then fixed the responsibility for them both upon Webster's New England. But New England was actually a late and reluctant convert to the protective policy. Webster's denial of Yankee responsibility for the tariffs of 1824 and 1828 was the literal truth. Neither was framed with regard to New England interests, and neither was passed by New England votes. Jacksonian New York and Pennsylvania escaped the imprecations that Benton and Hayne rained down on National Republican New England. Yet in 1824 and again in 1828 New York and Pennsylvania each cast more House votes for the tariff than all the New England states combined, while at the head of Jackson's cabinet sat a New Yorker who bore more responsibility for the "tariff of abominations" than Daniel Webster and all his minions.[24]

By 1828 New England was turning rapidly from seafaring to manufacturing, and hence to support for the tariff. But New England had converted to internal improvements *before* converting to protection, and for reasons more subtle than a simple craving for higher textile duties. Both Adams and Webster saw New England's political salvation in a broad nationalistic policy. With its strength in Congress inescapably declining, the Federalist policy of parochialism threatened political isolation and impotence. By the mid-1820s many New Englanders saw what John Quincy Adams had grasped as early as 1813—that a West settled by Yankees and fostered by Yankee benevolence would strengthen rather than weaken New England's position in the Union. During Adams's tenure in the White House, regionalism and partisanship both summoned New England congressmen to sustain their president, who staked his administration on internal improvements, not on the tariff.[25]

As a further incentive to cooperate with the West, New England also profited from federal fortifications, lighthouses, and river and harbor improvements. Technically these did not fall under the rubric of "internal improvements." Even Southern strict constructionists admitted their constitutionality, though they voted against them anyway. But Westerners felt that federal largesse upon the seaboard required compensatory spending in the interior, and they threatened to withhold support from the former if they were denied the latter. During the Adams administration an ample Treasury provided for reciprocal generosity, as federal public works on the seaboard multiplied along with subsidies for interior roads and canals.[26]

On the other hand, there was the supposed responsibility of New England textile magnates for high land prices. First asserted by Thomas Hart Benton, it worked its way into the rhetoric of the Jackson party and eventually into the history books. Benton traced the motive of Foot's resolution to the tariff and land policies of Richard Rush, allegedly intended to ensure manufacturers a cheap and docile labor force. No one recalled that George McDuffie of South Carolina had offered a nearly identical resolution in 1825. New Englanders themselves indignantly denied Benton's insinuations, the *Lowell Journal* branding them "totally, and most ridiculously false." Admittedly this testimony does not rank as disinterested. But it raises the question: What evidence substantiated Benton's charges?[27]

Unable to find any, historian Raynor Wellington cautioned: "The fact that no letters from New England manufacturers to their Representatives in Washington are extant cannot be used as an argument against attributing Foot's resolution to the tariff interests." Yet the correspondence of Daniel Webster is both extant and full of confidential letters from Massachusetts businessmen. Webster and his correspondents did not mince words when discussing the impact of legislation upon their business affairs. With brutal candor Abbott Lawrence told Webster that the tariff of 1828 "will keep the South and West in debt to New England the next hundred years." But no letters of millowners imploring Webster to protect their labor pool have survived.[28]

No doubt New England industrialists did oppose cheaper land prices. But that they were the only ones who did so was a myth created by Thomas Hart Benton. Whatever influence textile interests exerted over New England politics in 1830, their writ did not run west of the Hudson, nor backward in time. Their desire to immobilize the laboring poor does not satisfactorily explain the opposition to cheap land in New England in 1830, and makes no pretense of explaining it elsewhere in 1830 or in New England itself a decade earlier, when manufacturing was in its infancy and Daniel Webster spoke for shippers, not industrialists. Yet the whole history of the land question showed that where partisan advantage or sectional tradeoffs did not intervene, every Atlantic state could be counted on to oppose cheaper lands. And this was just as much true in Virginia and South Carolina as it was in Massachusetts.

Benton's attack on New England industrialists served to obscure the Southeastern interest in preserving the current land system. Wellington, following Benton, observed that "except for loss in land values and population, the South Atlantic States occupied a neutral position in regard to the Western plans for the disposition of the public domain." But the loss of population and wealth was hardly a marginal consideration; it was the main reason for all Eastern opposition to graduation and cession. It was true, as Benton said, that a purely political motive

had also once impelled New England Federalists to oppose land policies designed to hasten the admission of Western Republican states.
But the demise of the Federalist party and cooperation in Congress
during the 1820s had done much to dispel ancient antagonisms between New England and the West. If the rapid growth of Ohio,
Indiana, and Illinois was dangerous to anyone in 1830, it was the Old
South.[29]

By 1830 the tariff so obsessed South Carolina's leading politicians
that they were willing to contemplate almost any sacrifice to destroy it.
Men willing to risk the Union did not blanch at giving away the public
lands. But other Southerners protested the folly of exchanging the
existing hardship for a worse one. James Madison thought the tariff
evil "vastly overrated"; in his view the first of "the great and radical
causes of the pervading embarrassments" was "the fall almost to pros-
tration in the price of land, evidently the effect of the quantity of cheap
Western land in the market." The *Carolina Observer* attributed "the
desolation and depopulation of our streets and lands" to the lure of
Western soils. Senator John Tyler of Virginia, approving Webster's
defense of the land system, dismissed Hayne's proposals as "ridiculous,
mischievous, or absurd." Even Calhoun in 1831 privately objected that
Hayne's plan "would at once unsettle the whole landed property of the
U.S."[30]

In Congress the projected alliance of South and West faced tactical
obstacles that had not arisen between Northeast and Northwest.
Tariffs always affected a welter of conflicting local interests even
among protectionists, but the key to resolving differences and amass-
ing majorities was to gather the various compromises and tradeoffs
into a single piece of legislation. The process was never better illustrated than in 1828, when specific concessions to New England textile
manufacturers and Missouri lead miners and fur traders induced
Daniel Webster and Thomas Hart Benton to vote for a bill which
neither really liked. The principle of the omnibus had been applied to
internal improvements too, but there it was less necessary. New England had no reason to favor the Cumberland Road, but no reason to
oppose it either, as long as funds remained to finance public works in
New England as well.

An alliance embracing Southeast and Northwest would have to function on a very different basis. The two regions could not combine to
enact measures of mutual benefit, for there were none such. Nor could
they exchange quid pro quos in a single compromise. Rather, each of
two regions with virtually nothing in common would have to act directly against its own interests on one issue in hope of reciprocation on

another. An alliance dependent upon such extraordinary trust was naturally liable to collapse at any moment.

An essential prerequisite for such a union was its promise of success. Neither party to the alliance was likely to risk the sacrifices without assurance of reaping the rewards. Together the thirteen Southern and Western states commanded 26 out of 48 votes in the Senate, but only 98 out of 213 in the House of Representatives, less than a majority. Given internal unity, South and West could still prevail with slight assistance from the New England and mid-Atlantic states. But that unity did not exist.

The scattering of Virginia National Republicans were out of the alliance from the start, and the entire North Carolina delegation was questionable. North Carolina suffered severely from emigration; its citizens worried as much about depopulation as about the tariff. North Carolina had been the first state to approve the Maryland proposition, and its congressmen had angrily rejected Indiana's claim to ownership of the public domain. Unlike South Carolina, North Carolina had no presidential prospects to promote by cultivating Western favor; unlike Georgia, it had no Indian lands to seize.[31]

But the weakest link in the alliance was Ohio. To Ohioans, exchanging the American System for cheap land meant trading something they all wanted very much for something many of them did not want at all. Ohio's senators had supported graduation in 1828, but the solidarity between old and new West was visibly cracking. In the Foot debate it broke, as Benton repudiated internal improvements and conceded that Foot's policy would actually benefit Ohio, whose lands were already in market. Western competition for population was driving Ohioans from lukewarm advocacy of graduation into open opposition. In December of 1830 Governor Allen Trimble denounced graduation as "ruinous" to Ohio and pled for a "steady adherence" to the American System. Ohio Jacksonians relinquished Western views on land policy less readily than did National Republicans, so by 1830 there were signs of an incipient party division on the issue. But given a flat choice between the American System and graduation, there was no doubt which one Ohioans of either party would choose. And Ohio fielded fourteen members in the House of Representatives, more than the other six public land states combined.[32]

Kentucky's sectional loyalties were also suspect. As slaveowners, Kentuckians had reason to be wary of aligning with the North and the Northern policy of the American System, though in the 1820s they had consistently done so. But if Western solidarity against the old states should disintegrate, they had even less reason to support graduation.

Kentucky had backed the Maryland proposition in 1822, and a resolution adopted as recently as 1829 showed that the legislature had not abandoned its hopes for a share of the public domain.[33]

The alliance of South and West thus had to overcome clashing interests, tactical impediments, and insufficient voting strength. It remains to be seen how that alliance fared in Congress.

The alliance at work: distribution and pre-emption

Even as Robert Hayne delivered his first speech on Foot's resolution in the Senate, the alliance of South and West underwent its first trial in the House of Representatives. The issue was Jonathan Hunt's proposal to distribute the land revenue to the states, in proportion to their congressional representation, for internal improvements and education. Westerners objected that the proposal discriminated in favor of the densely populated Atlantic states; Southerners complained that it diverted funds already pledged to the public debt, prolonging the tariff and riveting the American System upon the South. The roll call on the first portion of Hunt's motion, to appoint a select committee for inquiry, arrayed the frontier and most of the South against the Northeast:[34]

	For	*Against*
New England	31	1
Mid-Atlantic	56	12
Virginia, South Carolina, Georgia	2	25
West (except Kentucky and Ohio)	1	19
Ohio	6	7
Kentucky	9	2
North Carolina	8	4
	113	70

The *National Intelligencer* hailed the vote as a victory for distribution itself, but shortly had to retract. Contingents from New York and Pennsylvania joined distribution's Western and Southern foes against two subsequent motions specifying the content of the inquiry, and defeated one of them. The House took no further action on distribution. But the episode launched the alliance of South and West; it also illustrated its essential weakness. Though the sectional issue was clearly drawn, Ohio, Kentucky, and North Carolina cast 23 votes against the alliance.[35]

The distribution debate also underscored the latent antagonism of the two allies. The *St. Louis Beacon* thanked "our brother republicans" in the South for their aid against distribution. But Southern cooperation did not originate in "friendly spirit," as the *Beacon* alleged, but in sectional self-interest. Westerners opposed distribution as the foil to graduation and cession. But Southerners opposed it for diverting the land revenue. No Southern speakers promised support for graduation, and they ridiculed the Western claim to ownership of the public domain.[36]

One Southerner went even further. William Martin of South Carolina opposed distribution altogether, but he thought that if the land proceeds were to be divided up, the "incalculable" giveaways to the new states should be counted in, and he introduced an amendment to that effect. Here was the Maryland proposition all over again. Martin's demand "that those States which have hitherto received no lands shall have their allotment of lands or money, in the same proportion as those that have hitherto received them" echoed right out of Virgil Maxcy's pamphlets.[37]

Though the House dumped Martin's amendment by a large margin, the amendment exposed the gulf between West and South. Southern strict constructionists might join the West against distribution—the *Richmond Enquirer* branded federal subsidies for education and internal improvements "obnoxious to all the *principles* of the Constitution"—but in the same breath and for the same reason they denounced all the other land projects pouring in on Congress, including those from the West. The Milledgeville *Southern Recorder* reminded Westerners that the public lands were "the great common stock fund of the Union." Back home in South Carolina, William Martin called for resistance to the "preposterous claims" of the new states. The *Richmond Enquirer* condemned distribution along with the tariff, internal improvements, land grants, and the Western "claims and schemes" to seize the public domain. The *Enquirer*'s columns carried no hint that the portfolio of states' rights included ownership of the public lands; nor, in Congress, did any Southeasterner sustain the pretensions set forth by Indiana and Mississippi. State sovereignty, one may conclude, meant different things east and west of the mountains.[38]

With distribution defeated, South and West turned to another issue—pre-emption. Ever since Confederation days the status of the unauthorized settler on public lands—the "squatter"—had plagued federal land officials and provoked a running feud between the government and frontiersmen. Federal land laws clearly prohibited settlement before purchase. Under a law of 1807, still on the books in 1830, squatters on government land, far from acquiring any "right, title or claim" thereto, incurred criminal penalties of fine and imprisonment.[39]

Yet from the beginning Congress had allowed some settlers special dispensations. Squatters in ceded or purchased territories who had settled before they came under federal jurisdiction were allowed the privilege of pre-emption—the preferential right to purchase the lands they occupied from the United States, without competition and at the minimum price. But the distinction between prior residents and mere trespassers was quickly lost, as an assortment of pre-emption laws extended the privilege to settlers who had clearly intruded on lands already belonging to the United States. Altogether Congress passed more than thirty such acts between 1800 and 1830.[40]

All the pre-emption acts thus far applied only to specific frontier locales, and all were retrospective. They granted pre-emption rights only to those who had already settled before the acts were passed. A typical law, of April 1826, allowed pre-emption to Florida Territory occupants who had settled before January 1, 1825. Under such restrictions not much land was sold through the pre-emption system, perhaps a million acres all told before 1830.[41]

There was no consistency in pre-emption policy. The pre-emption laws rewarded the frontiersman for precisely the same behavior which exposed him to a hundred-dollar fine and six months in jail. Madison's proclamation in 1815 testified to the futility of prohibiting trespassing. Yet Congress refused to remove the 1807 law from the statute books. One attempt in the Senate in 1824 was easily rebuffed. Congress thus preserved a distinction: since squatting was still illegal, occasional retrospective pre-emption acts neither sanctioned trespass on the public domain nor provided precedent for future leniency.[42]

It was a nice exercise in logic, but that was all it was. Frontiersmen paid it no mind. They swarmed over the lands and then demanded pre-emption as minimal payment for their services to the nation. "A liberal and enlarged policy on the part of the general Government points to the improvement of the public lands, of the Territory as an event whose importance bears no comparison with that of disposing of these lands for a price," explained the Florida legislative council in 1824. "Urged on by a spirit of enterprise which no obstacles or danger could subdue," pioneers had opened up the territory "at great expense and loss." Petitioners celebrated what the Arkansas territorial assembly called "their valour and perseverance in venturing alone and defenceless in the forest, and in cultivating the Soil." Having fought off the Indians and improved the land, to the great benefit of the United

States and at great cost to themselves, they asked in return protection for their homes from the merciless land speculator.[43]

Pre-emption petitions never failed to contrast the heroic poverty of the hardy pioneer with the cruel greed of the speculator. By 1820 these twin themes were joined by a third—the settled practice of the United States government. The petitioners argued that by its pre-emption acts Congress itself had voided the law against trespassing as surely as by formal repeal. The Mississippi legislature pronounced pre-emption "the well-considered and settled policy of the government," while Arkansas pioneers, claiming their settlement "has never been prohibited, but approbated and encouraged," demanded "the same protection" accorded settlers elsewhere. The Louisiana legislature asked pre-emption for all who "have settled in good faith," implying that the good faith of the government, rather than the legality of the settlement, was in question.[44]

Most federal officials frowned on the squatters, who squandered government timber and fomented endless trouble with the Indians. The tribes often complained of settlers' intrusions, and the task of removing them westward became immensely complicated when Indians arrived at their new homeland to find it already covered with squatters. Indian superintendent Thomas McKenney sputtered furiously at the insolence of the pioneers, while General Land Office commissioner Josiah Meigs lamented in 1821 that "the existing laws in favor of pre-emption rather *encourage*, than forbid intrusion." House and Senate public lands committees periodically denounced the squatters and called for enforcement of the law against trespassing.[45]

Given the antipathy of the federal bureaucracy, the wonder is that any pre-emption laws passed at all. In fact most of them slipped through Congress virtually unnoticed. In 1822 a pre-emption bill that did attract attention in the Senate was defeated by lopsided majorities from the old states; yet even after that five more such acts passed Congress before 1830, none of them occasioning a division in either house, and only one provoking any reported debate.[46]

Few signs indicated any imminent change in pre-emption policy in Jackson's first Congress. Congress had entertained no general pre-emption measure since Ninian Edwards tried to tack one onto the Land Act of 1820, though in 1828 the House Public Lands Committee did report two special pre-emption bills with arguments that for the first time defended pre-emption on general principles. The public land states memorialized for pre-emption in the later 1820s, but usually as an afterthought to their main demands for graduation or cession. It was on these, not on pre-emption, that Westerners expected Congress to move.[47]

The swiftness of events in the Twenty-first Congress thus strongly suggests previous concert out-of-doors. On December 23, 1829, the Senate Public Lands Committee reported a bill granting preferential right of purchase at the minimum price to all current occupants of public lands. A brief debate followed, and on January 13, still six days before Hayne's first speech on Foot's resolution, pre-emption passed the Senate, with South and West unanimously in favor.[48]

Pre-emption also slipped quietly through the House, though there it took a little longer. Several postponements gave General Land Office commissioner George Graham (a holdover from the Adams administration) a chance to condemn the bill as an administrative nightmare and a craven capitulation to lawless squatters, who reportedly were threatening to shoot anyone who dared bid against them at auction. Graham's expostulations notwithstanding, the House took up the bill on May 29, passed it, and sent it to Jackson, who signed it the same day. In the midst of all the debate over graduation, cession, and distribution, Congress had enacted, without prior preparation and virtually without discussion, the most important land measure since the Relief Act of 1821.[49]

Another decade would pass before the ramifications of the General Pre-emption Act of 1830 became fully apparent. Like its predecessors, it was retrospective, applying only to settlers in residence on the day it became law. It did not repeal the anti-trespassing statute of 1807, or authorize squatting in the future. Of course pre-emption undercut the auction, but the settler still had to purchase at the minimum price, which, as proponents of the bill pointed out, was rarely exceeded at the auction anyway. Attempts by land officials to stimulate competitive bidding were nearly always futile.

But though technically it did not bind Congress to pre-emption as a permanent policy, the law of 1830 started the system down a road from which it was impossible to turn back. It destroyed the fragile fiction that pre-emption was a special favor granted to recognize particular services and sufferings. The sanctions against squatting, already moribund, were now dead beyond hope of resurrection. Future settlers would demand the same treatment, and Congress, having passed the law of 1830 as a general policy measure, could offer no fair grounds for refusal. Prospective pre-emption and the formal legalization of squatting were just a matter of time.

On pre-emption the alliance of West and South scored its first real triumph. The roll call underscored the hybrid nature of the alliance—half-sectional, half-partisan (see table 5.1). Although Southerners provided the West's main backing and no state divided along clear party lines, Jacksonians gave stronger support to pre-emption than did the opposition men in all the Atlantic regions. Whether they would also support a more drastic revision of the land system was shortly to be

TABLE 5.1
GENERAL PRE-EMPTION, 1830

SENATE

	Jackson		Opposition		Total	
	For	*Against*	*For*	*Against*	*For*	*Against*
New England	1		4	6	5	6
Mid-Atlantic	3	2	1	4	4	6
South Atlantic	5				5	
Ohio			1		1	
Other West	12		2		14	
Total	21	2	8	10	29	12

HOUSE

	Jackson		Opposition		Total	
	For	*Against*	*For*	*Against*	*For*	*Against*
New England	6	1	12	10	18	11
Mid-Atlantic	15	16	8	12	23	28
South Atlantic	24	7	1	7	25	14
Ohio	6	1	2	4	8	5
Other West	23		3		26	
Total	74	25	26	33	100	58

Sources: Senate Journal, 21st Cong., 1st sess., p. 83; *House Journal*, 21st Cong., 1st sess., pp. 779–780. Partisan affiliations for senators are derived from the contemporary public record, voting behavior on strictly defined party issues, and various secondary accounts. Partisan affiliations for representatives are derived from electoral data in the contemporary press, especially *Niles' Weekly Register*, and the *Congressional Quarterly's Guide to U.S. Elections* (Washington, D.C., 1975), pp. 551–553. The Jackson column includes those who ran for Congress or were otherwise publicly identified as Jackson men; "opposition" includes those variously identified as "Adams," "Clay," "anti-Jackson," or "opposition."

seen. For the pre-emption bill, hurriedly passed and scarcely noticed, did not in the least slake the thirst of the West for graduation.

The alliance falls short: graduation and cession

The auspices never seemed brighter for graduation than in the spring of 1830. The West was "loud and unequivocal" in demanding it with an "almost unanimous voice," the *St. Louis Beacon* observed. With a thus-far neutral but Western president installed in place of Adams, an administration majority in both houses of Congress, and a tender of Southern assistance from Robert Hayne, Benton and his confederates predicted easy passage of his bill.[50]

The Senate debate on graduation (which spilled liberally over into debate on Senator Foot's still-pending resolution) focused on the huge quantity of unpurchased land on the market. Benton produced estimates from census marshals and land officials to show that while more than 140,000 Westerners owned no property, the real market value of unsold federal lands was less than 50¢ per acre in four of the frontier states and only 3½¢ in Arkansas Territory. These statistics sustained Benton's contention that the government was demanding an impossible price for lands "of inferior value, consisting of a few acres only fit for cultivation, the rest worthless and sterile." But graduation's opponents pointed to the high valuations and rapid sales of leftover lands in the oldest Ohio districts, buttressing the conclusion of General Land Office commissioner George Graham that "population and improvement," not fertility, gave value to land. The discussion eventually drifted off into moral archetypes, with the character of the squatters at issue. According to how one felt about the graduation bill, they were brave pioneers clinging to "broken and inferior tracts" or "intruders— mere trespassers, who have selected and seized upon the best and most eligible of the public lands."[51]

Benton's bill stipulated annual price reductions of 25¢ per acre on lands untaken at the auction, with an additional 25¢ discount for actual settlers at each price level. Poor families could receive free donations of eighty acres. After a year in market at the bottom price of 25¢ per acre (and at a nominal 5¢ for actual settlers), the unsold residue would be ceded to the state for education and internal improvement. Thus all the acreage put in market would be out of federal hands, one way or another, within five years.

On the Senate floor Benton's friends proceeded to dismember his bill. Hayne, hinting at constitutional objections, struck out the cession for education and internal improvement, and also the third and fourth

annual price reductions (to 50¢ and 25¢ per acre, respectively). Levi
Woodbury of New Hampshire, New England's sole Jacksonian senator
and Benton's ally in the Foot debate, next struck out the donation
clause and the second price reduction. All that remained was the initial
reduction to $1.00 per acre and 75¢ for settlers, and to make the bill
more palatable John McKinley of Alabama moved to restrict it to lands
offered at auction before June of 1827. By this time, taunted David
Barton, Benton's bill was even weaker than his own modest
alternatives.[52]

The coalition of South and West, along with Woodbury of New
Hampshire, put the truncated graduation bill through the Senate over
the opposition of New England National Republicans and mid-Atlantic
senators of both parties. Though John Tyler of Virginia, William
Smith of South Carolina, and Jacob Burnet of Ohio aligned with the
opposition, the alliance squeaked the bill through its third reading and
passage on identical votes of 24 to 22.

The House of Representatives, preoccupied with other matters,
finally took up graduation two days before adjournment, only to table
it, 82 to 68. With no time for debate amid the usual press of closing
business, graduation men denied that the vote was a test of strength.
But the bill as it left the Senate embraced only one simple provision, the
principles of which had been amply discussed both in and out of
Congress for years. The voting pattern in the House mirrored that in
the Senate. Jacksonism's "scattering reinforcements" in New England
and 10 votes from Maryland and New York counterbalanced the few
Southern defections from the South–West coalition. Yet neither New
England nor the National Republicans alone determined the outcome,
for had the West been unanimous the bill would have survived. Eight
members from Ohio, three of them Jacksonian, killed graduation in
the House (see table 5.2).

Now here was a cruel paradox for the West. From the moment of
their admission to the Union, the new states hungered for the power to
control their own destiny. Their favorite policies—cheap lands and
internal improvements—would hasten the day when the West might
appear in Congress not as supplicant but as lawgiver. For Ohio that day
was near. With fourteen seats in the House—fourth behind Pennsylvania, New York, and Virginia—Ohio was a power in the Union. Having
achieved the maturity the new states awaited so impatiently, Ohio
could demand an amelioration of the land laws, and many in the old
states were apparently willing to yield it. But strangely Ohio no longer
wanted it, and was ready to deny it to its western neighbors. Something
had happened to Ohio. The state that led the West against the Mary-

land proposition in 1822 now marched in Eastern step. In growing powerful, Ohio had ceased to be Western. On the very eve of its realization, the vision of Western preeminence proved a mirage, receding endlessly before its relentless pursuers.

At the second session the following winter, lame-duck David Barton reintroduced the weakened graduation bill, explaining to Missourians that if they had asked for something reasonable instead of Benton's extravagant original bill, they might have obtained their object long before. But an impeachment trial ate up most of the Senate session, and neither house found time for major land legislation. In March 1831 the Twenty-first Congress adjourned, and graduation men again returned home empty-handed.[53]

TABLE 5.2
GRADUATION, 1830

SENATE

	Jackson		Opposition		Total	
	For	*Against*	*For*	*Against*	*For*	*Against*
New England	1			11	1	11
Mid-Atlantic		4		4		8
South Atlantic	6	2			6	2
Ohio			1	1	1	1
Other West	13		3		16	
Total	20	6	4	16	24	22

HOUSE[a]

	Jackson		Opposition		Total	
	For	*Against*	*For*	*Against*	*For*	*Against*
New England	4			23	4	23
Mid-Atlantic	9	24	1	16	10	40
South Atlantic	22	4	1	7	23	11
Ohio	3	3	1	5	4	8
Other West	24		3		27	
Total	62	31	6	51	68	82

Sources: Senate Journal, 21st Cong., 1st sess., pp. 291–292; *House Journal,* 21st Cong., 1st sess., pp. 780–781.

[a]The vote was to table; "for" indicates nay.

While graduation encountered rough sailing in Jackson's first Congress, the Western claim to ownership of the public lands sank like a stone. Even many graduation men shunned it. The House again signalled its disapproval by squelching the plan to cede the government's Tennessee lands. Davy Crockett, taking charge of the Tennessee bill, disclaimed any connection with the general cession project, but to no avail. Illinois representative Joseph Duncan concluded that the cession struggle in Congress was hopeless; worse yet, the prejudice against it there was sabotaging efforts for more modest reform.[54]

Indeed, Atlantic politicians were unanimous in rejecting the states' rights argument for cession. A North Carolina congressman spoke for his colleagues when he branded it "one of the most extravagant pretensions that could possibly be urged." Yet two states, Indiana and Mississippi, had now officially urged that pretension. In a third, Illinois, a bitter campaign to succeed Ninian Edwards as governor zeroed in on the land issue, one candidate favoring graduation and the other cession. The cession candidate won. Good evidence supported John Quincy Adams's prediction that Georgia's defiance of the federal government over the Indians "will be imitated by other States, and with regard to other national interests—perhaps the tariff—still more probably the public lands."[55]

Though the expectation of a showdown over the public domain continued to influence actions in Congress for several more years, by 1831 that perception was actually out of date. Indiana and Mississippi, having asserted their rights, did nothing to vindicate them. The new governor of Illinois, John Reynolds, elected with Edwards's backing on a cession plank, promptly softened his tone upon taking office. Edwards himself was through. Champion of the West against the Land Act of 1820 and the Maryland proposition, he was the first to discern the political possibilities of the land issue. But his erratic temper and faulty judgment ruined him for the role of Western chief, so it was Benton who trod the road that Edwards discovered. By 1830 Edwards's control of Illinois politics was shattered, and his attempt to restructure it and regain leadership of the land reform movement with the cession issue did more to sully its reputation than to advance his fortunes. In 1832 a bid for Congress failed, and a year later Edwards died. For all practical purposes, the cession campaign died with him.[56]

It died because the Twenty-first Congress opened Western eyes to certain political realities. The aversion of most congressmen to cession was so "pertinaciously obstinate," as one Indianan put it, that no amount of argument or bombast could shake it. Even the Ohio delegation opposed cession unanimously; though through it Ohio would acquire nearly five million acres of land. When Atlantic congressmen vowed to oppose all Western land measures until Edwards's pretensions were renounced, Westerners realized that cession was doing them more harm than good.[57]

Westerners had much to lose by intransigence on the land issue. Their central dilemma, like that of Southerners over the tariff, was whether to seek drastic or ameliorative measures, and whether to adopt militant or conciliatory tactics. Extremism might frighten Congress into action—or stiffen its resistance. To simply antagonize Congress was self-defeating, for while Western states demanded the whole domain, they continued to beg for other favors: still more relief for debtors who had purchased land under the credit system, preemption, exchange of poor-quality internal improvement and school donation lands for better ones, the right to tax federal lands immediately after sale (still denied them despite the abolition of the credit system), and land grants for everything under the sun—hospitals, deaf-and-dumb asylums, schools, academies, prisons, courthouses, roads, canals, river improvements, and railroads. Eastern politicians were becoming frankly disgusted at the number of these requests and at their schizophrenic language—haughty and threatening in one memorial, unctuous and flattering in the next. Moreover, the experiment with internal improvement grants under John Quincy Adams indicated that the Westerners' real purpose was not to build roads and canals but simply to subvert the federal land system. Only Ohio, which began work before receiving a land grant, had made any progress on its canals. Indiana put its donation lands up for sale at one-fourth down and seventeen years to pay, while an Alabama commission recommended selling its 400,000 acres of prime cotton lands at nominal prices. Looking at these results of past generosity, many Atlantic congressmen compared the pleas of Westerners to the whinings of a spoiled child. Hence Westerners like Joseph Duncan thought it foolish to offend Congress further with the extravagant cession demand.

As for graduation, an anti-Benton paper in Missouri confessed a hope that it "was at rest forever—we are sick even to nausea at the bare mention of it." But compared to cession it had fared well, and graduation men did not despair; instead they looked for someone to blame. Barton and Benton exchanged a final round of insults and accusations. The *St. Louis Beacon* and *United States Telegraph* railed at graduation's New England foes, while Barton's friends toasted "The 'bargain'—As the 'generous south' has failed to give the public lands to the west for a 'pepper-corn,' *we* are not bound to repeal the tariff of 1828." None of the recriminations could disguise the cold fact that after years of preparation and with the full cooperation of Jacksonians in the Old South and New England, a dismembered version of Benton's graduation bill had barely survived the Senate and had been summarily dismissed in the House of Representatives.[58]

North and West: the American System alliance in jeopardy

If Southerners expected Westerners to abandon the American System in return for Southern votes for graduation and pre-emption, their illusions were shortly dispelled. On Southern propositions in Congress to roll back the tariff to the levels of 1816 and 1824 the tariff coalition of mid-Atlantic and Northwestern states held firm, bolstered by increasing support from industrializing New England.[59]

If they could not destroy the protective system directly, Southerners hoped to accomplish it indirectly by cutting federal spending. They could hasten the retirement of the national debt by applying surplus revenue to debt service instead of public works. Paying the debt would release ten million dollars annually, leaving the government with revenues nearly double its ordinary expenses. As no Congress would dare to amass unneeded millions in the Treasury, if the line could be held on spending the tariff must come down. "Destroy the tariff and you will leave no means of carrying on internal improvement," said South Carolina senator William Smith; "destroy internal improvement and you leave no motive for the tariff." "You ought to keep an eye to all the measures *looking to the distribution of the natl.* funds," advised Robert Hayne, "whether by direct appropriation of money, or for Roads and Canals, Schools, Pension Bills, or in any other way—and every decision in favor of such projects ought to be noticed and condemned."[60]

In April 1830 the House of Representatives rejected a bill to begin a new national road from Buffalo to New Orleans, sending Southerners into paroxysms of joy. Philip Barbour, observing that "the House had done enough for glory for one day," moved an adjournment, and the next day Samuel Carson of North Carolina resumed the celebration:[61]

> Yes, sir, it was a victory over a monster which has been lapping the life-blood of the South. Yesterday, sir, we harpooned the monster, and made his blood spout gloriously. . . . We have won the victory once—we have got the monster down—he is struggling and ready to expire, and I, for one, will keep my foot upon his neck, and hope to witness his expiring gasp.

Carson rejoiced too soon. Road and canal men still had the upper hand in Congress, as they soon proved by authorizing new internal improvement surveys, a $200,000 appropriation for the Cumberland Road, and stock purchases for three private ventures—the Louisville and Portland Canal around the falls of the Ohio, the Washington Turnpike from the capital to Frederick, Maryland (with connections to the Cumberland Road), and the Maysville Road. The last, running some sixty miles through Kentucky, followed part of the route of yet another projected national road, from Zanesville, Ohio, to Florence, Alabama. Henry Clay was particularly interested in the Maysville Road, and, perhaps with his eye on the 1832 presidential campaign, he begged his New England friends "not to deprive us of the benefit of this weapon." Clay thought New England support for the road would "be worth a thousand of Benton's speeches."[62]

A look at the supporters and opponents of these measures shows no substantial deviation from the pattern of the previous Congress (see table 5.3). The internal improvement coalition still functioned—a coalition of all the mid-Atlantic and Northwestern tariff states except New York, New England except for the Jacksonians, and about half the anti-tariff Southwest as well. It was the same combination that upheld the tariff, except in New York, where some protectionists opposed roads and canals, and in the Southwest, where some anti-protectionists supported them.

Measured by Southern expectations, the congressional alliance of South and West had failed utterly in 1830. Southern votes for land reform did not weaken the West's attachment to the American System coalition with the Northeast. The alternatives presented in the Webster–Hayne debate were further demonstrated in the voting, where Atlantic congressmen separated into two nearly exclusive camps on internal improvements and graduation. But Westerners simply refused to choose, voting as they always had for both cheap land and roads and canals. Southern aid on graduation and pre-emption had not won a single Western convert against the "general bribery system" —not even Benton, who voted, quietly, for internal improvements.

The first successful blow against the American System came not from Congress but from the White House. Jackson in his opening message to Congress had not directly opposed internal improvements, though he preferred distributing surplus revenue to the states in order to avoid chronic congressional wrangling. Some National Republicans ascribed the defeat of the Buffalo Road to administration influence, but the roll calls show that it was not the votes of Jacksonians but of opposition men who doubted the road's practicability which produced that debacle. The president's veto of the Maysville Road bill four days before the session's end thus caught internal improvement men off

TABLE 5.3
INTERNAL IMPROVEMENTS, 1830

HOUSE[a]

	Jackson		Opposition		Total	
	For	*Against*	*For*	*Against*	*For*	*Against*
New England		7	19		19	7
Mid-Atlantic	21	10	14	1	35	11
South Atlantic		30	3	3	3	33
Northwest	11	1	9		20	1
Southwest	5	7	1		6	7
Total	37	55	46	4	83	59

SENATE[b]

	Jackson		Opposition		Total	
	For	*Against*	*For*	*Against*	*For*	*Against*
New England		1	6	1	6	2
Mid-Atlantic	2	2	4		6	2
South Atlantic		7				7
Northwest	3		4		7	
Southwest	2	3	1		3	3
Total	7	13	15	1	22	14

Sources: *House Journal*, 21st Cong., 1st sess., pp. 486–487, 533–534, 540–543, 582–583, 585–587, 763–764, and 800–805; *Senate Journal*, 21st Cong., 1st sess., pp. 184, 247–248, 250–251, 295, 304, and 306.

[a]House tabulation is based on twelve roll calls concerning the survey bill, Louisville Canal, Washington Turnpike, Buffalo Road, and Maysville Road. The twelve roll calls make up a Guttman scale with a coefficient of reproducibility of .97. Missing data and contrived items have been handled according to the procedures outlined in Anderson et al., *Legislative Roll-Call Analysis*, chap. 6. The scale divides the legislators into five scale types, of which the table shows the two extremes: those who voted consistently for or against internal improvements. They constituted 72% of the 198 members on the scale.

[b]Senate tabulation is based on six roll calls concerning the survey bill, Louisville Canal, Washington Turnpike, Maysville Road, and Cumberland Road. These roll calls do not scale, but fully three-quarters of the senators voted the same way on all of them. The twelve who did not are omitted from the table.

guard. Immediately following came vetoes of the Louisville and Portland Canal, the Washington Turnpike, and a lighthouse and coastal improvement bill. The survey bill and the Cumberland Road appropriation were allowed to stand.[63]

The Maysville Road veto message harkened back to the internal improvement vetoes of Madison and Monroe without precisely assuming their ground. Jackson followed them in denying federal jurisdiction over internal improvements within the states, a power never successfully asserted in Congress since Monroe's veto of the Cumberland Road tollgate bill. Like Monroe in his latitudinarian phase, Jackson conceded, though reluctantly, a right of appropriation for national works. But he rejected congressional authority to subsidize a purely local improvement like the Maysville Road.

Jackson acknowledged that the distinction between national and local improvements was an imprecise and at bottom arbitrary criterion furnishing no clear guide to either executive or congressional conduct. He therefore requested a clarifying constitutional amendment, urging Congress in the meantime to refrain from "irregular, improvident, and unequal" expenditures delaying the retirement of the national debt.[64]

The veto message was a hodgepodge of constitutional and expedient arguments, but in its very logical fuzziness lay its political strength. The nebulous distinction between national and local works stung American System men to fury, for it freed Jackson to decide on individual bills precisely as he chose—a freedom he exploited to the utmost. None of his predecessors enjoyed such flexibility. Madison and Monroe, until the latter's change of heart in 1822, felt constrained to veto everything except Cumberland Road bills. Under Adams internal improvement had flourished, but its advocates never reduced it in practice to what they claimed it to be, a "general system" of planned national works. In the absence of some comprehensive plan or durable administrative apparatus, internal improvements proceeded through the Adams congresses via random appropriations and land grants. The need to defend the policy's constitutionality and to reward its supporters prevented Adams and congressional leaders from picking and choosing among individual projects. Nothing could be safely refused. Under such conditions the opportunities for what Jackson called "flagicious *logg-rolling legislation*" were very real indeed.[65]

Jackson's Maysville Road veto and his first two annual messages steered a middle course between Northern American System men and Southern strict constructionists. His suggestions for a moderate reduction of the tariff and the distribution of the surplus revenue to the states satisfied neither of the extremes. Southern anti-tariff men reacted violently to distribution, Calhoun calling it "the most danger- ous, unconstitutional and absurd project ever devised by any govern- ment." They thought it even worse than "that gangrene on the body politic," internal improvement; for while road and canal bills could be fought and sometimes beaten one by one, distribution would fasten the protective system like some great leech upon the South, forever draw- ing off Southern wealth to fill Northern coffers. Jackson's statement that no tariff revision "upon principles satisfactory to the people of the Union will until a remote period, if ever, leave the Government with- out a considerable surplus in the Treasury" baldly assumed what Cahounites would never concede—the right to levy unnecessary taxes solely to protect American industry.[66]

Outside of the South opinion on Jackson's distribution proposal divided along partisan lines. All but the most extreme antiprotection- ists agreed that any acceptable tariff would still yield surpluses, so the question was whether they should be expended at Washington or thrown back upon the states. The National Republican press attacked distribution as unconstitutional and a "subterfuge" for opposing inter- nal improvements. The *National Intelligencer* protested that distribu- tion "would disarm the general government of the means of doing general good." On the other hand the *Globe*, Jackson's new Washington organ, explained that distribution would "prevent partiality, log- rolling, corruption and a dangerous extension of executive patronage."[67]

Nothing came of Jackson's suggestion to distribute the surplus. Internal improvement men, including Western Jacksonians, did not want to forgo direct federal subsidies, though Jackson termed the present nonsystem "perhaps, the worse that could exist"; and Jackson's own doubts of distribution's constitutionality warned off those who knew they could not procure an amendment. A House committee chaired by James Polk, as loyal a Jacksonian as there was in Congress, approved distribution only in the most equivocal terms. The matter died there.[68]

The Maysville Road veto alarmed Western Jacksonians. Richard M. Johnson rushed to the White House, exclaiming "you will crush your friends in Kentucky if you veto that Bill!" According to Martin Van Buren, Western Jackson men all believed the veto would "destroy his popularity." They were wrong. Jackson's star stood as high as ever, though the opposition press shouted that the West was "deceived and betrayed" in going for him as an internal improvement man in 1828. A Clay corresponding committee warned that "this administration is anti-tariff, anti-internal improvement, anti-western, anti-northern, and a real southern administration." But most administration presses dutifully followed the president's lead. Western Jackson papers seized eagerly on his distinction between national and local works, pointing to his signature on the Cumberland Road bill as proof of his favor for truly national projects. The *St. Louis Beacon* said the veto principle would protect the West, which "has been voting millions for the East of the Alleganies and getting nothing for itself," from being "any longer cheated, duped, defrauded, and imposed upon."[69]

Though the veto took no measurable toll of Jackson's own popularity in the West, it embarrassed his congressional partisans. Northwestern Jacksonians had accepted in good faith the pledges of his campaign managers in 1828. Their own devotion to the American System remained unshaken, as did that of voters, who evidently did not consider Jacksonism and internal improvements incompatible. The Jackson label was the touchstone of political success in the West, but few dared to follow the president's lead against internal improvements. When the vetoed bills returned to Congress, nearly all their original supporters, including Benton, voted for them again. Since they could not command the two-thirds majority needed to override Jackson's veto, these votes did not matter, but they revealed the unwillingness of Western Jacksonians to follow the president blindly against sectional interests.[70]

Some Westerners, like Representative William Stanbery of Ohio, found Jacksonism incompatible with the American System and decamped to the National Republicans. Most stayed with the president, but without relinquishing their fondness for internal improvement. These American System Jacksonians remained curious fixtures of Northwestern politics for many years afterward—men who bore the Jackson label but voted for internal improvements and, later, for the Bank of the United States. Some, like Joseph Duncan of Illinois and William Ashley of Missouri, eventually went over to the opposition; others, like John Tipton of Indiana, despite disillusionments, did not.[71]

Looking back, Van Buren recalled the veto as "the entering wedge to the course of action by which that powerful combination known as the Internal Improvement party was broken asunder and finally annihilated." The veto was not the end, but it was the beginning of the end. In the 1830–1831 session Jackson employed his maneuverability to the fullest, signing several internal improvement bills. He was still a long way from the Southerners, and the congressional internal improvement phalanx showed no signs of weakening. But in the same session Jackson confirmed his opposition to stock purchases, the chief vehicle for road and canal funding since 1824; and though a House committee disputed his reasoning, the dependence of the internal improvement policy upon the will of a president who doubted its constitutionality and expediency could not have been more completely demonstrated. Road and canal men had never commanded enough strength to override presidential vetoes. And Jackson, having to his satisfaction been sustained by public opinion in his first blow at the internal improvement system, vowed to carry on the campaign.[72]

Jackson's first Congress began with Northerners and Southerners courting the West with promises of cheap lands and internal improvements. It ended with the graduation campaign mired in futility, and with internal improvements retreating before a hostile executive. Disappointed in their hopes for Jackson, Southern anti-tariffites and Western graduation men now expected the imminent retirement of the national debt to either consummate their plans or banish all hope forever. As the New York *Courier and Enquirer* remarked, the surplus revenue question promised to sweep "every great question which has been separately shaking the country for the last twenty years"—including the public lands—into its vortex. Americans had long awaited their liberation from national indebtedness, but in 1830 the *Courier* could see only that payment of the debt would precipitate "a fearful and important crisis."[73]

CHAPTER 6
CRISIS AND COMPROMISE
1832–1833

The stand taken by South Carolina against the *tariff*, may be taken by Illinois concerning the *public lands* and so on, by other states, through the whole catalogue of their *supposed* interests. . . . THERE IS NO END TO THE DOCTRINE.

Niles' Weekly Register
November 10, 1832

Benton versus Clay

Americans eagerly anticipated the discharge of the national debt. The young Republic's ability to throw off the costs of two wars while European monarchies wallowed in debt provided a pleasing text for patriotic orators. Yet the triumphant moment had been long postponed, so that while Americans calculated the day of its arrival they hardly dared hope that war or depression would not again defer their dreams. Now the great event was suddenly at hand. The Treasury paid off more than $16 million in 1831, leaving a debt of only $24 million, most of it redeemable at the pleasure of the government and paying well below prevailing interest rates. In substance the debt was paid, but President Jackson wanted more than the substance. Economy in government was central to the old Republican creed; as the heir of Jefferson, Jackson craved to see the last nickel of indebtedness wiped out under his tenure. Treasury secretary Louis McLane thought this could be done by March 4, 1833, terminal date of Jackson's term and of the Twenty-Second Congress.[1]

Restructuring the national finances, then, could no longer be postponed. Recent receipts, including about $2 million from public lands, had averaged $25 to $30 million annually, with expenses other than debt service at about $15 million. Clearly the tariff, which furnished nine-tenths of the revenue, would have to come down. But how far, how fast, and on what principles? Jackson's answer came with his message to Congress of December 1831, urging "a reduction of our

143

revenue to the wants of the Government." Before this he had favored retaining some duties solely for protection. As Jackson explained it to Martin Van Buren, his reversal was precautionary. Frustrated in their hopes for relief from Congress, South Carolina extremists now contemplated nullifying the tariff as unconstitutional and forcibly preventing its collection—a remedy that threatened civil war. By taking their position on the tariff, Jackson hoped to "annihilate the Nullifiers as they will be left without any pretext of Complaint." Of course, a revenue tariff would leave no surplus to spend or return to the states. Distribution of the surplus revenue, itself so objectionable to Southerners, silently vanished from Jackson's program, never to reappear.[2]

Treasury secretary McLane went one step further. Noting that the land revenue would shortly be redundant, and that the land system furnished "gradually accumulating causes of inquietude and difficulty," if not of complaint" between the West and the federal government, McLane proposed to sell the domain on credit to the states in which it lay. Proceeds of the sale could be divided among all the states for education and internal improvement.[3]

A mixed reaction greeted McLane's proposal. Jackson did not endorse it. The Alabama legislature approved the plan, and the *St. Louis Beacon*, Benton's mouthpiece, declared it the "best mode ever presented to Congress" for settling the land question. But some Westerners wanted to see details first, and others were against it from the start. A caucus of congressmen from the new states, convened to plot strategy on land reform, refused to endorse McLane's project. Few Westerners were willing to contract large state debts, burdening their citizens with high land prices or heavy taxation.[4]

Henry Clay asked, "was there ever a wilder scheme than that respecting the public lands?" Even the favorable responses to McLane's project underscored its impracticability. The *Richmond Enquirer*, praising it as the practical expression of Hayne's ideas in the Foot debate, exulted over the great sums the sale would generate for the old states. A sale of 300 million acres, even at only 50¢ per acre, would yield $150 million. Virginia's portion would be at least $15 million, or, if invested at interest, $800,000 per annum. "What might not Virginia do with an annual dividend of $800,000—or even the half of it? How many miles of road might she not complete? How many schools establish? How many of her degraded population might she not transport to the shores of Africa?" The prospect was so heady that the *Enquirer* nearly forgot its scruples against federal subsidies for such purposes. But it suggested that the peculiar constitutional footing of the land fund might justify an exception.[5]

The *United States Telegraph*, now the voice of the Calhoun faction but still sympathetic to the West, pinpointed the flaw in the plan. McLane had not specified a price for the lands. No figure could satisfy both old and new states. Westerners complained of the two or three million dollars sent eastward through land sales each year; where on earth would they get a hundred million, or even the interest on such a sum? Indiana contained sixteen million acres of federal land, worth, at fifty cents per acre, eight million dollars. The entire state budget for 1831 was $174,000.[6]

The *Richmond Enquirer* thought fifty cents per acre a low price for lands. Atlantic congressmen cited fifty cents, or even a dollar; none went lower than twenty cents. But at the Western caucus, only Joseph Duncan of Illinois was willing to pledge more than three cents per acre. Representative Franklin Plummer considered even one cent too high for much of the federal land in Mississippi. The House Public Lands Committee concluded that any price acceptable to the old states "would paralyze the growth and prosperity" of the new ones. McLane's proposal quickly foundered on the rock that had wrecked every other major land measure—the absolute inability of West and East to agree on what constituted a reasonable price for public lands.[7]

Less than ever were Westerners willing to compromise, for they scented victory in the impending retirement of the national debt. Would Congress dare to reduce the tariff but refuse relief to land buyers, who also contributed to the Treasury? "Now is the favourable time for us of the new States to make a stand," said Senator John Robinson of Illinois, for if the tariff was lowered without changing the land system, "it will be a kind of estoppel to any future relief on this subject. I say relief, for the present land system is a burthen of the most onerous character to all the new States." Missouri congressional candidate James Birch hailed the coming downfall of the present "arbitrary, unjust, oppressive, and absurd" land system. The release of the lands from their pledge to the public creditor made possible "an essential change" in the land system, an Illinois Jackson meeting declared. Senator Gabriel Moore of Alabama, a cession advocate, anticipated "some great and important change" in the land system, while the Washington *Globe* thought the "critical period" was at hand when land policy must take a new course. "Whether that destination shall be disastrous, or felicitous, for the new States, is now to be decided."[8]

Henry Clay, back in Washington as senator from Kentucky and National Republican presidential candidate, also planned to revamp the nation's finances—and to save the American System, which the discharge of the debt exposed to imminent peril. Clay's idea, embodied in resolutions submitted to the Senate, was to reduce or abolish duties on noncompetitive items, lopping off seven million dollars of revenue while leaving protection intact. In debate, Clay also urged Congress to resist "all the mad and wild schemes . . . for squandering the public domain," and to allocate the land revenue for roads and canals, thus preserving the land system and internal improvements.[9]

Clay's resolutions offered an opening to the promoters of the South–West alliance. His tariff proposal, which would still leave a large surplus, antagonized Southerners who wanted a pure revenue tariff with uniform duties across the board. Westerners, of course, wanted land prices reduced. The *Richmond Enquirer* urged South and West to unite for a lower tariff and cheap lands: "Both are connected; both must go together. The strength which is gained to the Tariff cause, by connecting it with Internal Improvement, must be counteracted by connecting the Tariff relief with the relief to the purchasers of the public lands."[10]

Still, there were signs that a union of South and West would prove no easier to achieve in 1832 than in 1830. South Atlantic senators invariably began their reckoning on the tariff with two or three million dollars of annual land income; but Westerners objected that a revenue tariff calculated on that basis would foreclose lowering land prices, as there would be no money to spare. Benton and the Southwesterners urged reducing the tariff and land prices together, but Elias Kane of Illinois declared himself "incomparably more interested in a change of the land system of the United States, than in any conceivable adjustment of the tariff," while some Southerners, including Hayne's South Carolina colleague Stephen Miller, opposed any more land concessions to the West.[11]

Protectionists wanted Clay's tariff resolutions consigned to the Committee on Manufactures, of which Clay was the guiding spirit and Mahlon Dickerson of New Jersey the chairman. Tariff reformers preferred the moderate Committee on Finance. The outcome was foretold early in the session, when protectionists steered Thomas Hart Benton's bills to reduce duties on salt and Indian blankets to the Manufactures Committee, over his objections. On March 22, 1832, the tariff coalition of all the National Republicans and nine Jacksonians from the mid-Atlantic and Northwestern states sent Clay's resolutions to the Manufactures Committee as well.[12]

The tariff referral vote was a test of protective principle; hence the sectional split among the Jacksonians. But sectionalism could also be turned to Jacksonian advantage. Clay was the National Republican candidate for president. If by Jacksonian disharmony he was to be allowed control of the tariff, why not embarrass him with the land question as well? Western Jacksonians immediately moved to refer the land issue to the Committee on Manufactures. Clay and the National Republicans protested the idiosyncratic reference, but to no avail. Benton had his revenge; the referral passed, 26 to 20. The division exactly reversed that on the tariff, except that seven of the nine protectionist Jacksonians voted yea on both, making the land referral almost a pure party question.[13]

Clay was now in a predicament. His opposition to Benton's land policies, though fixed and no doubt known to the Senate, was not yet a matter of public record. To proclaim it now would certainly hurt him in the West in the presidential election, only seven months away. But not only the election was at stake. To Clay, the maneuvers in the Senate offered proof of "a scheme which I have long since suspected—that certain portions of the South were disposed to purchase support to the anti-Tariff doctrines, by a total sacrifice of the public lands to States within which they are situated. A more stupendous, and more flagitious project was never conceived." But Clay saw a way to escape the trap they had set for him and rescue the American System as well.[14]

The Manufactures Committee reported a tariff bill based on Clay's resolutions on March 30, prompting Benton to ask what had become of the public lands. Two weeks later that report appeared, bearing Clay's signature. The report faced cession and graduation squarely, and repudiated both. Against cession Clay invoked the obligation to conserve the lands as a common fund for all the states. He dismissed Treasury secretary McLane's plan as impractical, even dangerous, for by indebting the Western states to the nation it would revive all the dangers to the Union stilled by the Land Act of 1820.

But the crux of Clay's report was its refutation of Benton's graduation arguments. Clay summoned all the old objections, added some new twists of his own, and wove the whole into a composition that challenged the Bentonian critique of the land system at every point. "Whilst the spirit of free emigration should not be checked or counteracted, it stands in no need of any fresh stimulus," said Clay. In the last decade the population of the seven public land states had increased by 85 percent; in the other seventeen states, by only 25 percent. The five fastest-growing states in the Union were Illinois, Alabama, Indiana, Missouri, and Mississippi. Ohio was seventh, Louisiana ninth. Annual land sales had tripled in three years, to three million dollars in 1831. It was "incredible to suppose that the amount of sales would have risen to so large a sum if the price had been unreasonably high." Like graduation's earlier critics, Clay argued that millions of acres remained unsold only because "the power of emigration has been totally incompetent to absorb" the glut of lands generously thrown open at Western behest. Deftly Clay exploited the growing rift between old and new West, naming Kentucky, Tennessee, and Ohio as the chief suppliers of migrants. For them graduation meant declining property values, population, and wealth, while on the frontier it threatened to produce a rampage of speculation, to the ultimate detriment of the actual settler.[15]

Clay's solution to the land dilemma was that Western anathema, distribution of the land revenue to the states according to population— but distribution with a difference. In the "spirit of liberality" he proposed a direct rebate of 10 percent of the land proceeds to the states from which they came, beyond the 5 percent allocated for roads under the admission compacts. To the two traditional objects of distribution, internal improvements and education, he added a third, colonization of free Negroes. Like Virgil Maxcy a decade earlier, Clay closed with a list of the sums due each state under his plan.

Though it followed six years later, Clay's report was the logical counterpart to Benton's Senate speech of 1826. Each definitively stated its side of the land question. Clay's friends greeted his report enthusiastically. The *National Intelligencer* called it "one of the most luminous and comprehensive documents to which American Legislation has ever given birth . . . ; a paper for history and for posterity." A correspondent of the Louisville *Journal and Focus* said it was "unsurpassed by any document on record" for the "liberality and expansiveness of its views and its strength of argument." "The subject was grappled by a fearless and a master hand—*and is subdued*," concluded *Niles' Register*. Richard Rush and Chief Justice John Marshall tendered personal compliments.[16]

Clay's enemies, on the other hand, showed no sign of being "subdued" by his report. Southern and Western Jacksonians, with Vice-President Calhoun casting the deciding vote, referred his distribution bill to the Committee on Public Lands, dominated by Jackson men from the new states. That committee pronounced its "decisive condemnation" on Clay's bill, and submitted in its stead a price-reduction and graduation bill, with a 15 percent rebate to the new states to outbid Clay's offer of 10 percent. Concluding that "the new States have grown up, not so much by the aid of the present system as in spite of it," the committee's report recited all the old arguments for cheap land and against distribution. The signature on the report was that of committee chairman William King of Alabama, but the phrasing, the statistics, and the quotations all betrayed its true parent: Thomas Hart Benton.[17]

As in 1830 the issue was now clearly drawn, but with one essential difference. The West could go for graduation, or through distribution it could cling to internal improvements and the American System, but it could no longer do both. Dressed up as it was, Clay's distribution was still distribution, a program concocted explicitly to frustrate the Western desire for cheap lands. It was futile to deny that graduation and distribution were mutually exclusive.

Distribution: the creation of a party platform

Clay's report elevated land revenue distribution from a sectional land proposition to a great national program. Like his more famous compromises, Clay's distribution plan was an agglomeration of disparate provisions, each appealing frankly to someone's self-interest but collectively conforming to no policy principle beyond the principle of compromise itself. Like his other compromises also, distribution had something in it for everyone.

The idea of basing internal improvements on the land revenue had been in many minds at the opening of the Twenty-second Congress. Clay contemplated it at least as early as October of 1831. Quite independently, so did Calhoun. "Should there be a disposition to close the present controversy," he remarked to Samuel Ingham in July 1831, "the question of internal improvement might to the mutual advantage of all be closed by pledging the publick lands after the discharge of the debt, as a fund for that purpose. Without something of the kind the West will never be satisfied." Duff Green broached the idea to Ninian Edwards, while still encouraging his cession crusade. James Madison told Martin Van Buren apropos the Maysville Road veto that "if Congress do not mean to throw away the rich fund inherited in the public lands," their proceeds might be "aptly appropriated" to internal improvements upon retirement of the national debt.[18]

Linking internal improvements to land proceeds would solve two problems at once. Few Easterners were willing to grant the radical revision of the land system demanded by the West. On this even the South Carolina member of Clay's Manufactures Committee concurred. Given a chance, the new states would no doubt begin a bidding war for settlers, competing with cheap prices and easy terms and triggering a land scramble that, in Calhoun's words, "would at once unsettle the whole landed property of the U.S." Calhoun was willing perhaps to relinquish the land revenue, but not to depopulate and impoverish South Carolina into the bargain.[19]

The best way to reconcile Westerners to the existing system was to apply land proceeds to internal improvement, itself a favorite Western policy. The arrangement might also quell Western demands for direct road and canal spending, thus, in Calhoun's hopes if not Clay's, loosening the West from its attachment to the American System. Like acid and base, lands and internal improvements could be combined to produce a neutral solution. Neither by itself "will ever be settled down," thought Calhoun, and "till they are both fixed, our political system will be subject to violent discord and vibrations."[20]

Southerners like Calhoun who damned Jackson's earlier plan to distribute the general surplus could face land revenue distribution with relative equanimity; for though it too diverted revenue and so sustained the tariff, the size of the diversion was fixed and fairly small. Jackson's distribution, by contrast, was open-ended, with an infinite capacity to absorb surplus receipts. From Clay's point of view, land revenue distribution sheltered a remnant of the internal improvement policy from Jackson's vetoes, without preventing a return to direct spending should the Hero be ousted in the 1832 election.

By adding colonization of free blacks to distribution's objects, Clay also appealed to reformers, North and South, who sought a moderate solution to the slavery dilemma. The idea of using land proceeds to colonize blacks had been raised before in Congress, once by Senator Rufus King of New York. Both Jefferson and Madison had favored it. Colonization appealed especially to older Southerners like Charles Fenton Mercer of Virginia and Clay himself, who were schooled to oppose slavery in principle but to accept it in practice. By 1832 moral intransigence was eroding colonization's constituency in both North and South. Younger Southerners, not sharing Clay's qualms about slavery, considered colonization an attack on the institution itself, while Northern abolitionists rejected it because it failed to address slavery's fundamental immorality. But Clay, a border-state man who learned his politics at the school of the Jeffersonian Enlightenment, never lost his faith in colonization. He had been active in the American Colonization Society since its founding in 1816, and would later serve as its president.[21]

Strict constructionists had always gagged at propositions to subsidize education and internal improvement, to say nothing of Negro colonization. But the peculiar status of the land revenue suggested a way around this obstacle. Clay himself found "not the slightest authority" in the Constitution for such a general distribution as Jackson had proposed. But Congress's constitutional right to "dispose of, and make all needful Rules and Regulations respecting the Territory or other Property belonging to the United States" entailed a plenary power over land receipts. The state deeds of cession, which antedated the Constitution and controlled its interpretation, could be construed to allow or even require distribution. Virginia's said the lands should be "a common fund for the use and benefit of such of the United States as have become, or shall become, members of the Confederation or federal alliance of the said States, Virginia inclusive, according to their usual respective proportions in the general charge and expenditure." That this obligation was still current no one doubted, but its meaning was dubious. In 1784 "United States" was a plural noun, and federal revenues came from requisitions upon the individual states. The clear intent of the ceding states and the Confederation Congress to apply the lands to the national debt had made interpretation unnecessary for half a century. But now the debt was paid. Clay argued that the federal government held the lands as trustee for the individual states. With the proceeds of the trust no longer needed for any common purpose, its terms permitted, even required, distribution of the dividends to the owners. The Constitution itself defined "usual respective proportions in the general charge and expenditure" by specifying population (calculated according to the three-fifths clause) as the basis for apportioning direct taxes.[22]

Clay's distribution offered benefits for everyone: for Westerners, guaranteed subsidies for internal improvement; for Easterners, a safeguard against destabilization of the land system; for reformers and improvers everywhere, a constitutionally safe fund for education and Negro colonization. But distribution also denied graduation to the West, hinted of antislavery, indirectly buttressed the protective tariff, and steered federal funds to purposes which many critics still thought unconstitutional. But most important for the immediate reception of Clay's program was the fact that it was Clay's. His name on the report enlisted behind land revenue distribution the power and prestige of a national politician; thenceforward distribution was known simply as "Mr. Clay's land bill." Jacksonians denounced it as a shameless bid for votes in the presidential election. Dropped into an electioneering congressional session by an aspirant for the presidency, distribution was promptly swept into the maelstrom of partisan politics.

Western Jacksonians berated Clay for betraying his section. "He is no longer a Westerner, either in feeling or policy; he has deserted the West," judged the *St. Louis Beacon*. The Vincennes *Western Sun* said that "fear" of rapid Western growth was "the pivot upon which the whole report turns," and accused Clay of sacrificing "the honest, highhearted yeomanry of the nation with their families, to the remorseless cupidity of a few pampered monopolists of the North." Illinois Jacksonians called the report "a reiteration of the odious doctrines" of Richard Rush, which had "retarded to an inconceivable extent the population and improvement" of the West. The *Illinois Advocate* warned that Clay "is endeavoring, like Nebuchadnezzar, to bind the new states hand and foot and throw them into the 'firey furnace' of the American system." The *Frankfort Argus* hoped the West "will award to him the just condemnation for his treachery."[23]

These partisan attacks masked the ambivalence of the Western response. Like other distribution schemes stretching back to the Maryland proposition of 1821, Clay's plan blocked the way to cheap land. But unlike them it offered compensation. Its advantages did not compare to those expected from graduation or cession, but still they were there, and tangible. By comparison graduation was a vision, and cession a chimera. What had the West to show for years of pursuing them both? Clay's distribution offered more than the West now received, which was nothing. Was distribution in the hand worth graduation in the bush? For the first time Westerners faced something close to a balanced alternative.

Before the dictates of party took hold, even Jackson men were unsure which way to turn. Jacksonian senator John Tipton of Indiana, like many Westerners, had resolved to salvage what he could from the existing land system. "We will try to procure a portion of the money arriseing from the sales of land for internal improvement within the new states provided the present land system remains," he confided the day before Clay submitted his report. But later in the session Tipton turned against distribution because it was an "entirely new and a very important question *thrown into the senate by party.*" Still, he expected to support it the next year. Even the *St. Louis Beacon* at first was "at an entire loss" to understand Benton's opposition to distribution; surely some "judicious arrangement" of the land system was preferable to fruitless pursuit of the cession "phantom." But within a month the *Beacon*, without quite rejecting distribution, was calling Clay a traitor to the West for proposing it.[24]

While Clay's distribution plan held attractions even for Jacksonians, his repudiation of graduation and cession was difficult for his own Western adherents to swallow. In Indiana and Illinois, hotbeds of land reform sentiment, National Republican papers greeted Clay's report uneasily, begging readers to lay aside sectional prejudice and give it a "candid examination." But soon they were trumpeting the advantages of distribution over "the schemes of demagogues which could never be adopted." Outside the frontier West, National Republicans backed Clay's project from the start.[25]

In Senate debate on distribution Clay and Benton took the lead, sneering and jibing at each other before packed galleries. A new and striking manifestation of partisanship appeared in the early roll calls. Two years earlier a truncated graduation bill had passed the Senate, but now Benton's attempts to graft graduation onto distribution failed, 21 to 27 and 20 to 28. On these votes John Tyler of Virginia, Stephen Miller of South Carolina, and Jacksonians from the mid-Atlantic states joined Eastern National Republicans against graduation. This was as before. But Benton's coalition of South and West suffered its crucial losses in the West itself. All five Western National Republicans—not only Clay and the Ohioans, but both Louisianians as well—voted with graduation's Atlantic foes. The rest of the West lined up for Benton's amendments, but it was not enough. Western solidarity had been a staple of graduation voting since the first roll call in 1828, and that solidarity, with Southern help, had squeezed a bill through the Senate in 1830. Suddenly it was gone.[26]

On the Senate floor the friends of distribution sweetened the concoction for Western palates. They inserted a stipulation that distribution should not prevent graduation or cession. They raised the rebate on land sales from 10 percent to 12½, after rejecting a frontier bid for the Public Land Committee's figure of 15. Next they tacked on a massive internal improvement land grant of 500,000 acres each to Mississippi, Louisiana, and Missouri, 100,000 to Alabama, 20,000 to Illinois, and 115,272 to Indiana, which, together with previous donations under Adams, equalled the 500,000 acres granted for the Ohio canal in 1828. Only a handful of distribution's Western foes, Benton not among them, resisted these enticements, though Southeastern senators opposed them all.[27]

Altogether distribution went through twenty-four Senate roll calls. The twenty National Republicans, East and West, voted in column, joined usually by some mid-Atlantic Jacksonians. In the West, independent William Hendricks of Indiana and states' righter George Poindexter of Mississippi supported distribution. Tipton of Indiana wavered, but voted against it in the end.[28]

Thus a new national coalition appeared to challenge Benton's alliance of Southerners, Westerners, and New England Jacksonians. Like Benton's, it was sectionally based; nineteen of the twenty-six Senate votes for distribution were Northeastern. But also like Benton's, Clay's coalition seduced support from its traditional sectional enemies.

As Benton's appeals to the poor against the rich and to "Republicans" against "Federalists" had won over Jacksonians in New England (and to a much lesser extent in the mid-Atlantic states), so devotion to Henry Clay and the promise of rich subsidies rallied many Westerners to distribution. The Senate passage of distribution showed the extent to which partisanship had undermined Western sectional solidarity (see table 6.1).

Distribution won no recruits in the Old South. The *Charleston Mercury* classified it with internal improvement and other spending bills as "parts of a grand system of tyranny, by which the South is to be fleeced and trampled, for the benefit of the North and West." The embellishments which helped to reconcile Westerners to distribution made it even more offensive to the South. Some of Calhoun's skeptical South Carolina confederates viewed his own distribution idea not as a compromise to save the Union but as a wild scheme to promote his dubious

TABLE 6.1
DISTRIBUTION, SENATE, 1832

	Jackson and Calhoun[a]		National Republican		Total	
	For	*Against*	*For*	*Against*	*For*	*Against*
New England		1	11		11	1
Mid-Atlantic	4	2	4		8	2
South Atlantic		8				8
West	1	9	5		7[b]	9
Total	5	20	20		26	20

Source: Senate Journal, 22d Cong., 1st sess., pp. 392, 394.

Note: Table 6.1 combines roll calls on third reading and passage, with a cohesion of 100% (see note to table 2.1).

[a]Tables in chapter 6 group Calhoun's Southern states' rights faction with the Jacksonians (for the method of determining party affiliation, see note to table 5.1). Despite the two men's personal feud and their differences over nullification, Calhounites remained essentially indistinguishable from Southern Jacksonians in their opposition to the tariff and hence to distribution.

[b]William Hendricks of Indiana is not shown in the party columns. A political trimmer, Hendricks had defended the Adams administration, and now called himself a Democrat but admired Henry Clay. For contemporary uncertainty as to his affiliation, see the *Baton Rouge Gazette*, January 29, 1831; *Illinois Advocate*, November 4, 1831, and January 13, 1832; Henry Clay to J. S. Johnston, November 1, 1830, in Clay papers, LC.

presidential prospects. But the circumstances of distribution's introduction in the Senate made it unacceptable even to Calhoun. The key to Southern sentiment was the tariff; until it was lowered, no Southerner would abide a bill that bolstered protection by drawing three million dollars annually out of the Treasury. While the Senate debated distribution, a tariff bill waited in the wings, having already passed the House. Though framed as a compromise, it fell far short of the South Carolina standard, and the Senate Manufactures Committee reported it out with a string of protective amendments the very day before the final vote on distribution. The South had divided its tariff votes in the House, but the amendments drove Southern senators into solid opposition. Benton, seeing his opening, played on distribution as "an ultra tariff measure." On cue, all eight Southeastern senators lined up against distribution.[29]

Distribution arrived in the House of Representatives at the tail end of a long session and failed to obtain a hearing. A move to kill the bill by postponement carried 91 to 88, and reconsideration failed by 100 to 88. Both were party votes, National Republicans unanimously for the bill and Jacksonians outside of Pennsylvania and Ohio almost equally united against it.[30]

Given a choice between graduation and a suddenly attractive distribution, Westerners again returned home with neither. But again they did not go empty-handed. While the party battles raged, they quietly secured another minor land reform, the right to purchase public lands in forty-acre tracts after the auction. Like pre-emption, the forty-acre law was a staple, though secondary, request of Western petitioners, who stepped up their agitation just before the meeting of Congress. Though the floor debate vented sectional animosity, the measure passed the Senate without a division and the House by 118 to 44. Eastern Jacksonians gave the bill stronger support than did National Republicans, especially in New England.[31]

At the beginning of the session Benton had seen "all the indications" as favorable to graduation; at its end he was farther from his object than he had been two years before. The session marked the emergence of a partisan alternative to Benton's land bill, and the elevation of two old Western rivals to leadership in their respective camps. Webster and Hayne sank into the background; it was Clay, candidate for the presidency, and Benton, now recognized as Jackson's spokesman, who battled over the lands, the Bank of the United States, and the tariff. Together they dominated the session, and it ended, fittingly, in a fiery altercation between the two Westerners before an aghast and scandalized Senate.[32]

Graduation versus distribution: the party line drawn

Both Clay and Jackson men employed the land issue in the 1832 presidential campaign. Clay's Atlantic followers publicized distribution's rich benefits, but even more emphatically they hailed it as the answer to "certain *demagogues* and *nullifiers* of the west." The land issue was already a "bone of contention" between East and West "and may be the cause of their ultimate separation" if not quieted, warned Rhode Island senator Asher Robbins and representative Tristam Burges; "of all subjects, it is already the most exciting of any we have in Congress, the most troublesome and difficult to deal with." *Niles' Register*, observing that the land question might "become, perhaps, among the most important which ever agitated the United States," touted Clay's bill as "the *bond of peace*." It "puts down all ideas of 'nullification' on account of the public lands, and seals the lips of boisterous pretenders to the people's confidence."[33]

Western Clay men lined up for distribution too, but with sentiments far removed from those of their Atlantic brethren. Western Clay papers took up the old argument of David Barton's party in Missouri: graduation would throw lands to speculators and thus obstruct the poor man's access to a farm, hindering, not hastening, the settlement of the West. But most Western converts to distribution abandoned the crusade for cheap land apologetically and reluctantly, and only from a conviction of its utter hopelessness. In 1830 Senator William Hendricks of Indiana, a cession advocate, likened the "wild scheme" of distribution to the old Maryland proposition. But in 1832, voicing "regret and surprise" at the "aversion" of the old states to the demands of the new, he voted for Clay's bill. A year later he called it "the only thing practicable, either at present, or in prospect." Hendricks told his constituents that "a preponderating power of the old States is against us" on land reform, and that "in contending for that which we prefer, but have no prospect of getting, we are losing every year large sums, which this bill would give us." Representative Jonathan McCarty of Indiana, "finding that all hope of any reduction of the price of the public lands had vanished," likewise converted to distribution in 1833, as the only measure "of which there was any hope of uniting a majority of Congress, perhaps, for years to come."[34]

Distribution's Western recruits offered such explanations partly to cover their political rear. They were wary of associating with distribution's Atlantic advocates, who touted it as the answer to the West's "extravagant calculations" and "unfounded pretensions." Yet the dilemma of men like Hendricks was real. Though he supported distribution in 1832, Hendricks did not, like the National Republicans, also turn against graduation. Neither did George Poindexter of Mississippi, who voted for distribution in the end after concluding that graduation was "hopeless." Distribution, in short, became a partisan measure in 1832, but it was able to attract a party following in the West only because it offered a defensible alternative to graduation. The proof of its innate attractiveness in the face of graduation's repeated failures lay in its ability to enlist men who were not Clay loyalists and who had not surrendered their first preference for graduation.[35]

The creation of an alternative in turn exposed Western graduation men, for the first time, to political counterattack from the National Republicans. Cheap lands were still the rage, but as one candidate who advocated them admitted, in "ten years fruitless legislation" graduation's friends "have ever found their exertions thrown away." It was therefore difficult to justify refusing the cash and land grants contained in Clay's bill. Internal improvement and education were still popular in the West, and the importance of state enterprise grew as the president throttled federal spending. In 1832 Jackson pocket-vetoed a rivers and harbors bill, prompting a Clayite friend of John Tipton's to ask, "Do not these two [the other was the Bank veto] take away all that we in the West have ever contended for, & struggled for, in aid of the progress of our country? and really it seems to me you cannot sustain the Hero unless you give these up." As an alternative or supplement to direct federal subsidies, distribution naturally inherited the internal improvement constituency.[36]

In the presidential campaign Clay's partisans pushed distribution along with direct federal improvements. The Jacksonian *Illinois Advocate*, on the other hand, urged voters to turn out "against the man who would prohibit emigration to the new States." Mingling sectional with class rhetoric, the Washington *Globe* and other Jackson presses accused Clay of selling out the West to the East, and the poor settler to the rich aristocrat. Anti-tariff Jacksonians like Senator Isaac Hill of New Hampshire faulted Clay for throwing away revenue to justify high duties.[37]

But though the campaign kept distribution before the public, it remained a secondary issue even in the West. From the start it competed for attention with the tariff and internal improvements. Jackson's veto of the recharter of the second Bank of the United States in July gave Clay, as he thought, better ammunition against the president than did the other American System issues. Down the final stretch the other issues were thrust aside and the talk was all of bank, bank, bank. The outcome, foreordained by the failure of Clay's National Republicans to coalesce with the anti-Masonic faction in the North and with disaffected Jacksonians in the South, was a repeat of 1828. Jackson won easily, taking all the West but Kentucky.

No one attributed the result to the land issue, even in part. But in local politics the issue remained potent. Westerners accustomed to acting together on land matters now parted company, and the partings were sometimes bitter. In Mississippi, Senator George Poindexter arraigned Jacksonian representative Franklin Plummer for his vote against distribution, a "surrender at the shrine of party discipline" that cost Mississippi two million dollars in cash and land grants. Poindexter's attack cost Plummer, by his own estimate, several thousand votes in his successful bid for reelection. Indiana governor Noah Noble, a National Republican, censured the state's representatives for opposing distribution and praised Senators Tipton and Hendricks for their support. His message drew fire from Representative Ratliff Boon, a Jackson and graduation man, and it embarrassed poor Tipton, who actually voted against the bill after cooperating with its friends on preliminary tests. Noble's misplaced praise drew scrutiny to Tipton's prevarications, subjecting him to a crossfire of complaint from both Clayites and Jacksonians.[38]

The use of the land issue in the 1832 presidential campaign accelerated its evolution from a sectional to a party question. But the process remained incomplete without direction from the White House. Jackson was the guiding light of the party that bore his name. His preferences shaped its policies; his popularity furnished its constituency. Thus far the president had noticed the public domain only as a source of revenue for his great goal of paying off the national debt.

In December 1832 Jackson broke his silence before the reconvened Twenty-second Congress. The public debt was paid, he said, and Congress was now at liberty to dispose of the lands as it saw fit. But a "liberal policy" was imperative, to ward off a sectional collision potentially "more dangerous to the harmony and union of the States than any other cause of discontent."

> It seems to me to be our true policy that the public lands shall cease as soon as practicable to be a source of revenue, and that they be sold to settlers in limited parcels at a price barely sufficient to reimburse to the United States the expense of the present system. . . . It is desirable . . . that in convenient time . . . the right of soil and the future disposition of it be surrendered to the States respectively in which it lies. . . . it cannot be expected that the new States will remain longer contented with the present policy after the payment of the public debt.[39]

Bentonism was now, officially and indisputably, Jacksonism. The word graduation nowhere appeared (having been excised from an earlier draft), but the policy was Bentonian, along with much of the accompanying argument. John Quincy Adams observed that Jackson "has cast away all the neutrality" he had hitherto maintained on sectional issues "and surrenders the whole Union to the nullifiers of the South and the land-robbers of the West." Jackson was no nullifier. But it was true that he had successively abandoned the outposts of the American System: internal improvements beginning in 1830, the protective tariff in 1831, the Bank in 1832, and now the land system. What was left was the states' rights, strict constructionist policy outlined by Benton and the propagators of the South–West alliance in the 1828 campaign.[40]

"Who shall now say that Gen. Jackson is not the friend of the West?" queried the *Louisville Public Advertiser*. Jackson "does not countenance and connive at the schemes of Webster & Co. to stint and cripple the growing population of the West," nor "recommend that the surplus population of the East, be 'cabined and cribbed' in manufactories, to lead a life of slavery, of moral and physical decrepitude and degradation." For its part, the *National Intelligencer* complained of Jackson's capitulation "to the apprehension of a *discontent* (which actually has no existence,)" in the West, just as he had surrendered the tariff to the blustering South. Western National Republicans maintained a discreet silence.[41]

At the head of the adherents of graduation and distribution now marched the leaders of the two great national parties; for Clay, though humiliated in the election, was still a power in the Senate and in the country. Should the government promote economic diversification and social progress with funds drawn from the land revenue, or encourage agricultural expansion by throwing open the Western domain at nominal prices? The winter legislative sessions soon yielded official reactions from the states.

Convening in November and December 1832, many state legislatures found on their tables resolutions adopted by Tennessee a year earlier (before Clay's bill and Jackson's message), requesting both graduation and distribution of the land proceeds to the states for education. Tennessee's two-faced posture reflected its borderline status in sectional politics, but its intrinsically difficult policy straddle had been rendered well-nigh impossible by events in the intervening year. In the states as in Washington, there were advocates of graduation and of distribution, but few who touted both.[42]

Within a month, the legislatures of four of the five mid-Atlantic states—Delaware, Maryland, New Jersey, and Pennsylvania—endorsed land revenue distribution. Sectionalism, not partisanship, governed the action; though specific praise of Clay and criticism of the president provoked Jacksonian dissent, all the resolutions eventually passed without opposition. Not one Jackson man in the four states defended the president's cheap land policy.[43]

The anti-Jackson Vermont legislature resolved for distribution without a division. So did Massachusetts, with an argument stressing the threat of cheap Western lands not to manufacturing but to New England agriculture. Both states praised Henry Clay. But in New Hampshire, where Jacksonism reigned, the legislature shunted aside distribution resolutions on a party vote. No one offered counterresolutions supporting the president's policy.[44]

In the legislatures as in Congress, partisanship on national issues had developed much further in New England than in the mid-Atlantic states by 1832. New England Jackson men dutifully followed the presidential lead against internal improvements, the tariff, and now distribution, while their co-partisans in Pennsylvania and Maryland refused to tread the party line. But even New England Jacksonians stopped short of endorsing cheaper land prices.

Alabama, Illinois, and Missouri echoed Jackson's message with new demands for graduation. The only opposition came from the remnant of the Barton faction in Missouri. Distribution thus made few inroads upon graduation's frontier constituency. But in the older West it was different. In Indiana, National Republican Governor Noah Noble espoused distribution. His message elicited conflicting committee reports and an untidy debate in the lower house of the legislature, where the urge to further Indiana's progress through internal improvements and education collided with the craving for accelerated migration and population growth. The result was confusion. Clay men took the lead for distribution, but party lines were still nebulous in Indiana (both sides claimed a majority in the legislature), and the discussion showed that advocates of neither policy were really willing to relinquish the benefits of the other. After thirteen roll calls, which suggested an unstable majority for both distribution and graduation, the house gave up.[45]

The Indiana debate provided the first evidence that Eastern views on land policy were seeping still further westward. One legislator, contrasting old and new West, linked Indiana with Ohio rather than Illinois. In Ohio itself, and in Kentucky, the contagion was already epidemic. Ohio National Republicans had greeted Clay's distribution bill enthusiastically and with none of the frontiersmen's qualms when it appeared in 1832. In February 1833 the Ohio senate debated distribution, a Clay man arguing that "it will unite Ohio with the older States," while cession would lure emigrants away, "curtail the increase of population, and finally stagnate the prosperity of the State." The vote on distribution followed strict party lines. In Kentucky the Clay legislature passed resolutions supporting distribution and opposing Western pretensions to ownership of the public domain; the Jacksonian governor vetoed them. The breakdown of a sectional posture on the land issue in the old West opened the way for party division, a development further marked by the intermingling of the land issue with other partisan concerns. An unsuccessful Ohio resolution praising Jackson cited the land message among his achievements. In Kentucky the distribution resolutions defended, while the veto message attacked, the Bank of the United States.[46]

From the seaboard South there was silence. Legislators there had graver matters on their minds, for as Congress reconvened in December 1832 the South teetered on the edge of rebellion over the tariff. Nullifiers commanded a majority only in South Carolina, but sharp dissent over remedies masked a fundamental unity of Southern resistance to the protectionist tariff "compromise" of 1832. Legislatures in Alabama, Mississippi, Virginia, and Georgia denied the constitutionality of duties levied solely for protective purposes. (Sugar-growing Louisiana hailed the tariff as constitutional and expedient.) Some Southern congressmen had voted for the tariff of 1832. But as the Alabama legislature explained, that tariff, though "unequal, unjust, oppressive, and against the spirit, true intent, and meaning of the constitution," was acceptable as, and only as, a "harbinger of better times—as a pledge that Congress will, at no distant period, abandon the principle of protection altogether." The same tariff led South Carolina's congressmen to conclude that hope of relief from Congress was "irrevocably gone." Southerners disagreed over whether the tariff of 1832 moved in the right direction, but they all knew what that direction was.[47]

Southern statements on distribution were therefore unnecessary. In 1832 Southern congressmen had lined up solidly against distribution—more solidly than Westerners—and for reasons having nothing to do with the public lands. The tariff controlled Southern response to the land issue.

Still there were indications that if it could somehow be disentangled from the tariff, distribution might quickly find a Southern following. In December 1831 the lower house of the North Carolina legislature protested the "great and unreasonable requests" of the West and demanded a "fair and equal application of the public lands," the "common property" of all the states. This was the language of distribution.[48]

The breakdown on distribution at the beginning of 1833 was then as follows: Clay's bill could expect bipartisan support from the mid-Atlantic states (New York perhaps excepted), partisan backing in New England and the Old West, opposition from the frontier, and a unanimous negative from the anti-tariff South until the tariff was reduced.

Prospects for graduation continued to dim despite Jackson's message. The winter legislative sessions brought no hint of approval from any North Atlantic state. Southern backing, never as strong as it appeared, had evaporated. The fragments of the alliance between Hayne's South and Benton's West lay strewn with the wreckage of Calhoun's presidential hopes. The congressional tariff-for-lands trade had failed in three straight sessions; Southerners, nullifiers or not, now looked to other remedies.

Benton, the master propagandist, wore a cheerful mask. Distribution threatened "a great outrage upon our rights," he warned on New Year's Day, but graduation was gaining with the president's help, and distribution was now "the sole obstacle to immediate success." But behind his brave front, Benton beat a steady retreat. The emasculation of his bill in the Senate in 1830 had chastened him. Subsequent versions stipulated smaller price reductions stretched over longer periods of time. By 1833 Benton's plan was closer to the Barton substitute he had hooted down in the Senate in 1828 than to his own original bill. Benton could play the land issue better than anyone else, but his efforts, unlike the histrionics of Ninian Edwards, were always aimed at practical results. He had refused to yoke himself to the cession campaign, correctly judging it hopeless. Now there was talk in the West of a blanket reduction to fifty cents per acre. Against that backdrop, the steady dilution of Benton's proposals spoke a telling commentary on the waning prospects for any great change in the land system.[49]

The Compromise of 1833

A week after Jackson's message in December 1832, Henry Clay resubmitted his distribution bill, and the Senate took up where it left off the previous spring. Meanwhile the tariff controversy built quickly to a crisis. In November South Carolina nullified the protective tariff as unconstitutional and forbade its collection; Jackson responded with a threat of force. But as the nullifiers drilled their volunteers and Jackson pondered strategies to repress rebellion, the Senate occupied itself by plodding through another distribution debate. Opponents hammered away at the tariff theme, Benton characterizing distribution as a device

> to keep up many millions of unnecessary revenue on imports, to the discontent and peril of the Union; to fill the new States with tenants, and the old ones with paupers; to make the new States the everlasting tributaries of countless millions to the old ones; and to gorge the high tariff States with the spoils of the West after having long fattened them upon the spoils of the South.[50]

Benton's strategy worked. South Atlantic senators stood firm against distribution. Calhoun himself, having resigned the vice-presidency for a seat in the Senate, spoke briefly against Clay's bill. But the positive side of Benton's South–West alliance, the commitment to a cheap land policy, collapsed completely. A Van Buren lieutenant in the House of Representatives observed that "the only real appearance of remaining regard for the Union among the nullifiers is found in the votes about the public lands. I had expected that these would be offered as a *donative* to squatters and states for recruits to nullification." Southeastern senators split evenly on a bid to substitute graduation for distribution, and voted 6 to 0 and 5 to 1 against George Poindexter's attempts to add it as an amendment. All three motions failed by large margins. Hayne was gone, and Calhoun, his replacement, voted against all three. With the partisan cleavage of his Western support and the collapse of his Southern wing, Benton's strength in the Senate was weaker than it had ever been before.[51]

Clay's distribution bill passed the Senate for the second time on January 25, 1833, by 24 to 21. Personnel changes aside, the vote was identical to that of the previous July (see table 6.2).

At this point no resolution of the nullification crisis was in sight. But during February, while distribution languished on the calendar of the House of Representatives, Congress moved toward a compromise on the tariff. The breakthrough came on February 12th, when Clay unveiled and Calhoun approved a bill providing for gradual reductions on protective duties until 1842 and a revenue tariff thereafter. On February 25 the House sidestepped its own more radical Ways and Means Committee bill, took up Clay's compromise, and pushed it quickly through its third reading and passage. Meanwhile the Senate passed the revenue collection, or "force," bill, designed to support President Jackson's warnings to the South Carolina nullifiers. On March 1 the House also passed the force bill, skipped over the rest of its

TABLE 6.2
DISTRIBUTION, SENATE, 1833

	Jackson and Calhoun[a]		National Republican		Total	
	For	*Against*	*For*	*Against*	*For*	*Against*
New England		1	10		10	1
Mid-Atlantic	4	2	3		7	2
South Atlantic		8				8
West	1	10	5		7[b]	10
Total	5	21	18		24	21

Source: *Senate Journal*, 22d Cong., 2d sess., p. 138.

[a]See note a to table 6.1.

[b]William Hendricks of Indiana is not shown in the party columns; see note b to table 6.1.

agenda, and took up distribution. Only a day and a half remained of the session.[52]

What one Washington pundit called a "great scheme of pacification" was taking shape, and distribution was in the middle of it. Clay explained the connection while introducing his compromise tariff: distribution would hedge against the accumulation of a treasury surplus during the nine years of gradual tariff reduction; after 1842, with the tariff fixed to a revenue standard, distribution would supply funds for internal improvements. Thus tandem passage of the tariff compromise and distribution would quiet all three of "the great questions which have agitated this country"—tariff, internal improvements, and public lands.[53]

Clay declined to unite his two bills in one, saying "each should stand or fall upon its own intrinsic merits." But the quid pro quo was plain, if unspoken: distribution was to be the price of tariff reduction. Some protectionists, including Webster, censured Clay for abandoning the American System, but they looked at the tariff alone. Taken together, land revenue distribution and Clay's tariff spelled a genuine accommodation, not a capitulation. Though the tariff would be reduced, diverting the land revenue into distribution would provide a protectionist cushion of about three million dollars annually. A long period of tariff adjustment (the largest reductions would begin in December 1841, more than eight years away) and the preservation of internal improvements through distribution would compensate American System men for sacrificing protection. Distribution itself already incorporated the principles of a compromise between East and West. As one Clay ally in the Senate later recalled, distribution and the tariff were "by us regarded *as part and parcel of one great revenue and financial system.*"[54]

Even before Clay introduced his tariff, feelers were out for a tariff-for-distribution trade. As the session neared its end, rumor warned that the Senate would refuse Clay's tariff unless the House of Representatives passed distribution. The same House had rejected it only eight months before; but, within hours after passing the force bill on March 1, the House jammed distribution through its third reading and passed it by 96 to 40. Clay's tariff passed the Senate the same day. Tariff, distribution, and the force bill went through, as the *National Intelligencer* said, "*pari passu,* and almost concurrently." "Contrary to almost universal belief three weeks ago," said *Niles' Register,* "the three great bills" had made it through Congress "by large and extraordinary majorities." "Sir," said Clay emerging from the Senate, "this has been the most proud and triumphant day of my life."[55]

His celebration was brief. On Saturday, March 2, Jackson returned the force and tariff bills with his signature, and Congress adjourned. On Sunday the 3d, the term of the Twenty-second Congress expired, and along with it Clay's distribution bill, unsigned.

Many omens foretold Jackson's pocket veto of distribution. Staunch Jackson papers everywhere had demanded it for weeks, while party lieutenants in Congress warned the president to be prepared. The *Globe,* Jackson's Washington press, did not predict a veto, but lavishly praised every floor speech for graduation and against distribution.[56]

Nevertheless the veto outraged distribution's advocates. They objected that Jackson had arbitrarily severed "part of the system of complete pacification, projected by the Senate," leaving unresolved a question which "would lead to distractions, dissensions and divisions, which would shake the integrity of our republic, and plunge us into all the dangers of anarchy and disunion." They also complained that Jackson's devious pocket veto avoided a nearly certain override in Congress. Some, including Clay, questioned the constitutionality of Jackson's maneuver, and a few ventured to suggest that the unsigned distribution bill was actually a law.[57]

This last was nonsense, of course. As James Madison told Henry Clay, a president's deliberate withholding of a bill from congressional reconsideration might justify impeachment, but that did not make the bill a law. Besides, the president was entitled to time for reflection. Jackson had had one day. In fact, as shortly became known, Jackson was ready with a veto message. But its objection was to the clause specifying internal improvements, education, and colonization as the purposes of distribution—a clause which the House struck from the bill just before passing it. Left with an obsolete message, and (according to Benton) with Calhoun and other likely sustainers absent from the hall, Jackson elected to sit on the bill instead.[58]

The assertion that a veto would have been overridden requires careful scrutiny, for it speaks to the nature of the compromise itself. John Quincy Adams later explained that the distribution bill "emanated from the same source, and was sanctioned by the same Congress, at the same time with the Compromise [tariff] Act, and although on another roll of parchment, as a system of administration, formed a part of it." Thus the veto "violated the principle of the Compromise at the very moment of approving and signing" the tariff. (Adams omitted to mention that he himself had voted for distribution but against Clay's tariff.) Clay also claimed a veto would have been overridden. Since distribution did not muster anything close to a two-thirds majority in either house in 1832, when it received no Southern support, the implication that it could now was plain: the South had been won over by the tariff compromise, and was prepared to fulfill its half of the bargain by sustaining distribution over Jackson's veto.[59]

Was such a deal struck? Certain evidence suggests it. Ten months before, the *Charleston Mercury*, Calhoun's homestate voice, was excoriating distribution as a scheme "to transfer annually millions upon millions of Southern tribute to those sections of the Union which have entered into an unholy combination to oppress the South." But the *Mercury*'s only comment when the bill passed was that it "will compensate the West, for any loss they may fancy themselves to have sustained from the surrender to the demands of South Carolina of the principle of protection." The Washington *Globe*, noting this abrupt reversal, branded it "one of the most extraordinary and enormous inconsistencies" to come out of the new Clay–Calhoun alliance. Duff Green's *United States Telegraph*, wholly devoted to Calhoun, did not endorse distribution, but it pronounced "the most decided condemnation" upon Jackson's pocket veto, and said the bill would have commanded two-thirds if returned.[60]

For proof that Jackson dodged a certain override, distribution men pointed to two votes: the 96 to 40 tally on final passage in the House, and the Senate concurrence late on March 1, by 23 to 5, with the House's amendment to strike the specific objects of distribution. The

Senate vote was actually meaningless. Seven former opponents of distribution, all from slave states, voted to accept the amendment, but not because they favored the bill. For them the amendment was an improvement, for it eliminated direct federal intervention in state concerns of internal improvement, education, and colonization. The seven senators had voted for a similar amendment during Senate consideration of the bill back in January. Having no chance now to defeat the bill, they seized their chance to make it less objectionable. Their approval of the amendment in no way committed them to distribution itself.[61]

The House of Representatives passed the distribution bill by more than a two-thirds majority. But it was two-thirds of a half-empty House. Full membership was 213, of which 205 (an extraordinarily large number) were present sometime on the afternoon of March 1. But only 136 remained to vote on distribution that night. The distribution vote came at the fag end of a continuous twelve-hour sitting, after a week of marathon labors which reduced many congressmen to a state of nervous exhaustion. Still, the attrition of so many members was surprising. Distribution was certainly important, it was not sprung on the House without prior warning, and an attempted filibuster allowed time for attending members to alert their wayward colleagues. The thin attendance becomes even more curious when one looks closely at who was absent.

Of the 69 representatives who were present earlier on March 1 but missed the distribution vote that night, 56 had been in attendance when distribution came before the House the previous July; and of those 56 members, 45 had then voted to kill the bill by postponement. The pattern of absenteeism, whether prearranged or not, was certainly far from random. Jacksonian foes of distribution who disappeared that evening included 5 members from Kentucky and Tennessee, 15 from the mid-Atlantic states, and the entire New Hampshire delegation. South Carolinians and Georgians vanished in a body, casting sixteen votes on the force bill and four on distribution.[62]

It was this group exodus, rather than any great change of front among those who remained, that permitted distribution to roll up its large majority. Eleven scattered votes for the bill came from members who had opposed it eight months before, but what really ensured its passage was the departure of its partisan opponents in the New England, mid-Atlantic, and old Western states and of Southern anti-tariffites, leaving Benton's frontier West to fight alone (see table 6.3).

It seems likely that an arrangement did exist between the Clay and Calhoun groups, allowing distribution to proceed unhindered after

TABLE 6.3
DISTRIBUTION, HOUSE, 1833

	Jackson and Calhoun[a]		National Republican		Total	
	For	Against	For	Against	For	Against
New England	1	2	20		21	2
Mid-Atlantic	22	6	22		44	6
South Atlantic	3	16	5		8	16
Ohio and Kentucky	7	3	11		18	3
Other West	1	13	4		5	13
Total	34	40	62		96	40

Source: *House Journal*, 22d Cong., 2d sess., pp. 460–461.
[a]See note a to table 6.1.

passage of the tariff compromise was assured. As the *Globe* noted, Calhoun could hardly go further. His followers could not easily turn around and vote for a bill they had just denounced in vitriolic terms and that Calhoun himself had spoken against earlier in the session. But they could, and most of them did, manage to be elsewhere when it came to a vote.[63]

The departure of the Jackson men, who were probably not privy to any understanding between Clay and Calhoun, is easily explained. The frontier Jacksonians, it should be noted, did not leave. With a passion, they hated distribution as the foil to graduation, and they fought it to the last with amendments and stalling tactics. But in the North Atlantic and old Western states, recent legislative proceedings had revealed the depth of popular sentiment for distribution as well as the dearth of sympathy for Jackson's land policy. Prominent Jackson men like Churchill Cambreleng of New York and Isaac Hill of New Hampshire had attacked distribution mainly as an obstacle to a tariff compromise. With that now secured and with Clay trounced in the 1832 election, the two main reasons to oppose distribution disappeared. So a few of its former foes, including some renegade Jacksonians from Pennsylvania and New York (among them Gulian Verplanck, antiprotectionist chairman of the House Ways and Means Committee), crossed over to the distribution ranks. Others, trapped between section and party, made themselves scarce. No doubt they had in mind constituents like Lucas Elmendorf, an old Jeffersonian who told Van Buren at about this time that Jackson's land policy would destroy the administration in New York state. Saying his own views were "so general and so deeprooted in interest as to be likely to become the popular creed of our native state," Elmendorf demanded a share of the land proceeds as the "least that is due" to New York "for all this adventitious Western Prosperity" purchased at Eastern expense. Jackson curtly dismissed Elmendorf's opinions as "too selfish" to consider, but Jackson was not up for reelection in Pennsylvania or New York.[64]

If there was a tacit bargain behind the passage of distribution in 1833, Clay got the worst of it. He sacrificed the protective tariff for sectional conciliation—and for distribution. He won the glory but not the prize. The absentees who permitted distribution to pass also washed their hands of responsibility for its fate. In no way did they commit themselves to uphold it against a veto. Nor could Clay justly complain of betrayal from the White House, for if distribution was central to Clay's idea of a compromise, it had never formed any part of Jackson's. Calhoun's apparent acquiescence constituted no recommendation to the president, who saw in the cooperation of Clay and Calhoun no great sectional pacification, but only "self agrandisement," vulgar ambition for the public lands and for a "splendid Scheme of internal improvements which was once, and still are their secrete hobby." The irony was that Jackson's estrangement from Calhoun allowed him to do what Calhoun was no longer free to do for himself—namely, kill distribution and escape with the benefits but not the burdens of the Compromise of 1833.[65]

The events of 1833 brought the curtain down on a phase of the land controversy that began nearly a decade before. The land issue had always been closely tied to internal improvements; since 1824 it had become progressively entwined with the tariff as well. The Compromise of 1833 resolved the tariff controversy and with it the nullification crisis. South Carolina accepted Clay's tariff, while nullifying the force bill in a final gesture of defiance. Carolina extremists claimed victory, but they would never attempt nullification again. For the next nine years the tariff of 1833 enjoyed an almost sacred inviolability as the act that saved the Union.

It was not immediately apparent that the land question had been settled as well. Through the summer, opposition papers criticized Jackson for blocking the resolution of this dangerous issue. Despite the tariff compromise, they worried that the land controversy still threatened the Union. Jackson agreed, though his solution was not theirs. His distribution veto message, delivered belatedly in December 1833 to the new Congress, said that "the harmony and union of the States" demanded an end to the "continued agitations" over the public lands. Graduation and eventual cession, said Jackson, would provide the quietus.[66]

But the truth was that the land issue was already as settled as if by positive legislation, though it was a settlement few desired and no one recognized. In recent years the adoption first of graduation, then of distribution, had appeared imminent. But by 1833 both were stymied. The first great hope for graduation fell with the South–West alliance, which had never functioned effectively but lost its very rationale with the tariff settlement of 1833. Benton's second hope collapsed when Eastern Jacksonians refused to follow the president into the graduation camp. Without partisan strength in the East and with its Western constituency fractured, Benton's campaign had passed its summit by 1833.

With an Eastern sectional following added to the National Republicans, distribution could command a majority in Congress. The Compromise of 1833 severed distribution from the tariff and cleared the way for the mobilization of its latent Southern strength, particularly in North Carolina. (In December 1833 Senator Willie Mangum, who had twice voted against distribution in the Twenty-second Congress, announced his conversion. By 1835 North Carolina was a hotbed of distribution sentiment.) But the majority for distribution, though real, was as powerless as the majority for internal improvements. Jackson blocked its path, backed by enough party loyalists, Western land reformers, and strict constructionist Southerners to uphold presidential vetoes.[67]

From the sectional tempest of Jackson's first presidential term the West had extracted general pre-emption and the forty-acre law, but these were mere trifles compared to other contemplated changes. Neither Benton's revolution of the land system nor Clay's counterrevolution could succeed. Originally sectional, each had been tailored to fit a national constituency—graduation with Benton's agrarian appeal to the farmers and workingmen of the East, distribution with its promise of land grants and subsidies for the West. But on reaching for the other's clientele, each had lost part of its own. The process of party division had far to go, but by 1833 it had progressed far enough so that no land measure could muster a solid sectional constituency; and thus, in the intricate matrix of political forces in Congress and the White House, none could succeed. No one acknowledged the futility of further struggle, and as the first session of the new Congress approached, gladiators in both camps armed in anticipation of battle and hope of victory. But Jackson's second term would bear out what his first had foretold: that until the delicate sectional and partisan balance was fundamentally disrupted, the federal land system would remain essentially as it was.

CHAPTER 7
THE VORTEX OF PARTY
1833–1837

The disposition of the public lands will occupy much of the public attention during the present winter; the more so, because the subject is evidently becoming political, and falling into the vortex of party politics.

Washington *Globe*
December 11, 1833

Stalemate

Through the summer of 1833 distribution and graduation men prepared for the next round of the struggle over the public domain. His defeat at Jackson's hands steeled an exhausted Clay to return to the Senate and introduce distribution again, "for the public lands will be lost to the country, without some such measure is adopted." In the West, speeches, resolutions, and newspaper pieces kept up the graduation fervor. In Danville, Illinois, on the Fourth of July, there were nine cheers for "*The Great West*—Her salubrious climate and fertile soil: nature gave the one freely, but Congress exacts a most unreasonable price for the other." The *Illinois Advocate* warned every man who was not "an enemy of State rights, an enemy to the poor, and a recreant to the West" that Clay's "corrupt scheme" would make them "wood hewers and water drawers" to "the aristocracy and monopolizers of the old States." The *Louisville Public Advertiser* denounced the plot "to prevent the emigration of people from the east to the west, and thus prevent this section of the Union from exerting the influence to which it is entitled in the national counsels."[1]

Such exhortations, by now a staple of Western rhetoric, worked to bolster spirits and prevent any more desertions to distribution by discouraged graduation men. The task of Jackson's Washington strategists was more difficult. In Congress in 1833 partisanship had worked against the Jacksonians but not for them. Clay took with him not only every National Republican, but many mid-Atlantic Jackso-

172

nians as well. The Democracy would have to be induced to rally around
Jackson's land policy as it had rallied around his veto of the recharter of
the Bank of the United States. To that end, an argument against
distribution was needed that could attract the East as well as the West.

A series of *Globe* articles and the veto message itself, delivered to the
new Twenty-third Congress in December 1833, spelled out the party
line on distribution. Both endorsed graduation, which Jackson now
mentioned by name. But alongside that endorsement and detachable
from it, they offered an argument against distribution that drew on
broad principles of national policy, yet also appealed to both Eastern
and Western sectional prejudices.

Against Clay's claim that distribution fulfilled the terms of the old
state deeds of cession, Jackson and the *Globe* said that the ceding states
had never contemplated state subsidies from the land revenue. Rather,
they meant the "common fund" to defray regular expenditures of the
Treasury. Where Clay set the land receipts constitutionally apart,
Jackson saw them as part of the general fund, and subject to the same
restrictions. The disagreement went straight back to the deeds of
cession, and to the interpretation of words written long before in a
confederacy that had since become a nation. To Clay the phrase
"United States," once assuredly plural, remained so still in the deeds of
cession, while to Jackson it had become singular.[2]

Jackson and the *Globe* masked this potentially confusing reversal of
form by putting their case in terms of strict construction. Since land
revenue was really federal money, not state money held in trust,
distribution meant a direct federal subsidy to state internal improvements, in violation of the Maysville Road veto principle. By collecting
money only to give it away, distribution threatened a "direct road to
consolidation." The *Globe* thundered that distribution would be "the
most fatal blow to our liberty ever yet struck," producing "a single,
wretched and uncontrollable general government" or "nullification,
anarchy, civil war and the establishment of petty military despotisms
among the mutilated and bloodstained ruins of our now glorious
confederacy."[3]

Even conceding the principle of surplus revenue distribution, Jackson and the *Globe* argued that Clay's bill made no sense. Jackson defended his own earlier distribution proposals, though constitutionally
dubious, as preferable to direct federal internal improvements. But
Clay proposed not to distribute a single surplus "accidentally or un-
avoidably" accumulated, but to create a perpetual pseudosurplus by
drawing off the land revenue and throwing all the accessory expenses
of the land system—surveys, acquisitions, Indian annuities—on the

general treasury. Since taxes would have to replace the distributed funds, the whole scheme amounted to a mere revolving door, through which the people were to be lured by glittering subsidies drawn from their own pockets.[4]

Clay's 12½ percent rebate on land proceeds also violated the cession compacts by diverting part of the common fund exclusively to the new states. But lest Westerners hastily presume that if distribution was unfair to the East it must be good for them, the *Globe* warned that the rebate was a "gilded bait" designed "to tempt them, by a small portion of the money exacted from emigrants, *to retard their own growth, cripple their own strength, diminish their own wealth.*" It was "a *bribe* . . . offered to the young giant to suffer himself to be *bandaged* and *crippled*, lest, perchance, he may become too strong, too rich, and too powerful."[5]

The *Globe* thus deftly addressed simultaneously the sectional prejudices of East and West. Distribution denied to the East its fair share, while for the West it preserved a "*tax upon emigration and settlement*" in the form of high land prices. The *Globe* series and Jackson's veto message integrated the administration's land policy further into its emerging philosophy of strict construction and limited government, and its appeal to the common man against the aristocracy. The intent was to unite the party behind Benton's and Jackson's land policies, but the effect was to reinforce the congressional stalemate by stimulating Eastern Jacksonians who would not support graduation to oppose distribution also.[6]

Many anticipated a revival of the land controversy in the Twenty-third Congress. "The long agitated question, of the disposition of the Public Lands, will we think, either be settled entirely, or brought to assume a shape, from which correct calculations can be drawn of its ultimate fate," a Missouri paper predicted, while an Illinoisan entertained "no doubt but there will be a change in the land system this winter." Letters from Washington promised that graduation would receive the "unanimous support" of Jacksonians. On the other side of the issue, as Martin Van Buren later recalled, distribution promised to be one of Clay's "great guns" against the administration. "If you can sustain the Bank against the President—& pass the land bill in spite of him," counseled a friend of Daniel Webster, "the dynasty will explode."[7]

Together the forces of Clay and Calhoun controlled the Senate. Their first move was to wrest the appointment of Senate committees from Vice-President Van Buren. No longer would Henry Clay have to fashion land policy from a seat on the Manufactures Committee. The coalition replaced two Western Jacksonians on the Public Lands Committee with Clay and George Poindexter of Mississippi. Other changes gave the old states a majority on the committee for the first time in eleven years.[8]

Clay resubmitted his distribution bill and presently produced a report condemning Jackson's veto. Benton brought in graduation, supported by the usual battery of Western state memorials. In the House of Representatives, Public Lands Committee chairman Clement Clay of Alabama also reported a graduation bill. The stage was all set.[9]

But the drama was never acted. The Senate did not even discuss distribution or graduation. In the House, though the West was numerically stronger than ever under the new apportionment, Clement Clay could not get his graduation bill to the floor. It was the same the next year. Again Benton and Clement Clay introduced graduation; again Henry Clay submitted distribution. Nothing happened. Though the governor of Missouri exhorted the graduation faithful to "never despair nor cease to urge it until the absolute impracticability of success is fully demonstrated," Congress was obviously deadlocked on the land question. There was still political capital to be made off the issue, so neither Benton nor Clay would let it drop. But neither pressed his bill. Jackson in the White House barred distribution, while the president's urging, the retirement of the national debt, and the increase in Western congressional strength together still could not produce a majority for graduation. Under the circumstances, trying to force the issue was a waste of time.[10]

But if graduation was hopeless, pre-emption was not. A bill to extend the General Pre-emption Act of 1830 to June of 1834 passed the Senate without debate or division and the House by 124 to 53. For the first time on a land bill, Jacksonians of the mid-Atlantic states toed a strict party line. All the opposition came from the old states, and most of it from foes of the administration. The lesson was clear: Jackson could carry the Eastern Democracy for pre-emption, but not for graduation.[11]

The Bank War and the triumph of partisanship

Something beyond its own evident futility explained the sudden disappearance of the land debate from Congress in 1834. For this was the famous "panic session," dominated by the struggle between President Andrew Jackson and the Bank of the United States. In the summer of 1833 what *Niles' Register* called a "pause-like state of affairs" had settled in over the political scene; with the nullification crisis resolved, there was for the moment "no peculiarly exciting subject before the public."

But then Jackson decided to remove the federal deposits from the Bank of the United States, whose original charter still had three years to run. The Bank retaliated with a financial contraction that brought sharp distress to businessmen, who in turn blamed Jackson and turned to Congress for relief. An orchestrated campaign produced an avalanche of protests against the president's action. Day after day the administration's opponents took the Senate floor to condemn the tyranny of King Andrew. The denunciations culminated on March 28, 1834, when the Senate adopted unprecedented resolutions censuring Jackson for having "assumed upon himself authority and power not conferred by the constitution and laws, but in derogation of both."[12]

In the heat of the Bank War all else, including the public domain, was forgotten. "Nobody talks or thinks of anything else," New York diarist Philip Hone recorded in January. Senator William Hendricks of Indiana found the land issue "wholly crowded out of view" by the "great exciting question" of the deposits and the Bank. Problems of banking and finance gripped national and state politics for years afterward, gradually pulling other economic issues into their orbit.[13]

The predominance of the bank issue in Jackson's second term marked a new phase in party development. Down to 1833, the motive thrust behind political controversy was sectional. Though the Bank briefly occupied the spotlight during the 1832 campaign, the central issue of Jackson's first term was the tariff. Closely tied to it were internal improvements and public land policy. All three were intrinsically sectional. Over the years the search for allies in presidential campaigns and in Congress had modified sectionalism in the direction of partisanship. But the process could not be completed through bargains over inherently sectional questions. Politicians dared not desert established sectional positions because they could invoke no higher loyalty or principle than sectionalism to justify their conduct. No Southerner could support the protective tariff, or Northwesterner oppose internal improvements, no matter what he expected in return; to do so was political suicide. At best a kind of quasi partisanship was achieved, a fragile alliance structure that broke down when crucial legislation came to a final vote in Congress.

The Bank War created a higher loyalty by forging true national parties out of sectional coalitions. For the Bank, unlike the tariff and the public lands, was not a sectional issue. Least of all was the Bank War a struggle of East and West. Benton clothed his senatorial tirades against the Bank in sectional rhetoric, but the Bank had plenty of Western defenders, including prominent American System Jacksonians like Joseph Duncan of Illinois and William Ashley of Missouri, both of whom left the party over the issue. Western Bank men argued cogently that the West, plagued by chronic currency problems, most required the national circulating medium provided by the Bank. Benton's dubious claim to represent Western sentiment on the Bank actually derived from his unchallenged leadership on the land issue. Trading on his status as spokesman for graduation, Benton phrased his partisan financial doctrines in the language of sectionalism.[14]

In the South, the Bank War accomplished what no disaffection with Jackson could achieve as long as the tariff occupied center stage: it drove his opponents into outright affiliation with the National Republicans in the new Whig party. Though the party has often been described as an expedient merger of essentially incompatible Northern nationalists and Southern states' righters, the two already shared important areas of agreement, especially on land policy. John Tyler of Virginia, Willie Mangum of North Carolina, and Hugh Lawson White of Tennessee, leaders of the Southern Whigs, had all opposed graduation and Benton's South–West alliance; now that the tariff was settled, they all favored distribution. And while some Southerners joined the Whigs only in order to resist Jackson's alleged usurpation of authority, others, like nullifier George McDuffie of South Carolina, were true-blue Bank men. Indeed the Bank, with its connotations of a well-regulated commerce and a stable national currency, possessed a natural Southern constituency among commercial interests, as did distribution among all who desired internal improvements or dreaded the effects of emigration. It required only the removal of the tariff issue to mobilize those Southerners in a perfectly rational combination with the Northern advocates of the Bank and distribution, the National Republicans. Some of the Southerners, like Calhoun and Tyler, never found a true home in the new party; but the majority, like Mangum, eventually embraced the whole of its program—including the tariff—and settled down as full-fledged Whigs. When Tyler later, as president, deserted the party's platform, he took few Southern Whigs with him. It was Mangum who offered the resolution reading him out of the party in 1841.[15]

Both Whigs and Democrats used the Bank War to draw party lines. Jacksonian leaders employed it to enforce conformity on loyal Democrats and to purge dissenters, including American System men, while Whigs rallied their following behind the new party standard. Much of the ammunition of the Bank War was expended in contending for sheer partisan advantage. The Whigs' crowning achievement in the panic session was the Senate resolution of censure—not an item of legislation, but a statement of the party's case against the president. In return, Democrats used Benton's resolution to expunge the censure to draw party lines in the state legislatures, then to force the resignations of Whig senators and thus to regain control of the Senate.[16]

To those outside the party maelstrom, the fury of the Bank War seemed disproportionate to its stakes. George M. Dallas wrote at the beginning of the panic session:

> The present session of Congress promises more of excitement than of real interest. The great questions which threatened the peace of the country are at rest:—and none but mere agitators will be disposed to disturb them anew. The coming Presidential canvass may probably soon produce fresh phases of party, and strange combinations of men: but I do not think that we shall be convulsed as we have been on fundamental and universal principles or systems. . . . The topic on which I anticipate most congressional heat is that of the Bank. It may be well, indeed, to take it up as a sort of safety valve, through which all the wordy ammunition of the opposition may be expended, and all our own fever let off, without any danger to the country, the government, the constitution, or the laws.[17]

But for those caught up in it, the Bank War assumed an importance far beyond its economic impact. Both sides saw themselves defending the American republican creed against sinister conspiratorialists. The vocabulary of the Bank War, both public and private, rang with phrases borrowed from America's Revolutionary struggle against British corruption and tyranny. To Jackson, the Bank was a "mammoth of corruption and power" that threatened to "destroy our republican institutions" by suborning the press, buying votes, and bribing legislators. To the Whigs, it was executive tyranny that threatened the Republic. In the Senate, Clay denounced Jackson's "open, palpable, and daring usurpation," and warned that "we are . . . rapidly tending towards a total change of the pure republican character of the Government, and to the concentration of all power in the hands of one man." The rhetoric linking the Bank War to America's Revolutionary tradition and to its basic political ideology served, for both Whigs and Democrats, to justify the imposition of party discipline and the elevation of partisan above sectional loyalty.[18]

The impact upon the land controversy was visible at once. Between 1833 and 1837 the land question cropped up in many of the state legislatures, and nearly everywhere party majorities determined the outcome. In Ohio a Democratic legislature praised Jackson's distribution veto and instructed the state's senators to oppose distribution— instructions which the Whigs promptly rescinded upon capturing the legislature a year later. In Missouri and Kentucky, North Carolina and New Hampshire, land resolutions arrayed Democrats and Whigs against each other.[19]

The merging of the land issue with the Bank War revealed its new function as a weapon in the party arsenals of Whigs and Democrats. The Ohio resolutions against distribution also condemned the Bank of the United States and applauded Jackson's removal of the deposits. In Missouri a chain of resolutions defending Jackson and demanding expunction of the Senate censure also praised graduation and denounced distribution. In Kentucky, distribution resolutions competed directly with expunging resolutions, Whigs supporting one and the Democrats the other. Vermont included distribution in its praise of the American System of Bank, tariff, and internal improvements, while New Hampshire condemned them all together.[20]

In North Carolina, the Whig land platform became the central rallying point for the party. More than anyone else on the seaboard, North Carolinians feared the competition of Western lands and resented the prosperity of the new states. Some North Carolinians also hoped internal improvements might lift the state from economic stagnation. The Compromise of 1833, severing distribution from the tariff, triggered a virtual stampede into the distribution camp. North Carolina Whigs seized the issue eagerly, though Jackson's land policy was so unpopular that even Democrats disavowed it. In legislative battles in 1835 and 1836, Jackson men tried to defend the national party line against distribution without alienating their constituents. They failed. What one authority terms their "downright disastrous" opposition to distribution contributed to Whig victory in the 1836 state elections and Whig dominance in North Carolina politics for years afterward.[21]

The intrusion of partisanship into the land controversy did not eradicate sectionalism. Though Whigs and Democrats contested land policy everywhere, the terms of the dispute varied from place to place. Frontier Whigs proclaimed their unabated ardor for graduation, espousing distribution only because Congress refused their first love. Frontier Democrats held firm for cheap lands, attributing Whig distribution sentiment to covert Eastern sympathies. By contrast, Democrats in the Atlantic and old Western states opposed distribution but offered nothing in its place, either explicitly repudiating Jackson's proposals or mouthing platitudinous sympathy for the settler. Only in New Hampshire, long an outpost of strict Jacksonian orthodoxy, did the legislature advocate reducing federal land prices. Legislative voting patterns also exhibited a lingering admixture of sectionalism. In

the West requests for graduation, when stripped of party entangle-
ments, still attracted Whig votes, while in the East a minority (or even
occasionally, as in Maryland, a majority) of Democrats joined the
unanimous Whig call for distribution.[22]

The seeds of party conflict over land policy can be traced back
through the Webster–Hayne debate and the presidential campaigns of
1832 and 1828. In fact never since 1824, when Thomas Hart Benton
first turned graduation against his Missouri rival David Barton, had the
issue been untouched by partisanship. As the land question was never
totally sectional, so it would never become completely partisan. Still,
though the line be indistinct it is possible and indeed necessary to draw
it. From its origins in the Great Migration and the panic of 1819 down
to the Compromise of 1833, the public land issue was a sectional
question increasingly colored by partisanship; from then until the
party system collapsed it was essentially a party issue modified by
sectionalism. Though the terms of party controversy in East and West
differed, the fact of controversy was unmistakable. By 1837 it was
impossible to put through a resolution on land policy in any state of the
Union without partisan opposition.

The public lands and the surplus revenue

In 1836, after a two-year hiatus, the land issue resurfaced in Congress
as an adjunct of the financial question. With the national debt paid, the
nation prosperous, and the compromise tariff schedules untouchable,
an embarrassing surplus had begun to accumulate in the Treasury.
Surprisingly, much of the excess revenue came from land sales, not
customs receipts, for the boom cycle of twenty years earlier had begun
again. In 1831 and 1832 land sales topped two million acres for the first
time since the panic of 1819. In 1833 they exceeded three million acres,
in 1834 four million. When Congress convened late in 1835, returns
for the first three quarters of the year showed sales of nearly seven
million acres, and receipts of more than $8 million.[23]

As in the postwar boom, sales rode a floodtide of emigration but then
surged ahead of it, as buyers anticipated the needs of settlers to come.
Again an abundance of paper money stimulated purchases, flowing
from the "pet banks" that held the federal surplus and from dozens of
tenuously capitalized satellites. In the mid-1830s large land companies
entered the market, backed by Eastern capital and fielding squads of
paid agents. But though trading in land was brisk and values multiplied rapidly, the government rarely netted more than the minimum

purchase price. Arrangements for suppressing competition at the auctions operated effectively throughout the West. Both squatters and nonresident purchasers employed them, and they enjoyed, despite their illegality, a universal sanction and an almost quasi-official status.[24]

Advocates of distribution and graduation both saw opportunity in the unwanted Treasury surplus, the former because distribution would get rid of it, the latter because graduation, together with Jackson's idea to allow sales only to "actual settlers," promised to reduce receipts. Accordingly, in 1836 both sides brought in their bills and secured favorable committee reports. But the surplus revenue problem also embraced a whole range of purely partisan concerns. Whigs charged that the surplus was a fount of executive corruption and a source of spoil for handpicked deposit banks; Democrats said distribution was a scheme to subvert the independence of the states. To foil distribution, Benton proposed to spend the entire surplus on coastal fortifications.[25]

Clay's bill to distribute the land revenue to the states passed the Senate for the third time in five years on May 4, 1836. It was nearly a pure party question. All the Clay Whigs supported the bill, joined by only four Democrats, two of them Pennsylvanians under legislative instructions. Calhoun, who considered distribution unconstitutional, preserved his principles by voting against it after siding with its friends on every test question; but most of the Southern Whigs stood with distribution to the end. The final roll call pitted party majorities against each other in every section of the Union (see table 7.1).[26]

TABLE 7.1
DISTRIBUTION, SENATE, 1836

	Whig		Democrat		Total	
	For	*Against*	*For*	*Against*	*For*	*Against*
New England	7			5	7	5
Mid-Atlantic	5		2	2	7	2
South Atlantic	3	1		4	3	5
West	6	1	2	8	8	9
Total	21	2	4	19	25	21

Source: *Senate Journal*, 24th Cong., 1st sess., pp. 317, 330-331.

Note: Table 7.1 combines the roll calls on third reading and passage, with a cohesion of 100% (see note to table 2.1).

Jackson had swung the Eastern Democracy around against distribution, completing its conversion to a party question, but he failed completely to marshal Eastern Democratic support for graduation. An exceedingly modest graduation amendment (reducing prices to $1.00 per acre on lands unsold after twenty years in market, then by another 10¢ every five years to a minimum of 50¢) picked up only two Eastern votes; curiously, these were from Daniel Webster, who may have been cultivating Western favor for his presidential prospects, and his Massachusetts colleague John Davis. The amendment was defeated, 27 to 16 (see table 7.2).[27]

Never before had graduation made so poor a showing. There were even signs that Benton himself had quietly dropped his crusade. For the first time in thirteen years he let a colleague, Robert Walker of Mississippi, introduce his bill, and his speeches against distribution were strangely silent on land prices. Where he had always juxtaposed distribution and graduation, Benton now spoke only of fortifications.[28]

Distribution never made it to a floor vote in the House of Representatives, where Democrats held a comfortable majority. On a procedural roll call, announced as a test of distribution strength, Democrats voted against it, 103 to 12, Whigs for it, 77 to 7.[29]

The House's action left Congress deadlocked, with the end of the session approaching and a large surplus, embarrassing to both parties, still undisposed of. It was an election year, and public pressure to return the surplus from the deposit banks to the people was rising, especially in several states which had just begun massive internal improvement projects. So two days after distribution failed its House test, Calhoun introduced, as an amendment to a bill regulating the federal

TABLE 7.2
GRADUATION, SENATE, 1836

	Whig		Democrat		Total	
	For	Against	For	Against	For	Against
New England	2	5		4	2	9
Mid-Atlantic		5		3		8
South Atlantic		4		3		7
Old West (Ky., Ohio, Tenn.)	1	3	2		3	3
New West	3			8	11	
Total	6	17	10	10	16	27

Source: Senate Journal, 24th Cong., 1st sess., pp. 313–314.

deposit banks, a proviso to "deposit" the Treasury surplus with the states according to their populations. Benton accurately described the measure as "in name, a deposite; in form, a loan; in essence and design, a distribution." Everyone understood that the deposit would never be returned and was, in fact, a gift. But Calhoun's amendment neatly sidestepped the constitutional objections to distribution, and it disentangled the problem of the Treasury surplus from that of the public lands. Democrats tried to divide the bill and defeat the deposit feature separately, but when this tactic failed most of them swallowed the package whole. "An Act to regulate the deposites of the public money," including a modification of Calhoun's proviso, passed the Senate easily, Benton among its six opponents.[30]

Jackson loathed the deposit measure as a flimsy disguise for Clay's bill, and he had Supreme Court chief justice Roger Taney prepare a veto message. But rather than risk an open party breach he settled in the end for a rewording of the bill to quiet some constitutional scruples. Thus amended, the deposit bill swept through Congress by overwhelming majorities, and Jackson signed it, though with "repugnance of feeling, and a recoil of judgment."[31]

The Deposit Act separated the financial issue from the land issue and distributed the surplus in time to neutralize its impact on the pending presidential election. The campaign itself exhibited the hardening of party lines on the land question. Van Buren, running as Jackson's heir, declared against distribution in all its forms, and favored "liberal facilities" for settlers. His silence on details allowed Democrats to interpret him as favoring either graduation or preemption. All the Whig candidates went for distribution. William Henry Harrison of Ohio, known as a frontier advocate from his early stint as a Northwest Territory congressional delegate, nonetheless defended the land system and recommended distribution either of the land proceeds or of the general surplus. As a Jackson senator, Hugh Lawson White of Tennessee had opposed distribution in 1832 and 1833, but as a Whig presidential candidate he supported it in 1836, providing campaign material for his new Whig friends in North Carolina and his new Democratic enemies in Tennessee. Webster of Massachusetts and Mangum, candidate of South Carolina, were both firm distribution men.[32]

The election returns reflected the shift from sectional to partisan politics since 1832. Dramatic gains by each party in the other's traditional strongholds produced tight races in many states and a nearly even division of the total popular vote. The close party balance in all sections heralded the rise of the Whigs, though in the electoral college Van Buren won handily.[33]

Financial problems again agitated Congress after the election, for the deluge of revenue continued to mount as the land boom gathered momentum. New Treasury statistics showed that government land sales for 1835 exceeded 12 million acres, bringing in almost $16 million. Already sales in the first three quarters of 1836 surpassed those fantastic figures, totalling close to 16 million acres with receipts of more than $20 million.[34]

For two decades Thomas Hart Benton had worked to speed federal land sales and lower prices. Now sales had accelerated beyond all imagining, and with receivable bank paper everywhere, government prices had in effect been reduced. The glut of capital sent values soaring, but buyers rarely lost their heads so far as to compete with each other at the auction, so the federal selling price did not budge. Yet Benton was appalled. For what had the spiralling sales to do with emigration? Benton expected a liberalized land policy to promote emigration and settlement, but the present boom in his eyes was doing rather the reverse. Huge tracts were passing not to Western farmers but to Eastern capitalists, and for speculation rather than cultivation. Instead of being given away to yeomen, the domain was being plundered by financiers.

Benton and Jackson blamed all the speculation on absentee capitalists and none on the hearty cultivators of the soil. That the dichotomy they posed was false is beside the point. For something had certainly gone wrong with the land system.

Benton and Jackson viewed the land bubble as part of a larger financial dysfunction, and their solution accordingly merged land policy with their developing assault on banking and paper money. Loose credit and flimsy currency had fed the boom in a cycle described by Jackson himself:

> The banks lent out their notes to speculators. They were paid to the [land office] receivers and immediately returned to the banks [as government deposits], to be lent out again and again, being mere instruments to transfer to speculators the most valuable public land and pay the Government by a credit on the books of the banks.

Thus a single paper dollar purchased lands over and over again as fast as it could shuttle back and forth between the land office and the depository bank.[35]

Jackson had acted before the election by promulgating the famous Specie Circular, initially floated by Benton in the Senate, and, after its rejection there, issued as a Treasury order. The circular directed land offices to accept only specie, in order, said Jackson, "to save the new States from a nonresident proprietorship" and "keep open the public lands for entry by emigrants at Government prices instead of their being compelled to purchase of speculators at double or triple prices."[36]

The monetary effects of this order and the long controversy ending in its rescision need not detain us here. They rightly belong to a history not of land policy but of national finance. Jackson contemplated no change in the land system, but an end to speculation and a return to the system as it had functioned before the disorders of the currency. His real purpose in issuing the Specie Circular was to strike a blow for hard money, not just in the land offices but everywhere. As Benton explained in the Senate,

> the currency is the object, and the lands the incident. The regulation of the currency is the great object; and as the lands, and not the custom-house, was the exciting cause of the swollen, bloated, and diseased state of the currency, the remedy was directed to the lands, and not to the customs. . . . Very rightly, then, did the Senator from Massachusetts [Webster] . . . declare this to be a currency question, and not a land question.

It was as a currency question, not a land question, that the circular was debated in ensuing sessions of Congress.[37]

The second Jacksonian cure for the paper money profusion and the Treasury surplus, propounded in the president's message of December 1836, was to sell lands only to actual settlers "for immediate settlement and cultivation," in limited quantities and at reduced prices. Jackson's preference for lower land prices was by now old news, as was the refusal of Atlantic Democrats to support it. Excluding nonresident purchasers was a new but logical extension of existing party policies. Democrats East and West had backed pre-emption in 1830 and 1834, and in 1836 an unsuccessful bid to extend it received trans-sectional party support in the Senate. Van Buren's campaign platform in 1836 promised aid to actual settlers, and the Specie Circular allowed them a temporary indulgence in the use of paper money. It was but one step further to exclude nonsettlers from the right to purchase at all.[38]

Democrat Robert Walker of Mississippi introduced a bill "to prohibit the sale of public lands, except to actual settlers in limited quantities"; it also included graduation and prospective pre-emption. It was clearly an administration measure, but it ran into trouble on the floor. Wishing to restrain Eastern buyers and encourage Western ones, the bill's advocates had to argue that lands were selling too fast and not fast enough, at prices simultaneously too low and too high. Easterners complained of the ban on nonresident purchases, while Westerners objected that a two-year residence requirement and a two-section limit on individual purchases restricted the settler's freedom and mobility. To compound the confusion, the enigmatic Calhoun suddenly offered to cede all the public domain to the Western states for a payment of one-third of the future proceeds. Westerners, stunned by Calhoun's proposition and mystified at its motives, recovered in time to vote for it, but few Easterners did, and it died a quick death.[39]

Walker's bill did not pass. In the Senate, Atlantic Democrats joined with most Whigs to delete graduation and prospective pre-emption. The margins were so decisive that Benton himself confessed "no hopes" for graduation in the near future. In the House of Representatives the same combination of seaboard Democrats and Whigs killed what remained of the bill. Three days later Martin Van Buren took the oath of office as president of the United States.[40]

Aftermath

By 1837 the land controversy and the Whig and Democratic parties had both emerged from a long period of evolution into an era of relative stability. Both parties had elucidated the programs and gathered the basic constituencies that would carry them through the 1840s. On the land issue, Old Hickory's second term had witnessed the crystallization of party positions along lines visible by 1833—the Whigs for distribution, the Democrats for pre-emption and, equivocally, for graduation. The parties continued to agitate the land issue furiously in later years, but without any substantive change in policies. From 1837 until the collapse of the party system, the course of land legislation was virtually predictable from the election returns.

Even at the zenith of party competition in the 1840s, the land issue still bore traces of its sectional origins. Graduation and pre-emption continued to attract frontier Whigs, while enough Atlantic Democrats shied away from graduation to prevent its enactment until 1854. But these were variations on an essentially partisan theme.

In the crisis year of 1833 a North Carolina Jacksonian had warned that Clay's distribution bill would excite "violent antipathies" in the new states "and possibly may produce in the end actual hostilities between the States East and West of the Alleghanies." In the same year John Quincy Adams called Jackson's land policy "a dissolution of the Union, an inextinguishable brand of civil war." Such rhetoric, almost commonplace from 1819 to 1833, was obsolete by 1837. President Van

Buren recognized the change. "All feared that they [the lands] would become a source of discord, and many carried their apprehensions so far as to see in them the seeds of a future dissolution of the Confederacy," he recalled in his first annual message to Congress. "But happily our experience has already been sufficient to quiet in a great degree all such apprehensions." There would be no crisis of union over the public domain.[41]

Van Buren himself, a New Yorker but a loyal Jackson man, lived up to his campaign pledges, repeatedly commending graduation and pre-emption to Congress. Under his urging Congress enacted retrospective pre-emption laws in 1838 and 1840. Graduation even revived, picking up enough Atlantic Democratic support to pass the Senate, but not the House of Representatives, in three successive years. Prospective pre-emption, the guarantee to future squatters of the preferential right to purchase, also failed for lack of Eastern support.[42]

The 1840 elections gave the Whigs control of Congress and the presidency for the first time. A special session of Congress convened, and within a few weeks it passed Clay's distribution bill. It was essentially the same bill as in 1832, with two important additions. To pacify the frontier Whigs, whose appetites were whetted by the recent near successes of graduation and pre-emption, permanent prospective pre-emption was inserted in the bill. The Southern Whigs—including John Tyler of Virginia, now president after William Henry Harrison's early death—also required reassurances. Southerners, it will be recalled, had steadfastly opposed distribution as long as it propped up the protective tariff. By fixing the tariff, the Compromise of 1833 released their latent support for distribution, a support reaffirmed by Tyler in his first message to Congress.[43] But the Compromise Act had only a year left to run, and Southerners feared, correctly, that Clay and the tariff Whigs planned to return to protection in 1842. This would put the Southerners back precisely where they had been in 1832. To calm their fears and prevent the impending tariff battle of 1842 from scuttling distribution in 1841, a proviso was inserted in the distribution bill to halt distribution whenever tariff duties were raised above the 20 percent level stipulated by the Compromise Act for 1842. Their Western and Southern flanks secured, the Whigs pushed distribution through Congress on a nearly perfect party division. Tyler signed it on September 4, 1841.

Distribution survived only a few months. The expiration of the Compromise Act of 1833 presented the Whigs with a choice between distribution and the protective tariff. In the logic of the American System and of sectional compromise the two were inseparable, but the suspending clause of the Distribution Act made them in fact mutually exclusive. It was a self-inflicted dilemma, arising from the party's undue haste to purchase the necessary votes for distribution regardless of consequences. The Whigs could not now enact one of their favorite measures without automatically cancelling another, unless the anti-tariffite in the White House would let them off the hook. Twice Congress tested Tyler's mettle with bills that raised the tariff and continued distribution; twice the president vetoed them. Forced to choose, the party chose the tariff, and distribution ceased less than a year after it began. But prospective pre-emption remained, a permanent feature of the land system and an ironic testimony to the twists of party politics: a measure urged by Democrats without success and finally enacted by a Whig Congress over the unanimous opposition of its own proponents.

Further changes in land policy awaited the decline of the Jacksonian party system and the restructuring of politics along new sectional lines. In the late 1840s agitation arose to grant free lands, now called homesteads, to actual settlers. Homesteads were popular not only in the West, but among Eastern radicals who favored a true agrarian law dividing the public domain into free but inalienable farm plots. In 1854, just thirty years after Benton first introduced it, graduation passed Congress as a byproduct of complex maneuvers over homesteads and the Kansas–Nebraska territorial organization bill. The law dropped land prices in the oldest districts to 12½¢ per acre and stimulated large sales before it was repealed in 1862.[44]

The alignments on homesteads and graduation in the early 1850s charted the disintegration of old party lines and the redefinition of the land issue as an adjunct of the slavery question. By the late 1850s homestead bills precipitated strict north-south divisions in Congress. President James Buchanan vetoed one in 1860. The new Northern sectional party, the Republicans, advocated homesteads, and during the Civil War Congress finally enacted a bill over border-state opposition. The Homestead Act of 1862 granted 160 acres free to settlers who fulfilled a five-year residency requirement. Curiously, the same Congress that enacted this originally Western measure also, on a vote pitting East against West, passed an act distributing nearly 10 million acres to the states, in proportion to their congressional representation, for agricultural colleges—a distant but direct descendant of the Maryland proposition of 1821.[45]

CHAPTER 8
THE PUBLIC LANDS AND THE PARTY SYSTEM

The land issue and party politics

In the generation after the War of 1812 the United States underwent one of the most fundamental political transformations in all of its history. A nonpartisan and poorly organized political structure, marked by low voter participation and uncontested presidential elections, gave way to one of the most highly organized, geographically balanced, and intensely competitive national party systems the country has ever seen. By 1840 two national parties had emerged, offering voters everywhere a choice of candidates, policies, and principles.

The political realignment originated in the rapid postwar national expansion and development that placed pressure upon inadequate resources of population and capital. The ensuing political struggle to control those resources first formed along geographic lines. Sectional groupings coalesced in the wake of the financial and slavery crises of 1819–1820, and then competed over the vital federal instruments for allocating wealth, population, and power—the tariff, internal improvement, and public land policies.

But sectional politics in turn held the seed of partisanship in the existence of alternative definitions of sectional interest and alternative strategies for pursuing it, and in the desire of sectional leaders to enlist support from outside their own sections in order to amass congressional majorities and elevate presidential candidates. In the 1820s trans-sectional coalitions arose. Each of them combined aspects of different sectional agendas and used sectional arguments and rhetoric in order to attract followers. Paradoxically, sectionalism helped draw people into these embryonic party organizations, which were able to gather constituents partly because they appeared as legitimate vehicles for pursuing sectional aspirations and expressing sectional grievances.

But just as they built upon sectionalism, the parties also supplanted it. They expanded and deepened their appeal by clothing themselves

189

in traditional republican ideology and by articulating alternative constitutional principles, governmental roles, and visions of the future.
The Compromise of 1833 removed the last obstacle to party organization; the Bank War immediately following completed the consolidation
of trans-sectional coalitions into national parties.

The Whig party sought to promote economic diversity and social
homogeneity by balancing agriculture with commerce and industry
and by elevating the educational and moral level of the populace.
Progress and improvement were the party's watchwords, government
action its method, broad construction of the Constitution its justification. Whigs were activists at all levels of government, but the party's
central instruments, and those around which it gathered its constituency, were federal: a national bank, a protective tariff, and distribution of the land revenue to the states for education, internal improvement, and Negro colonization.[1]

While the Whigs fixed their eyes on the future, the Democrats
looked back to the Jeffersonian republic of simplicity and virtue.
Holding to principles of strict construction and limited government,
the Democracy resisted Whig efforts to steer economic and social
development along centrally determined paths. Ironically, their lais-
sez-faire program, derived from Jefferson's vision of a yeoman republic, made the Democrats the champions of cultural pluralism and
aggressive entrepreneurialism in an increasingly mobile and heteroge-
nous society. But though the party threw the door open to industry and
commerce, it did not foster them; and its agrarian rhetoric, its land
policy, and its refusal to promote alternatives signified its preference
for what it continued to consider man's natural calling: agriculture.[2]

Land policy was an essential component of each party's program,
and an important expression of its fundamental ethos. The Whigs
viewed the Western domain essentially as a capital fund—not a source
of revenue for the Treasury, but an endowment for social and economic betterment. Seeing the key to future prosperity in commerce,
industry, and commercial farming, not in further expansion of a
primitive agriculture, the Whigs opposed land policies designed to lure
population to the subsistence frontier. The Whigs did not want to halt
westward migration, but to order and control it and thus prevent it
from monopolizing the nation's limited human resources. Believing
that law and social order were agents of civilization, Whigs also opposed policies that drew men beyond their restraining influence. Whig
rhetoric described the frontier as the seat of lawlessness and disorder,
and the squatter not as a heroic pathfinder but as a renegade and
outcast, a depredator of resources, and a trespasser upon the Indians.

The Democratic policies of cheap land and pre-emption tangibly expressed that party's commitment to individual freedom and opportunity, unfettered and unaided by government. Though in practice this meant an open field for speculators and town promoters as well as farmers, both Democratic land policy and the agrarian rhetoric that clothed it reflected party faith in the Jeffersonian vision of an agricultural republic.

Not only was land policy central to party programs and ideologies; it was also instrumental in the gathering of party constituencies. The metamorphosis from sectional blocs and coalitions into mass national parties was prolonged, exceedingly complex, and impervious to precise measurement. The personalities and public images of presidential candidates helped to mobilize party followings, but so did interests, ideologies, and principles. Jackson's personal magnetism, deftly exploited by his campaign managers, attracted thousands to his banner, but his subsequent clarifications of party policy drove many away again. Western American System men, Southern Bank advocates, and Atlantic opponents of giveaway land policies either modified their opinions or decamped to the Whigs. The elucidation of party programs and principles helped broaden constituent horizons beyond particular issues and candidates, encouraging the faithful to accept the party's discipline and its line on collateral issues. Martin Van Buren, a New Yorker attracted to Jackson partly by his strict constructionism, became a loyal Democrat and a dogged advocate of pre-emption and graduation, though he had never before shown much interest in the public lands. Westerners devoted to Henry Clay as the champion of the American System accepted distribution at his hands and followed him into the Whig party. Southern Bank men joined the Whigs and made their peace with the protective tariff.

As coherent parties emerged they extended their roots deeply into the electorate, drawing larger and larger numbers of citizens into the political process. The soaring voter turnouts of the 1820s and 1830s rested partly on new techniques of mass organization and publicity, partly on the mere existence of intensely competitive, closely matched political machines. But the parties could not have galvanized the electorate so spectacularly had they not spoken directly to pressing voter concerns. Tariff, internal improvement, banking, and public land policies not only impressed directly upon the welfare of communities and individuals, but expressed alternative—and attractive—visions of the national future. These visions were amplified as party organizations spread outward from Washington. State parties shaped themselves around national issues, linking them to local concerns. In state

legislatures, partisan competition appeared first over resolutions on
national affairs. As political warfare in Washington clarified party
policies, state politicians adopted parallel positions on comparable state
issues. The national controversies over banking and internal improvement in Jackson's administration were echoed in the states for many
years afterward.[3]

Once party formation was complete, the influence of issues upon
voter preference diminished. Individual issues were submerged in
essentially indivisible party programs. Voter attachments formed, then
stabilized, then hardened into traditions. But during the period of
party development, when political ties were still changeable, issues as
well as candidates were powerful recruiters to the party banner. Their
strength varied with circumstances, but at certain times and places
none was more important than the land issue. The crude indicators
available cannot measure the number of voters drawn to a party by any
one issue, and indeed voters themselves, could we have asked them,
might not have explained their preferences so simply. But the power of
the land issue is evident from the uses made of it by politicians, whose
very interest in political success gave them every reason to try to assess
the public mind accurately.

In the West, the land controversy entered into many campaigns and
dominated more than one. In printed circulars and public addresses,
Western candidates for national, state, and even local office stressed
their opinions on the public lands, sometimes to the exclusion of
everything else. An Indiana representative (later senator) recalled his
first campaign:

> The contest on my part looked at first almost hopeless. Stump
> speaking was just coming in fashion. The people met our appoint-
> ments by thousands. The judge had his high character to aid him, and
> I brought to my aid a strong voice, reaching to the very extremes of
> the largest crowds. The judge went for the graduation of the public
> lands, and I went for home gifts to actual settlers. My position was the
> most acceptable to the masses.[4]

On the frontier the land issue hurt the Whigs, helping to establish
the Democracy as the normal majority party in newly admitted states.
The refusal of frontier Whigs to follow the party leadership against
graduation shows their vulnerability on the issue, while its importance
to the Democrats appears in the letters of Western party workers
imploring New Yorker Martin Van Buren to adhere to Jackson's land
policy. Graduation's influence was most striking in Missouri, where it

enabled Thomas Hart Benton to establish a dominance in state politics that Whigs were long unable to challenge.[5]

In the Atlantic states the land issue was less powerful. The Democratic appeal to Eastern farm laborers and workingmen failed to mobilize much of a following for graduation. Distribution was popular, but it embraced so much of the Whig program and philosophy that its particular impact is difficult to assess. But in North Carolina, distribution was clearly the most potent weapon in the Whig arsenal and the main rallying point of the party.

In general, concentrations of party strength within the electorate reflected the programmatic alternatives proferred by the parties. Communities and groups interested in government sponsorship of social improvement and economic development gravitated to the Whigs. Rural backwaters resentful of metropolitan domination and ethnic and religious minorities resisting cultural homogenization inclined toward the Democrats. The Whigs were the party of cosmopolitanism, the Democrats of localism. The divisions were never absolute, and distinctive local conditions often obscured the general pattern; yet it still prevailed in such diverse places as Alabama, Missouri, North Carolina, New Hampshire, and the Ohio Valley.[6]

Whigs and Democrats incorporated local and regional as well as sectional divisions into their rivalry. Within states, concentrations of party strength sometimes reflected the antagonism of farm and city, or upcountry and delta. The two parties also continued to employ sectional appeals, but they did so within a political framework that remained stable because both programs attracted substantial support in every section. The Whigs refused cheap land to the West, but gave in its stead aid to education and transportation. In the South Democrats offered lower tariffs, but Whigs promised a stable currency and a growing industrial home market. The flexible ties between state and national organizations also freed politicians, where necessary, to deviate from the national line on matters of pressing local concern. Frontier Whigs backed graduation, while North Carolina Democrats opposed pre-emption.

A degree of sectional tension thus survived both between and within the parties, but it in no sense threatened their existence; it may have strengthened them. Through the 1840s the parties dealt successfully with the intrinsically sectional issues of the tariff, internal improvements, and public lands. Though they sometimes prevaricated, used different arguments in different places, and compromised their own positions in order to avoid antagonizing crucial voters, such expedients were not signs of weakness but of strength. Every durable American party has made similar accommodations in order to survive. Whigs and Democrats also managed to contain the new debate over Southwestern expansion and the cultural animosities produced by burgeoning Irish and German immigration within established channels of party competition.

Eventually the national party system collapsed. But neither sectionalism nor cultural conflict destroyed it; slavery did. In the 1850s the economic controversies that originally instigated party formation were not exhausted; nor were the parties doomed by ethnic and religious cleavages, which they had hitherto exploited to their benefit. Looking at the many similarities between the Whig and Democratic parties and their successors after the Civil War, it is difficult to see why the former were necessarily obsolete by the 1850s.[7]

There was only one subject Whigs and Democrats could not handle, and that was slavery. Once slavery came to dominate political discussion at every level, the parties as competitive national organizations were doomed. They continued to disagree on other issues, but found themselves locally in essential agreement, and therefore losing their distinctive identities, on the one subject that most mattered to the electorate. Furthermore, the slavery issue was inherently resistant to the kind of intersectional balancing by which Whigs and Democrats had erected a national political equilibrium upon a base of sectional economic issues. The power and intractability of the slavery controversy appeared in the way it reordered the rest of the political landscape. By 1860 homestead bills precipitated strict North–South sectional divisions in Congress. This made no sense. To the extent that it was sectional at all, homestead, like its predecessor graduation, was inherently an East–West issue. It became a North–South issue in the 1850s because Americans stopped perceiving it as a land question and began treating it as a slavery question. The sectionalism based on slavery that produced a party upheaval and a civil war was a sectionalism with which no genuinely national party system would have been able to cope.

Public land policy in Jacksonian America

Considering its central place in the Jacksonian debate over political economy, federal land policy did not change much during those years. The minimum purchase unit shrank from 160 to 40 acres. Sales for cash at a minimum price of $1.25 per acre (rarely exceeded) replaced sales on credit at $2.00 per acre. Pre-emption, or the option to settle on lands not yet offered for sale and then purchase them at the minimum price, evolved from an illegal but widespread custom to a legally guaranteed right. Compared to other revisions advocated by sectional interests and later by the Whig and Democratic parties, such changes were almost trivial. The lands were not given away, or sold at nominal prices, or ceded to the Western states; nor were the proceeds of land sales applied systematically to foster economic growth or social welfare. Except briefly in 1841, federal land revenue went into the general fund, where it merged with other receipts.

The images of the settler and the speculator permeated the contemporary debate over land policy. Newspapers, politicians, and petitioners told of an unending struggle between the wealthy capitalist and the poor but honest and hard-working settler. Both parties employed those images, the Democrats to greater effect. Whigs charged that reducing land prices would throw the public domain to speculators; Democrats argued that current high prices barred poor men from the market. The land speculations of prominent politicians of both parties were exposed by their opponents and held up for public condemnation.

Some twentieth-century historians have accepted the dichotomy of settler and speculator largely at face value because it comported with their own essentially agrarian precepts. In their view, a wise land policy would have furnished land at no cost to cultivators, blocked the acquisition of large holdings, and prohibited nonresident ownership. They have condemned the revenue policy for encouraging speculation and a train of attendant evils—large estates, tenancy, retarded agricultural development, dispersed population, and wasteful farming practices. To these historians the Land Act of 1820 was a backward step that crippled the settler's efforts to compete with the speculator. Preemption and homestead were settler triumphs, though fraud, the continuance of cash sales, and huge grants of land to canals and railroads largely vitiated their beneficial effects.[8]

Recent research calls into question the dichotomy of settler and speculator. In agrarian rhetoric, the defining difference between them was that the settler wanted to work the land, while the speculator acquired it only as a commodity to be held for profit. Yet the purchase of land for resale was commonplace throughout the West. The "actual settlers" who banded together to petition Congress for protection and to chase outsiders from the auction habitually claimed more land than they could farm. Small landholders along with great capitalists were swept up in the speculative booms of 1819 and 1836. Recent investigations also suggest that nonresident speculators, far from restraining settlement and cultivation, may have hastened it by enticing settlers westward, providing purchase credit and developmental capital, financing transportation improvements, and absorbing tax burdens.[9]

The distinction between settler and speculator also fails to illuminate political divisions on land issues. Daniel Webster, a Massachusetts Whig, speculated in Western lands and opposed graduation. Robert Walker, a Mississippi Democrat, speculated and favored graduation and the prohibition of sales except to "actual settlers." Speculation in lands, a common form of investment in the nineteenth century, attracted capital from men of means, including politicians, in both parties and all sections.

The one arena that threatened real conflict between the settler and the nonresident capitalist, or between purchasers of any kind, was the land auction. Squatters farming land they did not own had reason to fear that their improvements might attract outside bidders. In the boom of 1817–1819, bidding wars sometimes pushed prices far above the $2.00 per acre minimum. But the widespread advent of claims organizations in the 1820s and 1830s defused the potential for conflict. Though their rhetoric suggested otherwise, their real purpose was not so much to defend settlers from speculators as it was to protect all buyers from the folly of competitive bidding, which profited nobody but the federal government. Since the quantity of land offered for sale usually far exceeded the wants of purchasers, it was easy to make such combinations effective. Their recurrence and their membership, which included wealthy men as well as poor, revealed the possibilities for cooperation between "settlers" and "speculators." The failure of the government selling price to rise much above the $1.25 minimum during the land boom of the 1830s indicates their effectiveness.[10]

There were some true agrarians in Jacksonian America. George Henry Evans and a group of Eastern radicals wanted to give land to settlers, prohibit its alienation, and break up large estates. The agrarians' rhetoric was similar to that of Westerners. But their propositions contradicted the Western view of land as a commodity to be bought and sold, and when (as in 1837) they were introduced in Congress, they were rejected by Western votes. Through Horace Greeley's *New York Tribune*, Evans and his National Reform movement strengthened the later demand for homesteads, though the law of 1862 was not a true agrarian measure. But their influence on Jacksonian politics and land policy was negligible.[11]

The ubiquity of agrarian imagery in Jacksonian political dialogue suggests that it served some deeper societal need. The bucolic ideal had a stronger hold on men's imaginations than on their actions. The incessant denunciation of speculators by speculating politicians speaks of more than simple hypocrisy. It suggests, as Marvin Meyers has hypothesized, that agrarian rhetoric served as a sort of purgative, by which men reaffirmed their fidelity to an ideal they were perhaps all too conscious of violating. The settler ideal portrayed the American not as he was but as he wished to think of himself; the image of the speculator concentrated in an external figure the characteristics men did not want to acknowledge in themselves.[12]

Should the government have adopted a different land policy in the Jacksonian era? The twentieth-century critics have viewed land speculation, especially during the booms, as evidence of flaws in the system. As they see it, land should have been delivered directly to the cultivator, without intermediaries who raised its price and postponed its settlement.

That changes in the price or credit terms could have banished speculation seems doubtful. Land speculation was endemic throughout early American history, its volume determined more by general economic conditions and the availability of capital than by the details of the land system. Speculators operated under a wide variety of land-disposal arrangements from the colonial period through the Jacksonian land booms and beyond, despite the advent of pre-emption and homesteads. That speculative purchases slowed the rate of settlement is equally dubious. The evils attributed to speculation—dispersed population, wasteful farming methods, large estates—resulted rather from the great excess of land over population. The modern critics, like Thomas Hart Benton, have assumed that thousands of prospective emigrants were eager to move out onto the public domain but were shut out by high land prices. That assumption should be questioned. No direct link between the government price for land and the speed of settlement has been demonstrated. The Graduation Act of 1854 stimulated rapid purchases, but not necessarily more rapid settlement. Though thousands of pioneers took up land on the plains under the Homestead Act, equally impressive waves of migration had occurred earlier under more restrictive land-disposal systems. At all times, the initial price of undeveloped land was so small a fraction of the cost of farm-making that changes in it could only minimally affect the rate of settlement.

Benton and the modern critics assumed that settling as many Americans as possible on their own farms was desirable. But their arguments rested on agrarian postulates that historians are not required to accept. It was not necessarily to their own benefit or that of society—and certainly not that of the Indians—that Eastern tenants, farm laborers, and city dwellers be drawn westward to become frontier farmers. The placement of agriculture ahead of all other economic pursuits was a deliberate policy choice, not an axiomatic truth. The Whigs argued that industry and commerce deserved equal encouragement, and that geographic dispersion hindered even agricultural progress. A society composed entirely of freehold farmers was an agrarian ideal but not, according to Whigs, a desirable social goal. Their arguments deserve more consideration than they have received.

In the end, one is left with an appreciation of the narrow alternatives open to the government in the Jacksonian era. Ironically, the policies most conducive to immediate occupation of the land by actual cultivators may have been those advocated by Easterners like Senator Samuel Foot and rejected by all friends of the West. A carefully controlled opening of the public domain, with squatting prohibited and land titles withheld pending cultivation, might have eliminated the nonresident middleman, reduced the waste of capital on unproductive land purchases, and salvaged the government's Indian policy. But such a program was politically impossible and, even if enacted, unenforceable. The government's feeble efforts to control squatting and to prevent pre-emption and homestead frauds revealed its administrative incapacity to closely regulate the disposal of land. The historian of the General Land Office concludes that the system "never worked very well; at least, it never worked as precisely as it had been intended to work." Congress could raise or lower the price a little, offer credit or refuse it, praise squatters or denounce them, but it could not change the character of the American people or erase habits long engrained in American society. It could not prevent Americans from treating land as a commodity, or force them to migrate, or, within narrow limits, stop them from doing so. The abolition of the credit system, the adoption of pre-emption, and the Homestead Act probably affected the process of settlement much less than anyone thought. The Jacksonian debate over land policy, like that over the tariff, reveals that public faith in the government's capacity to direct great social and economic change outran its actual ability to do so.[13]

REFERENCE MATTER

A NOTE ON SOURCES

The major Washington papers—the *National Intelligencer, National Journal, United States Telegraph,* and *Globe*—published daily city editions and twice- or thrice-weekly country editions, ordinarily identical in content except for advertisements and local news. Most of my citations are to the country edition; a reader checking in the other edition will find the same items, but sometimes under a slightly different date.

I have made extensive use of state legislative journals and session law volumes, which were published under various and sometimes cumbersome titles. Rather than clutter up the notes with uselessly complex citations, I have cited them by generic names, i. e., Illinois *House Journal* or Mississippi *Session Laws.* This nomenclature conforms to the classification system of the Library of Congress microfilm collection of Early State Records, through which most of the volumes are readily accessible. I also use the short titles *House Journal* and *Senate Journal,* with Congress and session numbers, for the *Journal of the House of Representatives of the United States* and the *Journal of the Senate of the United States,* respectively.

The land data in this text are contemporary official figures annually presented to Congress by the secretary of the Treasury and the commissioner of the General Land Office. The General Land Office reported its transactions in fractions of a cent and hundredths of an acre; but in such a sprawling operation, where records were kept by hand and not always conscientiously, precision was an illusion. All land statistics, contemporary or modern, should be treated as rough estimates. For alternative data, some based on a different calendar, see Senate Document 246, 27th Cong., 3d sess., p. 6; Arthur H. Cole, "Cyclical and Sectional Variations in the Sale of Public Lands, 1816–1860," in Vernon Carstensen, ed., *The Public Lands* (Madison: University of Wisconsin Press, 1963), pp. 229–251; Malcolm J. Rohrbough, *The Land Office Business* (New York: Oxford University Press, 1968).

ABBREVIATIONS

AC   *Annals of Congress* (also titled *Debates and Proceedings in the Congress of the United States, 1789–1824*)

ASP   *American State Papers: Documents, Legislative and Executive*

GPO   Government Printing Office

LC   Library of Congress

OHS   Ohio Historical Society

RD   *Register of Debates in Congress, 1825–1837* (continuation of the *Annals of Congress*)

NOTES

Introduction

1 *RD*, 21st Cong., 1st sess., pp. 31–32. This was the speech that began the Webster–Hayne debate.

2 *RD*, 22d Cong., 1st sess., p. 1098.

3 James D. Richardson, ed., *A Compilation of the Messages and Papers of the Presidents, 1789–1897* (Washington: GPO, 1896–1899), 2:9.

4 For a contemporary picture of sectionalism in society, see Timothy Flint, *Recollections of the Last Ten Years* (Boston: Cummings, Hilliard, & Co., 1826); for the use of sectional imagery in politics, see John William Ward, *Andrew Jackson: Symbol for an Age* (New York: Oxford University Press, 1955).

5 On congressional voting in the 1840s, see Joel H. Silbey, *The Shrine of Party* (Pittsburgh: University of Pittsburgh Press, 1967); on elections, see Richard P. McCormick, "New Perspectives on Jacksonian Politics," *American Historical Review* 65 (January 1960): 288–301.

6 Frederick Jackson Turner, *Rise of the New West*, vol. 14 of the American Nation series (New York: Harper & Brothers, 1906); Frederick Jackson Turner, *The United States, 1830–1850* (New York: Henry Holt & Co., 1935).

7 Arthur M. Schlesinger, Jr., *The Age of Jackson* (Boston: Little, Brown & Co., 1945), p. 263.

8 Lee Benson, *The Concept of Jacksonian Democracy: New York as a Test Case* (Princeton: Princeton University Press, 1961), p. 165; Robert Kelley, *The Cultural Pattern in American Politics: The First Century* (New York: Alfred A. Knopf, 1979), pp. 6–7; Ronald P. Formisano, *The Birth of Mass Political Parties: Michigan, 1827–1861* (Princeton: Princeton University Press, 1971); Ronald P. Formisano, "Toward a Reorientation of Jacksonian Politics: A Review of the Literature," *Journal of American History* 63 (June 1976):42–65. Formisano's complaint, on page 59 of the latter, that the phrase "ethnocultural interpretation" is either a slur or a useless oversimplification surely applies equally to his own use of "economic determinism."

For critiques of the "ethnocultural interpretation," see James E. Wright, "The Ethnocultural Model of Voting: A Behavioral and Historical Critique," *American Behavioral Scientist* 16 (May–June 1973):653–674; Richard

205

L. McCormick, "Ethno-Cultural Interpretations of Nineteenth-Century American Voting Behavior," *Political Science Quarterly* 89 (June 1974):351–377; Morgan Kousser, "The 'New Political History': A Methodological Critique," *Reviews in American History* 4 (March 1976):1–14; Richard B. Latner and Peter Levine, "Perspectives on Antebellum Pietistic Politics," *Reviews in American History* 4 (March 1976):15–24.

9 Richard P. McCormick, in *The Second American Party System: Party Formation in the Jacksonian Era* (Chapel Hill: University of North Carolina Press, 1966), argues that national parties concerned more with winning elections than pursuing policies emerged out of essentially issueless presidential campaigns between candidates with strong regional identifications. McCormick concludes that the parties were "artificial" because they "could scarcely cope with the tariff or internal improvements issues," to say nothing of slavery (p. 353). But McCormick's analysis fails to acknowledge the connection between regional loyalties and alternative policy choices. For discussion of the McCormick thesis, see Robert E. Shalhope, "Jacksonian Politics in Missouri: A Comment on the McCormick Thesis," *Civil War History* 15 (September 1969):210–225; the exchange between Shalhope and McCormick in *Civil War History* 16 (March 1970):92–95; Donald J. Ratcliffe, "The Role of Voters and Issues in Party Formation: Ohio, 1824," *Journal of American History* 59 (March 1973):847–870; Donald J. Ratliffe, "Politics in Jacksonian Ohio: Reflections on the Ethnocultural Interpretation," *Ohio History* 88 (Winter 1979):5–36; Stephen C. Fox, "Politicians, Issues, and Voter Preference in Jacksonian Ohio: A Critique of an Interpretation," *Ohio History* 86 (Summer 1977):155–170.

James Sterling Young, in *The Washington Community, 1800–1828* (New York: Columbia University Press, 1966), describing the federal establishment as "government at a distance and out of sight," argues that "almost all of the things that republican governments do which affect the everyday lives and fortunes of their citizens, and therefore engage their interest, were in Jeffersonian times *not* done by the national government" (p. 31). The treatment of the period from 1800 to 1828 as a political unit is questionable. For a penetrating critique of Young's roll-call methodology and his handling of primary sources, see Allan G. Bogue and Mark Paul Marlaire, "Of Mess and Men: The Boardinghouse and Congressional Voting, 1821–1842," *American Journal of Political Science* 19 (May 1975):207–230.

10 *Niles' Weekly Register* 35 (September 20, 1828):55.

11 Harry L. Watson, *Jacksonian Politics and Community Conflict* (Baton Rouge: Louisiana State University Press, 1981) shows the use of national issues by local party organizers. On the partisan uses of national policy resolutions in state legislatures, see Rodney O. Davis, "Partisanship in Jacksonian State Politics: Party Divisions in the Illinois Legislature, 1834–1841," in *Quantification in American History: Theory and Research*, ed. Robert P. Swierenga (New York: Atheneum, 1970), pp. 149–162; Peter Levine, "State Legislative Parties in the Jacksonian Era: New Jersey, 1829–1844," *Journal of*

American History 62 (December 1975):591–608; Herbert Ershkowitz and William G. Shade, "Consensus or Conflict? Political Behavior in the State Legislatures During the Jacksonian Era," *Journal of American History* 58 (December 1971):591–621. Party competition in the legislatures appeared first over national issues, then over state issues such as banking that reflected national party policies, and lastly over local economic and social questions.

1. The national land system before 1815

1 For a more detailed treatment of the events in this chapter, see Payson Jackson Treat, *The National Land System, 1785–1820* (New York: E. B. Treat & Co., 1910), or Paul W. Gates, *History of Public Land Law Development* (Washington: GPO, 1968). Most of the crucial documents are collected in Thomas Donaldson, *The Public Domain* (Washington: GPO, 1884).

2 Worthington Chauncey Ford et al., eds., *Journals of the Continental Congress* (Washington: GPO, 1904–1937), 11:650; see also 14:619–622.

3 Ford et al., *Journals of the Continental Congress*, 9:807–808; 11:631–632, 636–637, 639, 648–651; 12:1162; 17:806–807; 19:138–139, 208–214; Donaldson, *Public Domain*, pp. 60–61. For a detailed treatment of these events, see Merrill Jensen, *The New Nation* (New York: Alfred A. Knopf, 1950).

4 Donaldson, *Public Domain*, pp. 64, 68–69.

5 On the recent "sagebrush rebellion," see Paul W. Gates, "Pressure Groups and Recent American Land Policies," *Agricultural History* 55 (April 1981): 103–127.

6 Donaldson, *Public Domain*, pp. 148–149, 153–156.

7 Ford et al., *Journals of the Continental Congress*, 24:256, 280; 26:315–317.

8 Treat, *National Land System*, pp. 395–400. I have omitted many details of the early land legislation that did not bear on developments after 1815.

9 *The Public Statutes at Large of the United States of America* (Boston: Little and Brown, 1845–1848) 1:144, 435.

10 Ibid., 1:464–469; 2:73–78, 277–283. Under the act of 1800, payments for credit purchases were figured as follows:

Payment number	Due date	Amounts due
1 & 2	Down and 40 days	50¢ per acre
3	2 years	50¢ plus 12% interest = 56¢
4	3 years	50¢ plus 18% interest = 59¢
5	4 years	50¢ plus 24% interest = 62¢

$2.27 per acre

For the purchaser who paid cash down, the three latter payments were discounted 16, 24, and 32 percent, reducing them respectively to 47¢, 45¢, and 42¢, for a total purchase price of $1.84 per acre. The legislation of 1804 waived interest for payments made when due, reducing the total price for the nondelinquent credit purchaser to a flat $2.00 per acre. Applying the same discount for early payment as before, the cash purchaser's payments were reduced to 50¢, 42¢, 38¢, and 34¢ respectively, for a total of $1.64 per acre.

11 *Statutes at Large*, 2:173–175, 225–227.

12 Adams to Alexander Everett, May 24, 1830, and September 18, 1831, *American Historical Review* 11 (January 1906): 340, 343.

13 Gallatin to William Branch Giles, February 13, 1802, *The Writings of Albert Gallatin*, ed. Henry Adams (Philadelphia: J. B. Lippincott & Co., 1879), 1:76–79; *AC*, 7th Cong., 1st sess., pp. 1097–1100. From the *AC* and the House and Senate journals it is impossible to determine when and under what circumstances the substitution was made. It was not debated. The drift of Gallatin's thinking at this time may be gathered from the fact that in April of 1802 he drew up a memo on the route of the Cumberland Road. This was while the Ohio Enabling Act was still before Congress, four years before the first appropriation to survey the road (Gallatin papers, New York University, microfilm ed.).

14 *Statutes at Large*, 2:641–643; 3:289–291, 348–349, 428–431, 489–492, 545–548. The compacts varied slightly in detail. For instance, in Illinois the 3 percent fund was designated for schools, not roads.

15 ASP *Public Lands*, 3:420.

16 ASP *Public Lands*, 1:183–184.

17 ASP *Public Lands*, 1:183–184.

18 ASP *Public Lands*, 1:182–184, 286–287, 909–910; 2:439–441, 730–731.

19 Calculated from the annual land statistics in ASP *Public Lands*, 3:420.

20 ASP *Public Lands*, 1:287.

2. The emergence of the new west, 1815–1821

1 Charles Royce, *Indian Land Cessions in the United States*, Eighteenth Annual Report of the Bureau of American Ethnology, pt. 2 (Washington: GPO, 1899), pp. 678–679.

2 Lewis Cecil Gray, *History of Agriculture in the Southern United States to 1860* (Washington: Carnegie Institution, 1933), 2:1027, 1039; Thomas Senior Berry, *Western Prices Before 1861* (Cambridge: Harvard University Press, 1943), p. 569.

3 Morris Birkbeck, *Notes on a Journey in America from the Coast of Virginia to the Territory of Illinois* (London: Severn & Co., 1818), p. 31; Jefferson to Albert Gallatin, November 24, 1818, *The Writings of Albert Gallatin*, ed. Henry Adams (Philadelphia: J. B. Lippincott & Co., 1879), 2:89 (hereafter cited as *Gallatin Writings*).

4 Bureau of the Census, *Historical Statistics of the United States: Colonial Times to 1970* (Washington: GPO, 1975), pp. 25–37.

5 William Sullivan to Virgil Maxcy, February 6, 1820, Galloway–Maxcy–Markoe papers, LC; *The Diary and Journal of Richard Clough Anderson, Jr.*, ed. Alfred Tischendorf and E. Taylor Parks (Durham: Duke University Press, 1964), p. 73.

6 James Graham to Thomas Ruffin, August 10, 1817, *The Papers of Thomas Ruffin*, ed. J. G. de Roulhac Hamilton (Raleigh: North Carolina Historical Commission, 1918–1920), 1:194–195 (hereafter cited as *Ruffin Papers*); legislative committee reports in *Niles' Weekly Register*, vol. 9, supp., pp. 150, 165–166. See also *Ruffin Papers*, 1:185, 198; the Washington *National Intelligencer*, July 30 and November 5, 1818; R. Carlyle Buley, *The Old Northwest* (Indianapolis: Indiana Historical Society, 1950), 1:14–15; "Nine Letters of Nathaniel Dike on the Western Country, 1816–1818," ed. Dwight L. Smith, *Ohio Historical Quarterly* 67 (July 1958):189–220.

7 ASP *Public Lands*, 3:420; this gives a compilation of figures from the annual Treasury reports. The reports themselves are in ASP *Finance*, vols. 2, 3.

8 William Rector to Josiah Meigs, July 7, 1817, in Clarence Edwin Carter, ed., *The Territorial Papers of the United States* (Washington: GPO, 1934–1962), 15:290; see also 15:283; 18:23–25; 19:65. For the operations and problems of the General Land Office during this period, see Malcolm J. Rohrbough, *The Land Office Business*, (New York: Oxford University Press, 1968), pp. 89–136.

9 Jackson to James Monroe, March 4, 1817, *Correspondence of Andrew Jackson*, ed. John Spencer Bassett (Washington: Carnegie Institution, 1926–1935), 2:277–278. See also Carter, *Territorial Papers*, 10:741, 759, 830–831.

10 James D. Richardson, ed., *A Compilation of the Messages and Papers of the Presidents, 1789–1897* (Washington: GPO, 1896–1899), 1:572.

11 Vincennes (Indiana) *Western Sun*, January 20, 1816. See also *Western Sun*, January 27 through February 24, 1816; Mississippi petition in Carter, *Territorial Papers*, 6:757–759; Jonathan Jennings letter in *Indiana Magazine of History* 39 (September 1943):290; Rohrbough, *Land Office Business*, pp. 93–96.

12 John Scott circular in Moses Austin and Stephen F. Austin, *The Austin Papers*, ed. Eugene C. Barker, Annual Report of the American Historical Association for the Year 1919, vol. 2 (Washington: GPO, 1924), pp. 255–258; legislative memorial in Carter, *Territorial Papers*, 15:502–505. See also Ninian Edwards circular in *Journal of the Illinois State Historical Society* 15 (April, 1922):539.

13 Crawford to Albert Gallatin, October 27, 1817, *Gallatin Writings*, 2:54; ASP *Public Lands*, 3:420.

14 Clay to William Thornton, December 6, 1817, *The Papers of Henry Clay*, ed. James F. Hopkins et al. (Lexington: University of Kentucky Press, 1959–) 2:407 (hereafter cited as *Clay Papers*).

15 Richardson, *Messages and Papers*, 2:9, 17.

16 Nathaniel Pope in the Kaskaskia (Illinois) *Western Intelligencer*, January 21, 1818; Lexington *Kentucky Reporter*, reprinted in *St. Louis Enquirer*, December 4, 1819; *Western Intelligencer*, January 14, 1818.

17 ASP *Public Lands*, 3:300–301.

18 Cincinnati *Western Spy*, March 28, 1818; Chillicothe (Ohio) *Scioto Gazette*, February 5, 1819. See also ASP *Finance*, 3:213, 232, 263, 266–269, 718–721; *Governors Messages and Letters*, vol. 12 of the Indiana Historical Collec-

tions (Indianapolis: Indiana Historical Commission, 1924), 3:68; Indiana legislative memorial in Corydon *Indiana Gazette,* January 9, 1819; *Western Spy,* April 4, 1818.

19 Thomas Ford, *A History of Illinois,* ed. Milo Quaife (1847; Chicago: R. R. Donnelley & Sons, 1945) pp. 46–47; Carter, *Territorial Papers,* 18:300; ASP *Public Lands,* 3:420.

20 *AC,* 15th Cong., 2d sess., pp. 77–79, 215–218. On Morrow's status in the Senate, see *Memoir, Autobiography, and Correspondence of Jeremiah Mason,* ed. G. J. Clark (Kansas City: Lawyer's International Publishing Co., 1917), p. 186; Jonathan Roberts, "Memoirs of a Senator from Pennsylvania," ed. Philip S. Klein, *Pennsylvania Magazine of History and Biography* 62 (July 1938):394; William Trimble to Allen Trimble, *Old Northwest Genealogical Quarterly* 10 (July 1907):261; eulogy by John McLean in *Old Northwest Genealogical Quarterly* 9 (April 1906):105; eulogy by Henry Clay in *RD,* 22d Cong., 1st sess., p. 1101.

21 *National Intelligencer,* February 23 and March 2, 1819; *AC,* 15th Cong., 2d sess., pp. 240–246.

22 The *AC,* which is very thin for this Senate session, does not mention this episode. It is described in several letters to Edwards printed in Ninian Wirt Edwards, *History of Illinois from 1778 to 1833; and Life and Times of Ninian Edwards* (Springfield: Illinois State Journal Co., 1870), pp. 510, 516–518. Edwards solicited these letters in 1832 to answer a campaign charge that he had opposed reducing land prices in 1819; see Edwards to John Jordan Crittenden, April 16, 1832, Crittenden papers, LC.

23 *National Intelligencer,* March 4 and 9, July 24, 1819.

24 Gray, *History of Agriculture,* 2:1027–1039; Berry, *Western Prices,* pp. 569–570; ASP *Finance,* 3:431–432, 560–562. In the last three calendar months of 1819 sales fell to 189,111 acres (an annual rate of less than a million acres) and the average sale price to $2.23 per acre.

25 St. Charles *Missourian,* June 24, 1820; *Albany* (New York) *Register,* reprinted in the *National Intelligencer,* August 11, 1819; "Franklin" in *National Intelligencer,* July 24, 1819; Tiffin to Josiah Meigs, October 31, 1819, in Rohrbough, *Land Office Business,* p. 142. See also *National Intelligencer,* August 4, 1819.

26 Philemon Beecher to Ethan Allen Brown, February 22, 1819, Brown papers, OHS (microfilm ed., roll 1, frame 331); "Franklin" in *National Intelligencer,* July 24, 1819; *National Intelligencer,* April 15, May 15, June 9, 1819; *Niles' Weekly Register* 18 (July 29, 1820):387–388.

27 St. Louis *Missouri Gazette,* April 28, 1819; *Kentucky Reporter,* reprinted in Jackson *Missouri Herald,* February 26, 1820; Cook letter in *Edwardsville* (Illinois) *Spectator,* April 25, 1820; Senate Document 67, 16th Cong., 1st sess.; *AC,* 16th Cong., 1st sess., p. 360.

28 Rankin in Natchez *Mississippi Republican,* April 25, 1820.

29 For the effects on the pre-emptioners, see Carter, *Territorial Papers,* 15:655–656 and 19:190–191.

30 Noble E. Cunningham, Jr., ed., *Circular Letters of Congressmen to Their*

Constituents, 1789–1829 (Chapel Hill: University of North Carolina Press, 1978), 3:1093; Chillicothe *Supporter*, May 26, 1819; *Kentucky Reporter*, reprinted in *St. Louis Enquirer*, December 4, 1819.

31 St. Louis *Missouri Gazette*, April 7, 1819; Barton in Franklin *Missouri Intelligencer*, January 29, 1821; *Missouri Intelligencer*, May 7, 1819.

32 Edwards and Thomas were "a tower of strength to the South throughout the Missouri Controversy" (Glover Moore, *The Missouri Controversy* [Lexington: University of Kentucky Press, 1953], p. 282). Even as far south as Alabama the antislavery campaign was sometimes seen as an attack on the West; see, for instance, the Huntsville *Democrat* of November 4 and 11, 1823. For more on the perceived relation between slavery and immigration, see the Franklin *Missouri Intelligencer*, July 2, 1819; St. Louis *Missouri Gazette*, June 2, 1819; *St. Louis Enquirer*, April 21, May 21, June 9, October 27, November 10, 1819.

In Illinois, the question of slavery's influence upon land values and immigration dominated the slavery debate in 1823. See the correspondence of Governor Edward Coles in Elihu B. Washburne, *Sketch of Edward Coles, Second Governor of Illinois, and of the Slavery Struggle of 1823–4* (Chicago: Jansen, McClurg & Co., 1882), pp. 143, 145, and in *Journal of Negro History* 3 (April 1918):174; Vandalia *Illinois Intelligencer*, May 24, 1823, January 30 and July 30, 1824; Shawneetown *Illinois Gazette*, July 5 and 26, 1823, January 10 and July 17, 1824; *Niles' Weekly Register* 25 (September 20, 1823): 39; Edward King to Rufus King, July 22, 1823, in *The Life and Correspondence of Rufus King*, ed. Charles R. King (New York: G. P. Putnam's Sons, 1894–1900), 6:532 (hereafter cited as *King Correspondence*); Ford, *History of Illinois*, pp. 57–58.

Missouri governor Alexander McNair complained that the postponement of statehood cost Missouri thousands of immigrants. See *The Messages and Proclamations of the Governors of the State of Missouri*, ed. Buel Leopard and Floyd Shoemaker (Columbia: State Historical Society of Missouri, 1922), 1:18, 21–22.

33 Clay to John Jordan Crittenden, January 29, 1820, *Clay Papers*, 2:769.

34 *AC*, 16th Cong., 1st sess., p. 445; ASP *Finance*, 3:562.

35 *AC*, 16th Cong., 1st sess., pp. 27, 32, 78, 81, 417, 426, 437–438, 444–452, 458, 463–466, 476–477, 481–487, 489; *National Intelligencer*, March 9, 1820. Waller Taylor of Indiana voted for the bill in violation of legislative instructions, for which he was excoriated in the Indiana press (Corydon *Indiana Gazette*, March 30, July 13 and 27, 1820).

36 *AC*, 16th Cong., 1st sess., pp. 1650, 1699–1700, 1862–1863, 1865–1887, 1889–1899, 1901; George Robertson, *An Outline of the Life of George Robertson, Written by Himself* (Lexington, Ky.: Transylvania Printing & Publishing Co., 1876), p. 55. Robertson's claim to have "initiated" the reform of the land system is without foundation.

37 *The Public Statutes at Large of the United States of America* (Boston: Little and Brown, 1845–1848) 3:566–567.

38 Edwards, *History of Illinois*, pp. 379–383. This speech is not in the AC.

39 Almost every editorial or speech on the credit system used one of these two arguments. See the *Albany* (New York) *Argus*, March 2, 1819; *Cincinnati Inquisitor Advertiser*, November 30, 1819; *National Intelligencer*, May 6, August 28, 1819; St. Louis *Missouri Gazette*, June 2, 1819. For Western denials of speculative buying during the boom, see the *National Intelligencer*, October 3 and 10, 1818; *St. Louis Enquirer*, December 22, 1819.

40 Morris Birkbeck, *Letters From Illinois* (1818; New York: Da Capo Press, 1970), p. 120; Solon Justus Buck, *Illinois in 1818*, sesquicentennial edition (Urbana: University of Illinois Press, 1967), p. 153.

41 ASP *Public Lands*, 3:413–414.

42 For the luring of Ohioans to greener frontier pastures, see the *National Intelligencer*, June 13, 1818. The details of King's maneuver are in chapter 3. Its effect is uncertain, though Ohio senator Benjamin Ruggles's vote for the cash bill in 1820 reversed his position of the previous session.

43 Sloane in *AC*, 16th Cong., 1st sess., pp. 1892–1893; James Campbell to Allen Trimble, February 11, 1819, in *Old Northwest Genealogical Quarterly* 10 (July, 1907):261; Levi Barber to Ethan Allen Brown, January 31, 1819, Brown papers, OHS (microfilm ed., roll 1, frame 304); Brown to Benjamin Ruggles, May 10, 1820, Brown papers (microfilm ed., roll 2, frames 371–372).

44 King to Christopher Gore, July 17, 1819, King to Jeremiah Mason, February 7, 1819, King to Gore, February 11, 1819 and April 9, 1820, in *King Correspondence*, 6:228, 207–208, 212, 328–329.

45 Cunningham, *Circular Letters*, 3:1075–1076.

46 Roane to James Monroe, February 16, 1820, in *Bulletin of the New York Public Library* 10 (March 1906): 175. On May 23, 1820, Monroe himself told Andrew Jackson that the Northeast had always shown "repugnance" toward the welfare of West and South (*The Writings of James Monroe*, ed. Stanislaus Murray Hamilton [New York: G. P. Putnam's Sons, 1898–1903], 6:126–128).

47 John McLean to Ninian Edwards, April 25, 1825, in Edwards, *History of Illinois*, p. 478.

48 Webster, quoted by John McLean to Ninian Edwards, April 25, 1825, in Edwards, *History of Illinois*, p. 478; Randolph in *RD*, 19th Cong., 1st sess., p. 354. Randolph was a member of the Sixteenth Congress but missed all the roll calls on land bills in 1820 and 1821. In 1806 he had argued strenuously against extensions of time for land debtors (ASP *Public Lands*, 1:284).

49 *National Intelligencer*, August 6, 1818, May 15 and 19, 1819; *Niles' Weekly Register* 15 (January 30, 1819):423–424; 17 (February 5, 1820):386–387.

50 Noble in Corydon *Indiana Gazette*, March 30, 1820; *Illinois Intelligencer*, reprinted in Jackson *Missouri Herald*, May 6, 1820; Hendricks circular in *Indiana Magazine of History* 70 (December 1974):334.

51 *Cincinnati Gazette*, reprinted in Vandalia *Illinois Intelligencer*, December 23, 1820; petitions in *AC*, 16th Cong., 2d sess., pp. 17, 19, 22, 28, 36, 39, 77, 99, 116, 126, 131, 134, 136, 142, 147, 153, 183, and in *Niles' Weekly Register* 19 (October 28, 1820):181–182. Legislative memorials in *AC*, 16th Cong., 2d

sess., pp. 212–213; Carter, *Territorial Papers*, 15:668–670; Senate Document 18, 16th Cong., 2d sess.; Ohio *Session Laws*, December 1820 sess., p. 204–205.

52 King to J. A. King, January 21, 1821, *King Correspondence*, 6:379; Richardson, *Messages and Papers*, 2:78; annual Treasury report in *AC*, 16th Cong., 2d sess., pp. 495–497; *National Intelligencer*, October 7, 1820.

53 *AC*, 16th Cong., 2d sess., pp. 170–174, 223–225; full Senate debate on pp. 133–134, 156–178, 213–236; House debate on pp. 1186–1189, 1221–1223, 1228–1236. See also *National Intelligencer*, October 11 and November 28, 1820.

54 King speech (misdated) in *King Correspondence*, 6:687–690; King to C. King, January 26, 1821, *King Correspondence*, 6:381. See also *AC*, 16th Cong., 2d sess., p. 1222; *National Intelligencer*, February 1, 1821.

55 *Senate Journal*, 16th Cong., 2d sess., pp. 164, 179–181; *House Journal*, 16th Cong., 2d sess., pp. 272–273, 282–284, 288–289; *Statutes at Large*, 3:612–614.

56 Edwards to James Findlay, February 13, 1821, in *Quarterly Publication of the Historical and Philosophical Society of Ohio* 6 (July 1911):50; Hendricks circular in *Indiana Magazine of History* 70 (December 1974):336–338; Walker in *National Intelligencer*, June 2, 1821; Cook letters in Vandalia *Illinois Intelligencer*, April 3, 1821, and Shawneetown *Illinois Gazette*, March 10, 1821. See also Alabama governor Israel Pickens in *National Intelligencer*, December 15, 1821; Calhoun to Charles Tait, April 23, 1821, in *The Papers of John C. Calhoun*, ed. Robert L. Meriwether et al. (Columbia: University of South Carolina Press, 1959–), 6:69.

57 *National Intelligencer*, reprinted in Chillicothe *Supporter and Scioto Gazette*, March 28, 1821.

58 *AC*, 16th Cong., 1st sess., pp. 1353–1354.

59 ASP *Public Lands*, 1:183.

3. Sectionalism, 1821–1825

1 Georgia *House Journal*, November 1821 sess., p. 17; Joseph Hobson Harrison, "The Internal Improvement Issue in the Politics of the Union, 1783–1825" (Ph.D. diss., University of Virginia, 1954), pp. 300, 339–340.

2 Annapolis *Maryland Gazette and Political Intelligencer*, December 23, 1819.

3 Maryland *Senate Journal*, December 1819 sess., pp. 46–47, and December 1820 sess., p. 52; Maryland report and resolutions in *AC*, 16th Cong., 2d sess., pp. 1772–1784.

4 *AC*, 16th Cong., 2d sess., pp. 1776, 1778, 1783.

5 *AC*, 16th Cong., 2d sess., p. 1778.

6 ASP *Public Lands*, 3:410–411, 496.

7 Verplanck report quoted in *Niles' Weekly Register* 20 (August 11, 1821):376–379; New Hampshire and Connecticut in ASP *Public Lands*, 3:499, 501; North Carolina *House Journal*, November 1820 sess., p. 102, and *Senate Journal*, November 1820 sess., pp. 78, 92; Virginia *House Journal*, December

1820 sess., p. 226; *Albany* (N.Y.) *Argus*, May 11, 1821; Chillicothe (Ohio) *Supporter and Scioto Gazette*, March 13, 1822.

8 *National Intelligencer*, April 26, May 4 and 23, September 19, October 31, November 13, 22, 24, December 8, 25, 1821; *Niles' Weekly Register* 21 (December 29, 1821):277; *North American Review* 13 (October 1821):310–342; Calhoun letters to Virgil Maxcy in *The Papers of John C. Calhoun*, ed. Robert L. Meriwether et al. (Columbia: University of South Carolina Press, 1959–), 6:42, 75–76, 487, 583, 595, 631; William Gaston to Bartlett Yancey, November 5, 1821, in *James Sprunt Historical Publications* (Chapel Hill: University of North Carolina Publications, 1900–), vol. 10, no. 2, p. 32. Aside from Calhoun, Maxcy's coadjutors included Gaston in North Carolina, Levi Maxcy in South Carolina, William Sullivan in Boston, Henry D. Sedgwick in New York, Benjamin Chew, Jr., in Philadelphia, and Robert Goodloe Harper, Joseph Kent, William Pinkney, and Jared Sparks in Maryland. Their correspondence with Maxcy from January 1821 to February 1823, in the Galloway–Maxcy–Markoe papers, LC, chronicles their extensive lobbying for the proposition.

9 Legislative resolutions are in ASP *Public Lands*, 3:500, 502–503, 509, 511, 514, and Georgia *House Journal*, November 1821 sess., pp. 253–254. For governors' messages, see Boston *Columbian Centinel*, January 12, 1822; New York *Senate Journal*, January 1822 sess., p. 10; and Virginia *House Journal*, December 1821 sess., p. 49. See also *Charleston* (South Carolina) *Courier*, December 18 and 19, 1821; Pennsylvania *Senate Journal*, December 1821 sess., pp. 73–76, 95.

10 Massachusetts report reprinted in Pennsylvania *House Journal*, December 1821 sess., pp. 716–728.

11 [Virgil Maxcy], *The Maryland Resolutions, and the Objections to Them Considered* (Baltimore: E. J. Coale & Co., 1822), published anonymously; Maxcy serialized the pamphlet under pseudonyms in the *National Intelligencer*, January 1, 5, 29, February 5, 14, March 7, 12, 1822. For the Virginia report, see Virginia *House Journal*, December 1821 sess., p. 156; *Richmond Enquirer*, December 25, 1821.

12 Indiana *House Journal*, November 1821 sess., pp. 321–324; Ohio *Senate Journal*, December 1821 sess., pp. 12–16. See also Tennessee's resolutions in *Niles' Weekly Register* 21 (January 5, 1822):299–300. Maxcy had counted Tennessee as a public land state, which it ostensibly was, though the federal land system had never operated there and the actual quantity of public domain was still undetermined in 1821. Accordingly, Tennessee criticized the Maryland proposition but also claimed a share of the distributed lands if the proposition succeeded.

13 Ohio *Senate Journal*, December 1821 sess., pp. 180–181; full report on pp. 174–191.

14 "Fact" in the *National Intelligencer*, December 25, 1821.

15 William Greene to Ethan Allen Brown, December 20, 1821 (quoted) and January 29, 1822, Brown papers, OHS (microfilm ed., roll 3, frames 384 and 464); Shawneetown *Illinois Gazette*, February 2 and March 9, 1822. See

also Charles Hammond to Ethan Allen Brown, Hammond papers, OHS (microfilm ed., roll 1, frame 198); Chillicothe *Supporter and Scioto Gazette*, January 23 and February 6, 1822.

16 *American Farmer* 3 (September 28, 1821): 215; *St. Louis Enquirer*, December 22, 1821; *Liberty Hall and Cincinnati Gazette*, reprinted in Cincinnati *Western Spy*, December 1, 1821.

17 *National Intelligencer*, January 17, 1822; communications in issues of December 22 and 25, 1821, January 16, February 28, 1822.

18 *Cincinnati Inquisitor Advertiser*, January 15, 1822; *National Intelligencer*, January 1, 1822; *AC*, 17th Cong., 1st sess., pp. 714–715.

19 St. Charles *Missourian*, December 13, 1821. The Missouri lower house adopted resolutions on November 28, 1821. In the senate on November 30, the word "agree" was substituted for "disagree" in the first resolution on a roll call vote, the phrase "provided such application is made in any of the Territories of the United States" was added to the same resolution, and the second resolution was struck in its entirety. The amended resolutions were referred to a committee on December 3. (Missouri *Senate Journal*, November 1821 sess., pp. 54–56, 61). No copy of the resolutions appears in the journal of either house. In its absence, the meaning of these transactions remains obscure.

20 Louisiana *House Journal*, January 1822 sess., pp. 6, 17–18, 28–29, and *Senate Journal*, January 1822 sess., pp. 42–44.

21 *AC*, 17th Cong., 1st sess., pp. 247–268.

22 James Blair to Edwards, April 12, 1822, and John Crowell to Edwards, April 27, 1822, in Ninian Wirt Edwards, *History of Illinois from 1778 to 1833; and Life and Times of Ninian Edwards* (Springfield: Illinois State Journal Co., 1870), p. 102; *Liberty Hall and Cincinnati Gazette*, reprinted in the *National Intelligencer*, May 18, 1822; *National Intelligencer*, November 19, 1822. See also Vandalia *Illinois Intelligencer*, August 10, 1822; Franklin *Missouri Intelligencer*, April 9 and July 2, 1822.

23 Mississippi *Senate Journal*, June 1822 sess., pp. 14–21, 106–107, and *House Journal*, June 1822 sess., p. 38; Alabama *House Journal*, November 1822 sess., p. 14; Illinois *Session Laws*, December 1822 sess., pp. 215–221.

24 Fletcher Harper Swift, *A History of Public Permanent Common School Funds in the United States* (New York: Henry Holt & Co., 1911), pp. 207–422.

25 Ohio *Senate Journal*, December 1821 sess., pp. 190–191. See also Franklin *Missouri Intelligencer*, January 15, 1822.

26 For detailed background on the early history of the internal improvement question in national politics, see Harrison, "Internal Improvement Issue." Gallatin's report was reprinted in House Report 8, 17th Cong., 1st sess.

27 *The Public Statutes at Large of the United States of America* (Boston: Little and Brown, 1845–1848), 2:173–175, 225–226, 357–359, 555–556, 661–662. On the general political history of the road, see Jeremiah Simeon Young, *A Political and Constitutional Study of the Cumberland Road* (Chicago: University of Chicago Press, 1904). A convenient list of all congressional Cumberland

Road appropriations appears as an appendix in Archer Butler Hulburt, *The Cumberland Road*, Historic Highways of America, vol. 10 (Cleveland: Arthur H. Clark Co., 1904).

28 James D. Richardson, ed., *A Compilation of the Messages and Papers of the Presidents, 1789–1897* (Washington: GPO, 1896–1899), 1:567–568, 576, 584–585. The bonus bill debate is in *AC*, 14th Cong., 2d sess., pp. 165–180, 851–870, 874–914, 916–923.

29 Richardson, *Messages and Papers*, 2:18; Lowndes resolutions in *House Journal*, 15th Cong., 1st sess., pp. 334–341; the debate is in *AC*, 15th Cong., 1st sess., pp. 1114–1180, 1185–1222, 1224–1250, 1268–1282, 1284–1384.

30 See Randolph's speech in *AC*, 14th Cong., 2d sess., pp. 464–468.

31 *Statutes at Large*, 2:730, 829; 3:206, 282, 289–291, 348–349.

32 ASP *Miscellaneous*, 2:443–447; *AC*, 15th Cong., 1st sess., pp. 1193–1197; Monroe to Madison, December 22, 1817, in *The Writings of James Monroe*, ed. Stanislaus Murray Hamilton (New York: G. P. Putnam's Sons, 1898–1903), 6:45–46. John Calhoun, Henry Clay, and John Quincy Adams all considered the Cumberland Road a governing precedent; see *AC*, 14th Cong., 2d sess., p. 856; *AC*, 15th Cong., 1st sess., pp. 1370–1371; *Memoirs of John Quincy Adams*, ed. Charles Francis Adams (Philadelphia: J. B. Lippincott & Co., 1874–1877), 5:156 (hereafter cited as *Adams Memoirs*).

33 Madison to Monroe, December 27, 1817, in *The Writings of James Madison*, ed. Gaillard Hunt (New York: G. P. Putnam's Sons, 1900–1910), 8:405–406. There is nothing to suggest that Jefferson felt misgivings over the road. See his letter of July 14, 1806 to Gallatin in *The Writings of Albert Gallatin*, ed. Henry Adams (Philadelphia: J. B. Lippincott & Co., 1879), 1:304–305.

34 Madison to Crawford, October 24, 1817, in *Letters and Other Writings of James Madison* (Philadelphia: J. B. Lippincott & Co., 1865), 3:49.

35 *Statutes at Large*, 3:426, 428–431, 489–492, 500–501, 545–548, 560, 604; ASP *Public Lands*, 3:717.

36 Harry N. Scheiber, *Ohio Canal Era* (Athens: Ohio University Press, 1969), pp. 3–11. In calendar 1817 the six Ohio land offices paid $1,094,749 into the Treasury (ASP *Finance*, 3:284).

37 Ohio *House Journal*, December 1819 sess., pp. 224–232, and Ohio *Session Laws*, December 1819 sess., pp. 142–143.

38 Brown to William Trimble, April 4, 1820, and Brown to Benjamin Ruggles, May 10, 1820, Brown papers, OHS (microfilm ed., roll 2, frames 343, 372).

39 William Trimble to Allen Trimble, February 12, 1820, in *Old Northwest Genealogical Quarterly* 10 (July, 1907):261; William Trimble to Ethan Allen Brown, April 29, 1820, Brown papers, OHS (microfilm ed., roll 2, frames 349–350). See also Trimble to Brown, March 11, May 3 and 10, 1820, Brown papers, OHS (microfilm ed., roll 2, frames 304–305, 357, 367); *AC*, 16th Cong., 1st sess., pp. 652, 682–684, 2221, 2231, 2241.

40 Trimble to Brown, April 29, 1820, Brown to Benjamin Ruggles, May 10, 1820, Brown to Trimble, May 12, 1820, Brown papers, OHS (microfilm ed., roll 2, frames 350–351, 372, 375–376).

41 U.S. *Senate Journal*, 16th Cong., 1st sess., p. 393, and 16th Cong., 2d sess., p. 111. Debate in *AC*, 16th Cong., 1st sess., pp. 682–683, and 16th Cong., 2d sess., pp. 144–146, 152–156.

42 *Statutes at Large*, 3:659–660. Compare the sentiments of two Illinois governors in the Illinois *Senate Journal*, December 1822 sess., pp. 14–15, 26–28.

43 *St. Louis Enquirer*, January 13, 1824; Chillicothe (Ohio) *Supporter*, June 2 and 16, 1819; Chillicothe *Supporter and Scioto Gazette*, January 2, 1822.

44 Illinois *Senate Journal*, December 1822 sess., p. 27; see also *Governors Messages and Letters*, vol. 12 of the Indiana Historical Collections (Indianapolis: Indiana Historical Commission, 1924), 3:515–516.

45 Jonathan Jennings to Samuel Milroy, December 28, 1822, in *Indiana Magazine of History* 39 (September 1943):293; Chillicothe *Supporter and Scioto Gazette*, February 22, 1823. See also James Campbell to Allen Trimble, February 11, 1819, in *Old Northwest Genealogical Quarterly* 10 (July 1907):261.

46 *AC*, 17th Cong., 1st sess., pp. 1479–1487, 1503–1514; *House Journal*, 17th Cong., 1st sess., pp. 496–500, 513–515; *Senate Journal*, 17th Cong., 1st sess., p. 331; Richardson, *Messages and Papers*, 2:142–143.

47 Richardson, *Messages and Papers*, 2:144–183, especially pp. 167, 170–171, 173, 175.

48 Ibid., p. 191; *AC*, 17th Cong., 2d sess., pp. 1030–1039, 1045–1051; *House Journal*, 17th Cong., 2d sess., pp. 246–247; *Senate Journal*, 17th Cong., 2d sess., pp. 68–69; *Statutes at Large*, 3:728.

49 Thomas Hart Benton, *Thirty Years' View* (New York: D. Appleton & Co., 1854), 1:22.

50 In 1818 the House of Representatives had requested reports on internal improvement from the secretaries of War and the Treasury. Calhoun's report is in ASP *Miscellaneous*, 2:533–537. Crawford made no report. See Harrison, "Internal Improvement Issue," pp. 461–462.

51 Glyndon G. Van Deusen, *The Life of Henry Clay* (Boston: Little, Brown & Co., 1937), pp. 46–48; *AC*, 14th Cong., 2d sess., pp. 1062–1063.

52 Wright to Clay, November 2, 1822, in *The Papers of Henry Clay*, ed. James F. Hopkins et al. (Lexington: University of Kentucky Press, 1959–), 3:308–309. See also Wright to Benjamin Tappan, March 29, 1824, and John Sloane to Tappan, December 25, 1823 and August 9, 1824, Tappan papers, LC.

53 *AC*, 18th Cong., 1st sess., pp. 1038–1040, 1298–1299, 1316–1317.

54 Indiana *Governors Messages*, 3:502–506; Indianapolis *Indiana Journal*, February 10, 1825. Mississippi *Session Laws*, November 1821 sess., p. 158; *Statutes at Large*, 4:47–48.

55 *Statutes at Large*, 3:727–728; ASP *Indian Affairs*, 1: 757; ASP *Miscellaneous*, 2:593–595; *AC*, 17th Cong., 2d sess., pp. 443–445, 547–553.

56 *Autobiography of Martin Van Buren*, ed. John C. Fitzpatrick, Annual Report of the American Historical Association for the Year 1918, vol. 2 (Washington: GPO, 1920), p. 116.

57 *Adams Memoirs*, 6:465; Indianapolis *Indiana Journal*, March 29, 1825. On

Ohio, see John C. Wright to Benjamin Tappan, December 18, 1824 and February 12, 1825, Tappan papers, LC; Wright to Charles Hammond, January 22, 1825, Hammond papers, OHS (microfilm ed., roll 1, frame 470); Anthony Walke to Duncan McArthur, January 28, 1825, and McArthur to Thomas McArthur, February 2, 1825, Duncan McArthur papers, LC; *Niles' Weekly Register* 28 (May 28, 1825):207.

58 *Adams Memoirs*, 5:326. In *John Quincy Adams and the Union* (New York: Alfred A. Knopf, 1956), p. 25, Samuel Flagg Bemis argued that Adams "proceeded to outstrip Henry Clay" in advocating internal improvements during the campaign. It is true that Adams's backers made him out to be an internal improvement man in quarters where it might do him good. Even the friends of William Crawford did the same. But like Crawford (and, to a lesser extent, Jackson), Adams had avoided public commitments. Martin Van Buren in his *Autobiography*, describing how Clay and Calhoun manipulated the internal improvement issue in their behalf, made no mention of Adams whatever—and with good reason. Calhoun and Clay put themselves on record with congressional votes and speeches and with executive reports. By contrast, Adams's opinions were so little known that while the election was pending in the House, James Barbour of Virginia called to ask where he stood on internal improvements—to which Adams returned an equivocal answer. One cannot imagine Barbour asking Henry Clay the same question (*Adams Memoirs*, 6:450–452).

Like Adams himself in his later years, Bemis claimed for Adams the title of "original sponsor of the American System," based on a resolution he introduced while in the Senate in 1807 (Bemis, *John Quincy Adams and the Foundations of American Foreign Policy* [New York: Alfred A. Knopf, 1956], p. 127). The claim is nonsensical. For a decisive refutation, see Harrison, "Internal Improvement Issue," pp. 181–199.

59 *St. Louis Enquirer*, April 19, 1823; *Indianapolis Gazette*, July 1, 1823, May 11 and 18, 1824; *United States Telegraph*, October 16 and 30, 1829.

60 Jackson to William B. Lewis, February 14, 1825, in *Correspondence of Andrew Jackson*, ed. John Spencer Bassett (Washington: Carnegie Institution, 1926–1935), 3:276. See also Huntsville (Alabama) *Democrat*, February 15 and 22, 1825; Robert P. Henry to J. F. Henry, January 17 and February 24, 1825, Short family papers, LC.

61 *AC*, 18th Cong., 1st sess., pp. 2201–2202, 2410–2411; William W. Freehling, *Prelude to Civil War* (New York: Harper & Row, 1966), pp. 106–107, 116–118.

62 *RD*, 18th Cong., 2d sess., pp. 251, 252, 254; entire debate on pp. 245–255.

63 Duncan McArthur to Thomas McArthur, February 2, 1825, Duncan McArthur papers, LC; Vincennes *Western Sun*, April 23, 1825; Joseph Vance to Webster, March 29, 1825, in *The Papers of Daniel Webster: Correspondence*, ed. Charles Wiltse et al. (Hanover: University Press of New England, 1974–), 2:39; William Plumer, Jr., "Reminiscences of Daniel Webster" in *The Writings and Speeches of Daniel Webster*, ed. Fletcher Webster (Boston: Little, Brown, & Co., 1903), 17:555–556.

64 *Statutes at Large*, 4:124, 128.
65 Vandalia *Illinois Intelligencer*, March 25, 1825; House Reports 53 and 78 and Senate Document 36, 18th Cong., 2d sess.
66 Malcolm J. Rohrbough, *The Land Office Business* (New York: Oxford University Press, 1968), pp. 144–151; *Statutes at Large*, 3:665–666, 781; ASP *Public Lands*, 3:629–630, 645.
67 *National Intelligencer*, December 20 and 22, 1821; *Niles' Weekly Register* 21 (December 29, 1821):277, and 25 (January 24, 1824):325.
68 *AC*, 17th Cong., 2d sess., pp. 224, 226; ASP *Public Lands*, 4:429, 794–795; *Statutes at Large*, 4:24–25, 60. The popularity of the Relief Act of 1821 was enlisted in behalf of William Crawford and Henry Clay as presidential candidates in 1824 and Richard M. Johnson as a vice-presidential candidate in 1832 (Jackson [Missouri] *Independent Patriot*, May 15, 1824; Shawneetown *Illinois Gazette*, June 26, 1824; Huntsville [Alabama] *Democrat*, October 5 and 12, 1824; Springfield [Illinois] *Sangamo Journal*, February 2, March 15, April 5, 1832).
69 ASP *Public Lands*, 4:429–430; *AC*, 18th Cong., 1st sess., pp. 325, 582–583, 809, 827.
70 William Nisbet Chambers, *Old Bullion Benton* (Boston: Little, Brown & Co., 1956), pp. 110–112, 129; St. Louis *Missouri Republican*, July 18, 1825; *St. Louis Enquirer*, October 27, 1819; *AC*, 17th Cong., 2d sess., pp. 237–243.
71 Benton, *Thirty Years' View*, 1:102–107; Chambers, *Old Bullion Benton*, p. 126; Perry McCandless, *A History of Missouri, 1820 to 1860*, Missouri sesquicentennial edition, vol. 2 (Columbia: University of Missouri Press, 1972), pp. 69–72.
72 *AC*, 18th Cong., 1st sess., pp. 656, 769.
73 Chambers, *Old Bullion Benton*, p. 126; Jackson (Missouri) *Independent Patriot*, November 27, 1824.
74 Vandalia *Illinois Intelligencer*, May 28, 1824. See also ASP *Public Lands*, 4:148 and 5:36; *Illinois Intelligencer*, January 16, 1824; Benton in *National Intelligencer*, June 16, 1825.
75 Chambers, *Old Bullion Benton*, pp. 128–131; McCandless, *History of Missouri*, pp. 72–76. The election episode is covered exhaustively in Alan S. Weiner, "John Scott, Thomas Hart Benton, David Barton and the Presidential Election of 1824: A Case Study in Pressure Politics," *Missouri Historical Review* 60 (July, 1966): 460–494.

4. Electioneering, 1825–1829

1 *Memoirs of John Quincy Adams*, ed. Charles Francis Adams (Philadelphia: J. B. Lippincott & Co., 1874–1877), 6: 474, 506 (hereafter cited as *Adams Memoirs*).
2 Vance to Clay, November 9, 1825, and Edwards to Clay, July 18, 1825, in *The Papers of Henry Clay*, ed. James F. Hopkins et al. (Lexington: University of Kentucky Press, 1959–), 4:807, 543 (hereafter cited as *Clay Papers*).
3 Finis Ewing to Clay, August 6, 1825, *Clay Papers*, 4:568–569.

4 James D. Richardson, ed., *A Compilation of the Messages and Papers of the Presidents, 1789–1897* (Washington: GPO, 1896–1899), 2:305, 311–316.

5 Annual Treasury report in *RD*, 19th Cong., 1st sess., Appendix pp. 24–26.

6 *AC*, 18th Cong., 1st sess., p. 1308.

7 Senate Document 95, 19th Cong., 1st session.

8 *RD*, 19th Cong., 1st sess., p. 704; 19th Cong., 2d sess., pp. 209–223, 1351–1352; 20th Cong., 1st sess., pp. 1639, 1678–1679, 1691–1692, 1705–1711; 20th Cong., 2d sess., pp. 28–42; William McCoy circular in Noble E. Cunningham, Jr., ed., *Circular Letters of Congressmen to Their Constituents, 1789–1829* (Chapel Hill: University of North Carolina Press, 1978), 3:1500–1501; *State of New York: Messages from the Governors*, ed. Charles Z. Lincoln (Albany: J. B. Lyon Co., 1909), 3:154–155; House Document 237, 20th Cong., 1st sess.

9 *RD*, 19th Cong., 1st sess., pp. 358–359, 762, 782.

10 *RD*, 19th Cong., 1st sess., p. 727; Benton's full speech is on pp. 720–749.

11 Fayette *Missouri Intelligencer*, August 24, 1826. See also the Vandalia *Illinois Intelligencer*, February 16, 1826; *Adams Memoirs*, 7:89.

12 *Adams Memoirs*, 7:194; see also 7:173.

13 *Letters of Hon. J. B. C. Lucas*, ed. John B. C. Lucas (St. Louis, 1905), p. 78; St. Louis *Missouri Republican*, September 28 and November 16, 1826; *Missouri Intelligencer*, July 6 and August 31, 1826; Jackson (Missouri) *Independent Patriot*, November 29, 1826; *Indianapolis Gazette*, June 27, 1826; Huntsville (Alabama) *Southern Advocate*, September 22, 1826.

14 For governors's messages, see *Governors Messages and Letters*, vol. 34 of Indiana Historical Collections (Indianapolis: Indiana Historical Bureau, 1954), 4:285–286; Louisiana *House Journal*, January 1827 sess., p. 8: Mississippi *House Journal*, January 1826 sess., p. 15, and *Senate Journal*, January 1827 sess., p. 14; Illinois *Senate Journal*, December 1826 sess., pp. 77–80; *The Messages and Proclamations of the Governors of the State of Missouri*, ed. Buel Leopard and Floyd Shoemaker (Columbia: The State Historical Society of Missouri, 1922), 1:118–119. For state memorials and resolutions, see Indiana *Session Laws*, December 1825 sess., pp. 87–88; ASP *Public Lands*, 4:871, 887, 892, and 5:37, 345, 350, 375, 445–446, 528–529, 582.

15 For examples of agitation of the land issue by politicians, see *Missouri Intelligencer*, January 25, 1827; *Mississippi Statesman and Natchez Gazette*, February 14 and March 8, 1827; *Illinois Intelligencer*, June 22, 1826 and January 6, 1827.

16 *RD*, 20th Cong., 1st sess., p. 160; *Woodville* (Mississippi) *Republican*, June 24, 1826; William Hendricks circulars in Cunningham, *Circular Letters*, 3:1380, 1432–1434; Vincennes (Indiana) *Western Sun*, September 9, 1826; Indiana *House Journal*, December 1827 sess., pp. 207–215; *Letters and Other Writings of James Madison* (Philadelphia: J. B. Lippincott & Co., 1865), 4:187–188; *The Correspondence of John Badollet and Albert Gallatin*, ed. Gayle Thornbrough (Indianapolis: Indiana Historical Society, 1963), pp. 285–286 (hereafter cited as *Badollet and Gallatin Correspondence*).

17 *Adams Memoirs*, 7:187–188, 194. On the Western mood before Benton's

speech, see the governor's messages in Louisiana *House Journal*, January 1823 sess., pp. 5–6, and January 1824 sess., pp. 7–9.

18 ASP *Public Lands*, 5:522–523; Barton in *RD*, 19th Cong., 1st sess., pp. 749–753, and 20th Cong., 1st sess., p. 484; *Missouri Republican*, March 16 and November 9, 1826. On the controversy in Missouri, see *Missouri Republican*, December 14, 1826; *Missouri Intelligencer*, November 30, December 7 and 21, 1826; February 8, 15, and 22, March 1, 8, 15, and 22, June 28, 1827; February 29, 1828.

19 *RD*, 19th Cong., 1st sess., pp. 1310–1320, 1429–1436; *Adams Memoirs*, 7:194.

20 Annual reports of the General Land Office from 1821 to 1828 (in chronological order) in Senate Document 8, 17th Cong., 2d sess., p. 25; Senate Document 16, 18th Cong., 1st sess., p. 18; ASP *Finance*, 5:160; Senate Document 6, 19th Cong., 1st sess., p. 24; ASP *Finance*, 5:529, 642; Senate Document 7, 20th Cong., 2d Sess., pp. 21–22; Senate Document 83, 21st Cong., 1st sess., p. 7. Aggregate statistics from ASP *Public Lands*, 5:527, and Senate Document 1, 20th Cong., 1st sess., pp. 264–265. As usual there were discrepancies in the various sets of statistics submitted by the General Land Office.

21 Computed from statistics in ASP *Public Lands*, 4:912–915, and 5:527.

22 Richardson, *Messages and Papers*, 2:391; ASP *Public Lands*, 5: 447–449; statistics computed from annual reports cited in note 20.

23 *National Intelligencer*, July 21, 1825. On the anti-Benton view, see also the *National Intelligencer*, July 9 and November 26, 1825; *Niles' Weekly Register* 29 (September 3, November 12, 1825):6, 162–163; *Missouri Republican*, June 6 and 20, August 22, 1825, and November 16, 1826.

24 *The Public Statutes at Large of the United States of America* (Boston: Little and Brown, 1845–1848), 4:151, 162, 169; *House Journal*, 19th Cong., 1st sess., pp. 333–334, 339–340, 573–574, 595–599, 636–637; *Senate Journal*, 19th Cong., 1st sess., pp. 189–190, 261, 317, 345, 365–366, 390–393; *RD*, 19th Cong., 1st sess., pp. 349–365, 590–597, 688–689, 697–698, 765, 786–788, 2632–2633, 2663–2664, 2688.

25 House Report 102, 19th Cong., 2d sess. On the agitation in Illinois and Indiana, see the *Illinois Intelligencer*, November 18, 1825, and March 23, 1826; ASP *Public Lands*, 4:437; Indiana *Session Laws*, December 1825 sess., pp. 90–91; Illinois *House Journal*, January 1826 sess., pp. 78–80, and Illinois *Senate Journal*, December 1826 sess., p. 27; Senate Document 46, 19th Cong., 2d sess.; Cunningham, *Circular Letters*, 3:1324–1325, 1341. Proponents of Western internal improvements invariably claimed that they would promote faster land sales at higher prices. For examples from the Nineteenth Congress, see Senate Document 47 and House Reports 144 and 147, 1st sess., and Senate Document 13, 2d sess.

26 *Statutes at Large*, 4:215, 216, 228, 234–236, 242; ASP *Indian Affairs*, 2:679.

27 Debate in *RD*, 19th Cong., 2d sess., pp. 55–58, 310–318, 337–338, 376–380, 488–491, 497–498, 1215–1238, 1397–1404, 1414–1418.

28 Senate figures in the text derive from the following table, showing votes on

internal improvements according to presidential affiliation. The table is based on the three roll calls shown in table 4.2, plus three others from the *Senate Journal*, 19th Cong., 2d sess., pp. 185, 196–197, 265. All but six senators voted consistently either for or against internal improvements on all these roll calls. Of the six, I have classified Henry Ridgely of Delaware and John Henry Eaton of Tennessee as internal improvement men; they voted consistently except on the survey roll call. Presidential affiliations for senators are taken from George R. Nielsen, "The Indispensable Institution: The Congressional Party During The Era of Good Feelings" (Ph.D. diss., University of Iowa, 1968), pp. 232–234.

	Adams			Jackson		
	For	*Against*	*Inconsistent*	*For*	*Against*	*Inconsistent*
New England	9		1		2	
Mid-Atlantic	3	2		2	3	
South Atlantic					8	
Northwest	6			3		1
Southwest	2			3	1	2
	20	2	1	8	14	3

29 The following table, based on the four roll calls in table 4.1, shows consistent supporters and opponents of internal improvements in the House of Representatives. Presidential affiliations are taken from Nielsen, "Indispensable Institution," pp. 243, 292. Inconsistent voters, those who missed two or more roll calls, and those whom Nielsen does not classify are not shown. (A congressman who voted the same way on three of the four roll calls is considered consistent. For absentees on the canal-grant roll call, a preceding motion to table has been substituted.)

	Adams		Jackson	
	For	*Against*	*For*	*Against*
New England	19	6		3
Mid-Atlantic	20	1	13	6
South Atlantic	5	3	1	26
Northwest	25		6	
Southwest	2		5	2
	71	10	25	37

30 On economic sectionalism and political partisanship in Virginia, see chapters 4 and 6 of Charles Henry Ambler, *Sectionalism in Virginia from 1776 to 1861* (Chicago: University of Chicago Press, 1910).

31 Scott circular in Cunningham, *Circular Letters*, 3:1342–1349. See also Bates letter in *Missouri Republican*, June 8, 1826.

32 On the graduation issue in Benton's election, see the *Missouri Intelligencer*, June 28, 1827, and June 27, 1828.

33 Edwards to Clay, September 21, 1826, in *Clay Papers*, 5:700–701; *Adams Memoirs*, 7:187–188: *Edwardsville* (Illinois) *Spectator*, May 27 and September 29, 1826; *Illinois Gazette*, July 15, 1826; *Illinois Intelligencer*, July 13 through August 3, 1826. On the land issue in Cook's earlier campaigns, see the *Illinois Intelligencer*, July 2 and 20, 1822; *Illinois Gazette*, August 5, 1820, June 29, July 27, and August 3, 1822, and July 17 and 31, 1824.

34 Hugh McKeen to John Tipton, March 2, 1827, *The John Tipton Papers*, ed. Nellie Armstrong Robertson and Dorothy Riker, vols. 24 to 26 of the Indiana Historical Collections (Indianapolis: Indiana Historical Bureau, 1942), 1:677; *Illinois Gazette*, July 22, 1826. See also the Columbus *Ohio State Journal*, November 8 and 29, 1827; William Hendricks circular in Cunningham, *Circular Letters*, 3:1324–1325; *Niles' Weekly Register* 31 (September 2, 1826):11; *Illinois Intelligencer*, January 20, 1827; *Indianapolis Gazette*, April 3 and 17, 1827.

35 *National Journal*, February 27, March 10 and 17, 1827. Calhoun's explanation of his casting votes is in *RD*, 20th Cong., 1st sess., pp. 632–633, 652–653.

36 *Indiana Journal*, March 14, 1826; *Illinois Gazette*, July 15, 1826; *Missouri Republican*, January 25, 1827. See also *Missouri Republican*, May 3, 1827; Francis Johnson to Webster, *The Papers of Daniel Webster: Correspondence*, ed. Charles M. Wiltse et al. (Hanover: University Press of New England, 1974–), 2:122 (hereafter cited as *Webster Papers: Correspondence*); James Brown Ray to David G. Mitchell, March 28, 1827, in Indiana *Governors Messages*, 4:212–213; Chillicothe *Supporter and Scioto Gazette*, August 3, 1826; *Illinois Intelligencer*, June 16 and 23, 1827; *Missouri Intelligencer*, November 16, 1826.

37 *Indiana Journal*, October 30, 1827. See also the *Missouri Intelligencer*, May 5, 1827; *Illinois Intelligencer*, March 17, April 21, July 28, 1827; *Indianapolis Gazette*, October 23, 1827.

38 Reed speech in *National Intelligencer*, December 7, 1826; Ellis speech in *Natchez Gazette*, December 23, 1826. On internal improvement in Southwestern state politics, see also *Natchez Gazette*, June 24, July 1 and 29, November 25, 1826; *Woodville* (Mississippi) *Republican*, April 29 and July 29, 1826; New Orleans *Louisiana Advertiser*, November 24, 1826; Louisiana *House Journal*, January 1826 sess., p. 8., Mississippi *House Journal*, January 1826 sess., pp. 45–46; Senate Document 4, 19th Congress, 2d sess.

39 Gurley to Clay, August 20, 1826, *Clay Papers*, 5:635. See also Natchez *Statesman and Gazette*, July 17, November 20 and 27, 1828.

40 *Louisiana Courier*, reprinted in *Louisiana Advertiser*, November 13, 1827; Alabama *Session Laws*, November 1826 sess., p. 121. See also Huntsville *Southern Advocate*, June 1, 1827; *Louisiana Advertiser*, June 4 and 7, 1827.

41 Ohio *House Journal*, December 1826 sess., pp. 97–98.

42 Polk circular in Cunningham, *Circular Letters*, 3:1385; *United States Telegraph*, March 7, 8, and 12, 1827; Duff Green to Ninian Edwards, December 29, 1826, in *The Edwards Papers*, ed. Elihu B. Washburne, vol. 3 of the

Chicago Historical Society Collections (Chicago: Fergus Printing Co., 1884), p. 267; *Louisiana Advertiser*, October 3, 1827; Vincennes *Western Sun*, March 24, 1827.

43 Natchez *Mississippi Statesman*, January 31 and February 7, 1827; Moore in *Bloomington* (Indiana) *Republican*, September 22, 1827. See also *Mississippi Statesman and Natchez Gazette*, April 19 and 26, 1827.

44 Samuel Milroy to John Tipton, December 10, 1827, in *Tipton Papers*, 1:819–821.

45 Huntsville *Southern Advocate*, November 23, 1827; N. Ewing to Thomas Ewing, December 8, 1827, Thomas Ewing papers, University of Notre Dame Archives (microfilm).

46 Clay to Webster, June 7, 1827, *Webster Papers: Correspondence*, 2: 215–216.

47 Richardson, *Messages and Papers*, 2:391.

48 *Adams Memoirs*, 7:362. State requests for the relief recommended by Adams are in ASP *Public Lands*, 4:921, and House Document 122, 19th Cong., 2d sess., p. 9.

49 Annual Treasury Report in *RD*, 20th Cong., 1st sess., pp. 2831–2833.

50 Madison to Nicholas Trist, January 26, 1828, *The Writings of James Madison*, ed. Gaillard Hunt (New York: G. P. Putnam's Sons, 1900–1910), 9:301–303; Jackson to L. H. Coleman, April 26, 1824, *Correspondence of Andrew Jackson*, ed. John Spencer Bassett (Washington: Carnegie Institution, 1926–1935), 3:250–251 (hereafter cited as *Jackson Correspondence*). Thomas Hart Benton conveniently omitted this passage from his discussion of Jackson's 1824 tariff views in *Thirty Years' View* (New York: D. Appleton & Co., 1854), 1:34. See also Madison to Henry Clay, April 24, 1824, *Clay Papers*, 3:740.

51 *Missouri Republican*, January 10, 1828; *Ohio State Journal*, December 29, 1827.

52 Van Buren quoted in Robert V. Remini, *Martin Van Buren and the Making of the Democratic Party* (New York: Columbia University Press, 1959), p. 131.

53 [Thomas Hart Benton], *Mr. Benton's Speeches on the Public Lands* (Washington: Green & Jarvis, 1828), pp. 34–41; *United States Telegraph*, December 31, 1827.

54 *Missouri Intelligencer*, April 25, 1828; *RD*, 20th Cong., 1st sess., pp. 23–28, 108–109, 384–385, 717–723; William Nisbet Chambers, *Old Bullion Benton* (Boston: Little, Brown & Co., 1956), pp. 138–139.

55 Ulrich Bonnell Phillips, *Georgia and State Rights*, Annual Report of the American Historical Association for the Year 1901, vol. 2 (Washington: GPO, 1902), pp. 53–72; Charles S. Sydnor, *The Development of Southern Sectionalism, 1819–1848* (Baton Rouge: Louisiana State University Press, 1948), pp. 182–185.

56 *RD*, 20th Cong., 1st sess., pp. 15–17, 23–29, 151–166, 483–505, 507–521, 529–532, 571–577. See also John Branch speech in *United States Telegraph*, February 12, 1828.

57 *RD*, 20th Cong., 1st sess., pp. 502, 518, 620–622; see also pp. 577–582, 609–619, 675–678.

58 *RD*, 20th Cong., 1st sess., pp. 653–656; *Senate Journal*, 20th Cong., 1st sess., pp. 296–297.

59 *RD*, 20th Cong., 1st sess., pp. 656–660, 665–667, 674–678; *Senate Journal*, 20th Cong., 1st sess., pp. 299–301, 306–309, 318–320, 323.

60 *Senate Journal*, 20th Cong., 1st sess., p. 418. The Old South's opposition to relief for land debtors had been shown a year earlier, in the Nineteenth Congress. A bill to allow relinquishers under the relief acts to repurchase their lands at a fixed price was advanced to its third reading on the following vote:

	For	Against
New England	8	2
Mid-Atlantic	10	
South Atlantic	2	4
West	16	1
	36	7

(Source: *Senate Journal*, 19th Cong., 2d sess., p. 165.) This bill did not become law. It was especially popular in Alabama, where large quantities of land purchased at inflated prices during the boom had been relinquished (*RD*, 19th Cong., 2d sess., pp. 308–309; House Document 122, 19th Cong., 2d sess.).

61 Debate is in *RD*, 20th Cong., 1st sess., pp. 102–111, 114–127, 1521–1522.

62 On the Chesapeake and Ohio Canal, see *RD*, 20th Cong., 1st sess., pp. 792–804, 2603–2640; *Senate Journal*, 20th Cong., 1st sess., pp. 448–449; *House Journal*, 20th Cong., 1st sess., pp. 712–714, 716–718. On the omnibus bill, see *RD*, 20th Cong., 1st sess., pp. 634–653, 1510–1512, 1609–1629, 1814–1818, 2494–2495; *House Journal*, 20th Cong., 1st sess., pp. 390–395. For the survey bill, see *RD*, 20th Cong., 1st sess., pp. 603–609, 631, 724–725, 734, 787, 1512–1517, 1630–1699, 1703–1717, 1797–1810, 2576–2577, 2580–2589, 2674, 2695.

63 Polk circular in Cunningham, *Circular Letters*, 3:1524; debate in *RD*, 20th Cong., 1st sess., pp. 453–458, 2743–2744.

64 *RD*, 20th Cong., 1st sess., pp. 809–810, 2732–2733, 2735–2743, 2767; *House Journal*, 20th Cong., 1st sess., pp. 48, 112, 188, 281, 631, 682, 691, 776–788, 790–792, 854, 863–866; *Senate Journal*, 20th Cong., 1st sess., pp. 441, 443, 449, 468–470; John C. Wright to Charles Hammond, May 20, 1828, Hammond papers, OHS (microfilm ed., roll 2, frames 308–310); *Ohio State Journal*, July 4 and September 25, 1828. Robert V. Remini, following Thomas Hart Benton via James Parton, incorrectly states that the Jackson bill was introduced first (*The Election of Andrew Jackson* [Philadelphia: J. B. Lippincott Co., 1963], pp. 170–171).

65 These figures were derived by combining the two roll calls on each of the bills (giving precedence to the second one in cases of discrepancy, since the party issue was then more clearly defined) and comparing them with the

final roll call on the combined bill after it came back from the Senate. Altogether 176 of the 194 congressmen who cast one or more votes on the Ohio bills were classifiable. Of those, 73 favored both bills (39 of them from the West), 59 opposed both, and 44 voted for one but not the other. There was also some evidence of partisanship in the Senate.

66 For the maneuvers behind the passage of the tariff of 1828, see Remini, *Martin Van Buren,* chap. 12.

67 Webster speech in *Niles' Weekly Register* 34 (June 21, 1828):275.

68 *Missouri Republican,* October 14, 1828. See also the Chillicothe *Scioto Gazette,* June 19 and August 28, 1828; *Indianapolis Gazette,* February 26, July 24, September 25, 1828; *Illinois Intelligencer,* March 8, April 5, May 3 and 24, 1828; *Indiana Journal,* October 23, 1828; Vincennes *Western Sun,* September 27, 1828.

69 *Western Sun,* January 26, 1828; *Illinois Intelligencer,* May 10 and June 21, 1828; Moore in *National Intelligencer,* January 22, 1831; *Western Sun,* April 26 and November 1, 1828. See also *Western Sun,* February 16, 1828; *United States Telegraph,* March 13, April 7 and 15, 1828.

70 Ray to Jackson, January 30, 1828, and Jackson to Ray, February 28, 1828, in Indiana *Governors Messages,* 4:319–328, 338–340; Benton to Jackson, February 22, 1827, Jackson papers, LC.

71 Haile in *Woodville* (Mississippi) *Republican,* May 27, 1828; *Missouri Monitor,* reprinted in *Illinois Intelligencer,* June 7, 1828; Finis Ewing to Jackson, October 4, 1828, Jackson papers, LC. See also *Benton's Speeches on Lands,* pp. 34–38; Chambers, *Old Bullion Benton,* p. 151.

72 Natchez *Statesman and Gazette,* September 25, 1828; *Louisiana Advertiser,* September 25, 1828; *United States Telegraph,* April 24, 1828.

73 King in Huntsville *Southern Advocate,* November 7, 1828. See also Montgomery *Alabama Journal,* August 29, 1828; *Woodville* (Mississippi) *Republican,* March 18, 1828.

74 *St. Louis Advertiser,* reprinted in *Louisiana Advertiser,* December 3, 1827; *Missouri Intelligencer,* May 23 and July 11, 1828; *Illinois Intelligencer,* March 8, April 19, June 7, 1828. See also *Missouri Intelligencer,* May 30, 1828; *Missouri Republican,* February 19 and July 29, 1828; *Illinois Intelligencer,* February 16, 1828.

75 Jennings circular in Indiana *Governors Messages,* 3:265–269. On the Illinois campaign, see *Niles' Weekly Register* 34 (August 23, 1828):411; *Illinois Intelligencer,* May 3, July 5 through 19, 1828; *Illinois Gazette,* July 19 and 26, 1828; Duncan circular in Cunningham, *Circular Letters,* 3:1465–1466. On Indiana, see *Indiana Journal,* July 24, 1828; *Western Sun,* June 28, 1828; *Indianapolis Gazette,* July 17, 1828. On Ohio, see *Scioto Gazette,* September 24 and October 15, 1828; *Ohio State Journal,* August 30 and September 13, 1827. On Mississippi, see *Woodville Republican,* July 15, 1828.

76 Benton to Van Buren, December 3, 1828, Van Buren papers, LC; *Missouri Republican,* December 2, 1828.

77 Webster to Samuel Bell, July 29, 1828, *Webster Papers: Correspondence,* 2:357; T. L. Hinde to Henry Clay, February 3, 1829, in Francis P. Weisen-

burger, *The Passing of the Frontier*, vol. 3 of *The History of the State of Ohio* (Columbus: Ohio State Archaeological and Historical Society, 1941), p. 236; Benton to Houston, August 15, 1829, in *The Writings of Sam Houston*, ed. Amelia W. Williams and Eugene C. Barker (Austin: University of Texas Press, 1938–1943), 1:140.

78 Remini, *Election of Andrew Jackson*, pp. 118–119, 187; Joseph George Tregle, Jr., "Louisiana and the Tariff, 1816–1846," *Louisiana Historical Quarterly* 25 (January 1942):51–52.

79 *Adams Memoirs*, 7:427; *United States Telegraph*, April 26, 1828.

80 Mississippi *House Journal*, January 1829 sess., p. 13; Louisiana *House Journal*, November 1828 sess., p. 8; Illinois *Senate Journal*, December 1828 sess., pp. 10–39.

81 Thomas Ford, *A History of Illinois*, ed. Milo Quaife (1847; Chicago: R. R. Donnelley & Sons, 1945), pp. 90–93; Clay in *Adams Memoirs*, 8: 87–88. See also John Badollet to Albert Gallatin, August 14, 1829, in *Badollet and Gallatin Correspondence*, p. 292.

82 Green to Edwards, January 6, 1829, in *Edwards Papers*, pp. 379–380; see also Green to Dr. H. Lane, December 28, 1828, in Duff Green letterbook, 1827–1830, LC, pp. 162–164.

83 *Illinois Gazette*, December 27, 1828. See also *United States Telegraph*, December 30, 1828; *Illinois Gazette*, November 22, December 6, 1828, and February 21 and 28, 1829; *Illinois Intelligencer*, February 21, March 7 and 14, April 18, 1829; *Edwards Papers*, pp. 378–379, 384; Illinois *Senate Journal*, December 1828 sess., pp. 109–112, and *House Journal*, December 1828 sess., pp. 99–100, 225–226; ASP *Public Lands*, 5:624.

84 ASP *Public Lands*, 5:630. See also Indianapolis *Indiana Journal*, December 13, 1828, through February 26, 1829; *United States Telegraph*, January 29, 1829; Indiana *House Journal*, December 1828 sess., pp. 256–259, 276–282; Indiana *Senate Journal*, December 1828 sess., pp. 70–71, 185, 191–192. The vote on adopting the resolutions in the Indiana legislature was as follows:

	Senate		House	
	For	Against	For	Against
Jackson	2		19	8
Anti-Jackson	14	2	12	10
Unidentified			3	5
	16	2	34	23

(Partisan affiliations are from *A Biographical Directory of the Indiana General Assembly* [Indianapolis: Indiana Historical Bureau, 1980], pp. 452–453.)

85 For Western criticism of the cession doctrine, see *RD*, 20th Cong., 1st sess., pp. 505–506, 577–582, and 20th Cong., 2d sess., pp. 58–59; Jennings in *Indiana Journal*, April 16, 1829; *National Journal*, January 22, 1829; *National Intelligencer*, April 11, 1829; *Illinois Gazette*, June 24, 1829. State resolutions

are in ASP *Public Lands*, 5:588, 621–622; Alabama *Session Laws*, November 1828 sess., pp. 103–104. For McKinley, see Huntsville *Southern Advocate*, July 18, 1828. See also Montgomery *Alabama Journal*, April 11, November 14 and 28, December 19, 1828, and January 2, 1829; William Hendricks circular in Cunningham, *Circular Letters*, 3:1543.

86 *RD*, 20th Cong., 2d sess., p. 165. See also *RD*, 20th Cong., 2d sess., pp. 161–167, 195–211; *National Journal*, January 6 and February 17, 1829; *National Intelligencer*, February 19, 1829; *Niles' Weekly Register* 35 (January 10, 1829): 313. The vote to table the Tennessee cession bill was 92 to 35 in the East, 10 to 2 in Ohio, and 1 to 26 in the rest of the West. A similar division had defeated the same measure the previous session (*House Journal*, 20th Cong., 2d sess., pp. 155–156; *House Journal*, 20th Cong., 1st sess., pp. 659–661).

87 *House Journal*, 20th Cong., 2d sess., pp. 153–154, 213, 215, 217; *National Intelligencer*, January 29 and 31, 1829. For earlier land revenue distribution proposals, see *AC*, 18th Cong., 1st sess., pp. 2594–2595; *RD*, 18th Cong., 2d sess., pp. 42 and 67, and 19th Cong., 1st sess., p. 861; King to Christopher Gore, April 9, 1820, in *The Life and Correspondence of Rufus King*, ed. Charles R. King (New York: G. P. Putnam's Sons, 1894–1900), 6:328–329.

88 ASP *Public Lands*, 5:793–797. A report by James Strong of New York a year earlier avowed a similar motive (ASP *Public Lands*, 4:750–753).

89 Jarvis in *National Journal*, October 15, 1829; Daniel Barringer circular in Cunningham, *Circular Letters*, 3:1551. See also *National Journal*, March 7 and April 11, 1829; *Niles' Weekly Register* 35 (January 31, 1829):379, and 35 (February 7, 1829):385; *Missouri Republican*, January 31, 1828; *United States Telegraph*, February 20, 1829; *Indiana Journal*, January 14, 1829; Cunningham, *Circular Letters*, 3:1408, 1490, 1495.

90 Calhoun to Littleton Waller Tazewell, July 1, 1827, in *The Papers of John C. Calhoun*, ed. Robert L. Meriwether et al. (Columbia: University of South Carolina Press, 1959–), 10:293 (hereafter cited as *Calhoun Papers*); *National Journal*, May 7, 1829. See also *Alabama Journal*, March 27 and June 12, 1829.

91 Calhoun to Bartlett Yancey, July 16, 1828, and Calhoun to William Campbell Preston, January 6, 1829, in *Calhoun Papers*, 10:401, 546; *Jackson Correspondence*, 4:12–13. The recommendation was excised from the final draft, but reappeared in Jackson's first annual message to Congress.

92 *Adams Memoirs*, 8:87–88; *National Journal*, January 27, 1829. Voting patterns on Cumberland Road appropriations and canal stock purchases in the session of Congress that met after the election showed no change from the previous session.

5. Sectional alliances, 1830–1831

1 *St. Louis Beacon*, reprinted in Vincennes (Indiana) *Western Sun*, October 31, 1829; *St. Louis Beacon*, July 11, 1829. See also *St. Louis Beacon*, July 18 and 25, September 5 and 9, October 7 through November 11, 1829.

2 *National Journal,* April 2, 1829; *RD,* 21st Cong., 1st sess., pp. 477–540.
3 *American Quarterly Review* 6 (December 1829):267; *United States Gazette,* reprinted in Indianapolis *Indiana Journal,* January 27, 1830; *Richmond* (Virginia) *Enquirer,* January 19, 1830; *North Carolina Journal,* reprinted in *St. Louis Beacon,* January 30, 1830; Milledgeville *Southern Recorder,* reprinted in *Richmond Enquirer,* January 19, 1830.
4 *RD,* 21st Cong., 1st sess., pp. 3–4. This is the resolution in its original form; it was later amended to include an inquiry into accelerating the sales and surveys.
5 In the Adams congresses Foot usually voted against internal improvements, an exception among New England Adams men. In the House in 1821 he voted against the Relief Act, and attempted to raise the cash price of public lands back up to $1.64 per acre, the level it had been under the credit system (*AC,* 16th Cong., 2d sess., pp. 1228–1229).

  The Essex Junto was a group of arch-Federalist New England politicians who planned to establish a separate Northern confederacy during Jefferson's administration. The Sedition Act of 1798, passed by a Federalist Congress under President John Adams, was assailed by Republicans as an unconstitutional infringement of civil liberties; its passage provoked the authoritative exposition of states' rights doctrine in the Virginia and Kentucky resolutions.
6 *RD,* 21st Cong., 1st sess., pp. 22–27.
7 *RD,* 21st Cong., 1st sess., pp. 31–35.
8 *RD,* 21st Cong., 1st sess., pp. 35–41.
9 *RD,* 21st Cong., 1st sess., p. 80; the Webster–Hayne exchange is on pp. 41–80.
10 Adams to Alexander Everett, April 15, 1830, in *American Historical Review,* 11 (January, 1906):335–336. See *RD,* 21st Cong., 1st sess., pp. 80–452 for later phases of the debate.
11 Smith and Barton speeches are in *RD,* 21st Cong., 1st sess., pp. 196–210, 146–159.
12 *United States Telegraph,* February 2, 1830; Concord *New Hampshire Patriot,* reprinted in *United States Telegraph,* February 6, 1830; *Morning Courier and New York Enquirer,* February 5, 1830; *Boston Statesman,* reprinted in *St. Louis Beacon,* June 10, 1830. See also Portland (Maine) *Eastern Argus,* reprinted in *St. Louis Beacon,* February 27, 1830.
13 *RD,* 21st Cong., 1st sess., pp. 51, 96, 101.
14 *National Journal,* February 6, 1830; Adams to Alexander Everett, April 15, 1830, *American Historical Review* 11 (January 1906):335–336. See also *National Journal,* February 13, 1830; Vance to Charles Hammond, January 29, 1830, Hammond papers, OHS (microfilm ed., roll 2, frame 445).
15 Indianapolis *Indiana State Gazette,* December 3, 1829; Green to Ninian Edwards, April 27, 1830, in *The Edwards Papers,* ed. Elihu B. Washburne, vol. 3 of the Chicago Historical Society Collections (Chicago: Fergus Printing Co., 1884), pp. 488–489. See also Green to James Hamilton, Jr., January 20, 1830, Duff Green papers, Southern Historical Collection,

University of North Carolina Library (microfilm, roll 24, vol. 4); and Green to Isaac Canby, May 14, 1830, Duff Green papers (microfilm, roll 24, vol. 5).

16 *St. Louis Beacon,* June 3, 1830; *United States Telegraph,* January 26, 1830; *Mobile Commercial Register,* reprinted in *National Journal,* March 9, 1830; Clay to Josiah Johnston, May 9, 1830, *The Works of Henry Clay,* vol. 4: *Private Correspondence,* ed. Calvin Colton (New York: G. P. Putnam's Sons, 1904), p. 267 (hereafter cited as *Clay Correspondence*). See also Clay to George Watterson, May 8, 1830, Clay papers, LC; *United States Telegraph,* January 23 and February 4, 1830.

17 Philadelphia *United States Gazette,* reprinted in *St. Louis Beacon,* March 11, 1830; *Memoirs of John Quincy Adams,* ed. Charles Francis Adams (Philadelphia: J. B. Lippincott & Co., 1874–1877), 8: 180 (hereafter cited as *Adams Memoirs*).

18 Mississippi *Session Laws,* January 1830 sess., pp. 181–188; Illinois *Senate Journal,* December 1830 sess., pp. 8–51.

19 *RD,* 21st Cong., 1st sess., pp. 115–116; Harry N. Scheiber, *Ohio Canal Era* (Athens: Ohio University Press, 1969), pp. 191–200.

20 Jackson's failure even to recommend the customary extension of the relief laws evoked bitter comment from his critics; see the Shawneetown *Illinois Gazette,* December 26, 1829; *National Journal,* March 27, 1830; *Woodville* (Mississippi) *Republican,* February 6, 1830.

21 Joel H. Silbey, *The Shrine of Party* (Pittsburgh: University of Pittsburgh Press, 1967). Chapter 10 reviews the historiography of the South–West alliance, which includes the works of Avery Craven, Ray Allen Billington, and Frank Owsley.

22 Raynor G. Wellington, *The Political and Sectional Influence of the Public Lands, 1828–1842* (Cambridge, Mass.: Riverside Press, 1914), pp. 9–10, 18; William W. Freehling, *Prelude to Civil War* (New York: Harper & Row, 1966), pp. 183–186. Two recent treatments of federal land policy follow Wellington: Paul W. Gates, *History of Public Land Law Development* (Washington: GPO, 1968), and Roy M. Robbins, *Our Landed Heritage,* 2d rev. ed. (Lincoln: University of Nebraska Press, 1976).

23 *RD,* 21st Cong., 1st sess., pp. 34–35.

24 For the vote on the tariff, see table 4.6. New England's contribution to the tariff of 1828, often overstated, was passive, not active. New Englanders delivered a necessary neutrality to a measure whose majorities came from elsewhere.

25 Adams to Benjamin Waterhouse, October 20, 1813, reprinted in *National Intelligencer,* May 31, 1827.

26 Appropriations for harbor improvements and coastal navigation aids, mostly in in the North Atlantic states, increased from $228,000 in the Eighteenth Congress to $545,000 in the Nineteenth and $1,070,000 in the Twentieth.

27 *Lowell* (Massachusetts) *Journal,* February 17, 1830. McDuffie's resolution is in *House Journal,* 18th Cong., 2d sess., p. 64.

28 Wellington, *Political and Sectional Influence,* pp. 27–28; Lawrence to Web-

ster, May 7, 1828, in *The Papers of Daniel Webster: Correspondence*, ed. Charles Wiltse et al. (Hanover: University Press of New England, 1974–), 2:342–343.

29 Wellington, *Political and Sectional Influence*, p. 9.

30 Madison to Reynolds Chapman, January 6, 1831, *The Writings of James Madison*, ed. Gaillard Hunt (New York: G. P. Putnam's Sons, 1900–1910), 9:429–432 (hereafter cited as *Madison Writings*); Fayetteville (North Carolina) *Carolina Observer*, reprinted in *National Intelligencer*, May 15, 1830; Tyler to Henry Curtis, February 22, 1830, Lyon G. Tyler, *The Letters and Times of the Tylers* (Richmond, Va.: Whittet & Shepperson, 1884), 1:407; James Hammond memorandum, March 18, 1831, in *American Historical Review*, 6 (July 1901):741–745.

31 For the impact of emigration upon North Carolina, see Harry L. Watson, *Jacksonian Politics and Community Conflict* (Baton Rouge: Louisiana State University Press, 1981), pp. 45–52.

32 Ohio *Senate Journal*, December 1830 sess., pp. 11–12. On party feeling on graduation see the *Ohio Monitor*, reprinted in the Indianapolis *Indiana Democrat and State Gazette*, June 3, 1830, and in the *St. Louis Beacon*, January 13, 1831; Columbus *Ohio State Journal*, May 27 and June 3, 1830.

33 Kentucky *Session Laws*, December 1828 sess., p. 192.

34 *House Journal*, 21st Cong., 1st sess., pp. 181–182. An earlier attempt to table exhibited a similar pattern (ibid., pp. 113–114). Debate is in *RD*, 21st Cong., 1st sess., pp. 477–540.

35 *National Intelligencer*, January 19 and 21, 1830; *House Journal*, 21st Cong., 1st sess., pp. 184–187. The distribution committee report is in ASP *Public Lands*, 6:163–166.

36 *St. Louis Beacon*, March 18, 1830.

37 *RD*, 21st Cong., 1st sess., pp. 477–478, 484–485.

38 *Richmond Enquirer*, January 23, 1830; *Southern Recorder*, reprinted in *Richmond Enquirer*, January 19, 1830; Martin speech in *Niles' Weekly Register* 38 (August 21, 1830):453–454; *Richmond Enquirer*, January 19, 1830. On Martin's amendment, see *House Journal*, 21st Cong., 1st sess., pp. 180–181.

39 *The Public Statutes at Large of the United States of America* (Boston: Little and Brown, 1845–1848), 2:445–446. For background on pre-emption see Gates, *History of Public Land Law Development*, chap. 10.

40 A list of pre-emption laws is in House Document 303, 25th Cong., 2d sess..

41 No complete figures on land sold under pre-emption laws exist. Partial statistics are in Gates, *History of Public Land Law Development*, pp. 223–224.

42 *AC*, 18th Cong., 1st sess., pp. 121–124, 130–132.

43 Clarence Edwin Carter, ed., *The Territorial Papers of the United States* (Washington: GPO, 1934–1962), 23:135–137, and 19:555–556.

44 ASP *Public Lands*, 5:791–792; Carter, *Territorial Papers*, 20:136–139; Louisiana *Session Laws*, January 1825 sess., p. 38.

45 Meigs to William H. Crawford, May 14, 1821, in Carter, *Territorial Papers*, 15:726; McKenney to James Barbour, ibid., 20:135–136. Committee reports are in ASP *Public Lands*, 3:300, 641, 719–721, and 4:82, 468, 958–959.

46 *Senate Journal*, 17th Cong., 1st sess., pp. 149–150, 174–176; *RD*, 19th Cong., 1st sess., pp. 1422–1436. The vote in 1822 was 12 to 4 in favor in the West (with two of the nays from Ohio), 22 to 6 against in the East.

47 ASP *Public Lands*, 5:400–401, 473.

48 *RD*, 21st Cong., 1st sess., pp. 8–9, 11.

49 Graham in ASP *Public Lands*, 6:186–188; *Statutes at Large*, 4:420–421. A move to table in the House provoked a sharper partisan division in New England and the mid-Atlantic states than on the final vote (*House Journal*, 21st Cong., 1st sess., pp. 768–769).

50 *St. Louis Beacon*, February 20, 1830. See also William Stanbery to Thomas Ewing, January 30, 1830, Ewing papers, LC.

51 *RD*, 21st Cong., 1st sess., pp. 406–407, 416; the complete debate is on pp. 405–427. Statistics are in ASP *Public Lands*, 5:595–596; Graham is in ASP *Public Lands*, 6:1–3.

52 *RD*, 21st Cong., 1st sess., pp. 413–414, 417, 421.

53 Barton in the Columbia *Missouri Intelligencer*, January 29, 1831.

54 House Report 137, 21st Cong., 1st sess.; *RD*, 21st Cong., 1st sess., pp. 474, 480–481, 869–870, 873; *House Journal*, 21st Cong., 1st sess., pp. 600–602; Duncan circular in Vandalia *Illinois Intelligencer*, April 16, 1831.

55 Lewis Williams circular in *National Intelligencer*, June 29, 1830; *Adams Memoirs*, 8:262. On the Illinois campaign, see the *Illinois Gazette*, June 12 through July 24, 1830; *Illinois Intelligencer*, March 20, June 5 through July 3, 1830; *Edwards Papers*, pp. 420–421, 463–464, 494–508, 512–513, 515.

56 Reynolds message in Illinois *Senate Journal*, December 1830 sess., pp. 60–61. On continuing cession agitation in Illinois, see the Springfield *Sangamo Journal*, April 19, 1832; Edwardsville *Illinois Advocate*, July 17, 1832; Vandalia *Illinois Advocate*, January 12 and 26, February 16 and 23, March 16, 1833.

57 John Wesley Davis address in the Vincennes *Western Sun*, January 8, 1831. See also Samuel Judah circular in *Western Sun*, September 17, 1831; *RD*, 21st Cong., 2d sess., pp. 413–414, 417–418; Joseph Duncan circular in *Illinois Intelligencer*, April 16, 1831; *Illinois Advocate*, June 3 and 10, July 1 and 29, 1831.

58 *St. Louis Times*, reprinted in the *National Journal*, December 9, 1830; toast at Barton dinner reported in *Niles' Weekly Register* 38 (July 17, 1830):372. See also Barton speech in *Missouri Intelligencer*, July 31, 1830; *St. Louis Beacon*, May 1 and September 23, 1830, March 24, 1831; *United States Telegraph*, May 11 and 13, October 15, 1830.

59 *House Journal*, 21st Cong., 1st sess., pp. 626–630, 642–646; *Senate Journal*, 21st Cong., 1st sess., p. 313; *House Journal*, 21st Cong., 2d sess., pp. 59–60, 166–167.

60 Smith address in *Niles' Weekly Register* 39 (December 4, 1830):245; Hayne to James Hammond, March 29, 1830, in *American Historical Review* 6 (July 1901):738.

61 *RD*, 21st Cong., 1st sess., pp. 791, 804; *House Journal*, 21st Cong., 1st sess., pp. 533–534, 540–543.

62 Clay to Josiah Johnston, May 9 and 10, 1830, *Clay Correspondence*, pp. 267–268.

63 James D. Richardson, ed., *A Compilation of the Messages and Papers of the Presidents, 1789–1897* (Washington: GPO, 1896–1899), 2:451–452, 483–494, 508–511. On the Buffalo Road, see the *Ohio State Journal*, May 6, 1830.

64 Richardson, *Messages and Papers*, 2:489.

65 Jackson to John Overton, December 31, 1829, *Correspondence of Andrew Jackson*, ed. John Spencer Bassett (Washington: Carnegie Institution, 1926–1935), 4:109.

66 "Fort Hill Address," July 26, 1831, in *The Papers of John C. Calhoun*, ed. Robert L. Meriwether et al. (Columbia: University of South Carolina Press, 1959–), 11:430 (hereafter cited as *Calhoun Papers*); Columbia (South Carolina) *Southern Times*, reprinted in *Niles' Weekly Register* 40 (April 9, 1831):105–106; Richardson, *Messages and Papers*, 2:451. See also *Calhoun Papers*, 11:116–118, 122, 226–229, 299, 395; Richardson, *Messages and Papers*, 2:512–517; *United States Telegraph*, February 9 and June 18, 1830, December 31, 1831; Woodville *Mississippi Democrat*, August 29, 1831.

67 *Ohio State Journal*, February 16, 1831; *National Intelligencer*, June 24, 1830; *Globe*, January 8, 1831.

68 Richardson, *Messages and Papers*, 2:517; House Report 51, 21st Cong., 2d sess. On Western reaction, see *Governors Messages and Letters*, vol. 12 of the Indiana Historical Collections (Indianapolis: Indiana Historical Commission, 1924), 3:417–418; *Illinois Intelligencer*, December 4, 1830; *Indiana Journal*, April 2, 1831.

69 *Autobiography of Martin Van Buren*, ed. John C. Fitzpatrick, Annual Report of the American Historical Association for the Year 1918, vol. 2 (Washington: GPO, 1920), pp. 323–326; *National Journal*, October 30, 1830; Clay committee address in *Niles' Weekly Register* 38 (July 31, 1830):412; *St. Louis Beacon*, June 17, 1830. See also the *Indiana Democrat and State Gazette*, June 17, 1830; Vincennes *Western Sun*, July 3 and 10, 1830; *United States Telegraph*, June 18, 1830.

70 *House Journal*, 21st Cong., 1st sess., pp. 763–764; *Senate Journal*, 21st Cong., 1st sess., p. 382.

71 On defections in response to the veto, see the *Ohio State Journal*, June 17 and, for Stanbery, August 5, 1830; *Indiana Journal*, July 7 and August 4, 1830; *Illinois Gazette*, November 27, 1830. American System Jacksonians sometimes received campaign backing from National Republicans and Whigs who were too outnumbered to elect a candidate bearing their own party label; see John Vollmer Mering, *The Whig Party in Missouri* (Columbia: University of Missouri Press, 1967), chaps. 2–4.

72 Van Buren, *Autobiography*, p. 327; Richardson, *Messages and Papers*, 2:508–514; House committee report in *RD*, 21st Cong., 2d sess., appendix pp. xxxv–xlii. In later years Congress partially circumvented Jackson's objections with river and harbor appropriations, though he sometimes vetoed them too. Cumberland Road appropriations, still tied to the 2 percent fund, also increased greatly. Nonetheless the Maysville Road veto throttled

"internal improvements" as the phrase was then understood. Under Jackson there were no more stock purchases or land grants and no new federal roads. Upon completion the Cumberland Road was relinquished to the states, releasing Congress from responsibility for its repair. Talk of a "general system" of federal improvements subsided so rapidly that by the close of Jackson's first term the phrase had virtually disappeared from the political lexicon. So although federal transportation spending did not cease and in some ways even increased under Jackson, the Gallatin–Clay–Adams project of a coordinated national transportation network was thoroughly quashed.

73 *Morning Courier and New York Enquirer*, February 19, 1830.

6. Crisis and compromise, 1832–1833

1 Annual Treasury report in *RD*, 22d Cong., 1st sess., appendix, pp. 25–27.
2 James D. Richardson, ed., *A Compilation of the Messages and Papers of the Presidents, 1789–1897* (Washington: GPO, 1896–1899), 2:556; Jackson to Van Buren, November 14, 1831, *Correspondence of Andrew Jackson*, ed. John Spencer Bassett (Washington: Carnegie Institution, 1926–1935), 4:374 (hereafter cited as *Jackson Correspondence*). Earlier drafts of Jackson's message by Amos Kendall and Andrew Jackson Donelson reiterated the earlier recommendations to distribute the surplus (Jackson papers, LC).
3 Annual Treasury report in *RD*, 22d Cong., 1st sess., appendix, pp. 29–30.
4 Alabama resolutions in ASP *Public Lands*, 6:385; *St. Louis Beacon*, December 29, 1831; Franklin Plummer and George Poindexter letters in the Vicksburg (Mississippi) *Advocate & Register*, January 9 and August 30, 1832; *RD*, 22d Cong., 1st sess., p. 1454. See also John Tipton correspondence in *Governors Messages and Letters*, vol. 38 of the Indiana Historical Collections (Indianapolis: Indiana Historical Bureau, 1958), 5:79–80; and *The John Tipton Papers*, ed. Nellie Armstrong Robertson and Dorothy Riker, vols. 24 to 26 of the Indiana Historical Collections (Indianapolis: Indiana Historical Bureau, 1942), 2:524, 535–536.
5 Clay to Francis Brooke, December 9, 1831, *The Works of Henry Clay*, vol. 4: *Private Correspondence*, ed. Calvin Colton (New York: G. P. Putnam's Sons, 1904), p. 321 (hereafter cited as *Clay Correspondence*); *Richmond Enquirer*, December 24, 1831.
6 *United States Telegraph*, January 17, 1832.
7 Committee report in ASP *Public Lands*, 6:451–454; Ratliff Boon letter in Vincennes *Western Sun*, May 5, 1832; Duncan in *RD*, 22d Cong., 1st sess., p. 1454; Plummer in Vicksburg *Advocate & Register*, January 9, 1832.
8 Robinson to Ninian Edwards, April 1, 1832, in *The Edwards Papers*, ed. Elihu B. Washburne, vol. 3 of the Chicago Historical Society Collections (Chicago: Fergus Printing Co., 1884), pp. 582–583; Birch letter in *St. Louis Beacon*, May 17, 1832; Jackson meeting address in Edwardsville *Illinois Advocate*, January 6, 1832; Moore to Ninian Edwards, December 31, 1831,

in Ninian Wirt Edwards, *History of Illinois from 1778 to 1833; and Life and Times of Ninian Edwards* (Springfield: Illinois State Journal Co., 1870), pp. 508–509; *Globe,* May 21, 1832.

9 *RD,* 22d Cong., 1st sess., pp. 66–75.

10 *Richmond Enquirer,* reprinted in Washington *Globe,* April 17, 1832. See also *RD,* 22d Cong., 1st sess., pp. 409, 563–565, 574–576, 628, 664–668.

11 *RD,* 22d Cong., 1st sess., pp. 626–627; see also pp. 439, 457–458, 615–616.

12 *RD,* 22d Cong., 1st sess., pp. 32–41, 49–53, 591–629.

13 *RD,* 22d Cong., 1st sess., pp. 629–638; *National Intelligencer,* July 7, 1832; *Niles' Weekly Register* 42 (June 23, 1832):297–298.

14 Clay to Francis Brooke, March 28, 1832, *Clay Correspondence,* pp. 330–331.

15 ASP *Public Lands,* 6:441–451.

16 *National Intelligencer,* April 17, 1832; Louisville *Daily Journal and Focus,* reprinted in Indianapolis *Indiana Journal,* July 21, 1832; *Niles' Weekly Register* 42 (April 21, 1832):122; Rush to Clay, April 23, 1832, in Clay papers, LC; Marshall to Clay, May 7, 1832, in *Clay Correspondence,* p. 339.

17 ASP *Public Lands,* 6:478–487. See also *RD,* 22d Cong., 1st sess., pp. 785–791, 870–872, 883–884, 901–907, 931.

18 Calhoun to Ingham, July 31, 1831, *The Papers of John C. Calhoun,* ed. Robert L. Meriwether et al. (Columbia: University of South Carolina Press, 1959–), 11:445 (hereafter cited as *Calhoun Papers*); Madison to Van Buren, July 5, 1830, in *Autobiography of Martin Van Buren,* ed. John C. Fitzpatrick, Annual Report of the American Historical Association for the Year 1918, vol. 2 (Washington: GPO, 1920), pp. 331–334. See also Green to Edwards, January 19, 1831 and January 14, 1832, in *Edwards Papers,* pp. 568, 577–579.

19 James Hammond memorandum, March 18, 1831, in *American Historical Review* 6 (July 1901):741–745.

20 Calhoun to Christopher Vandeventer, August 5, 1831, *Calhoun Papers,* 11:450–451.

21 Earlier colonization proposals are in *AC,* 16th Cong., 1st sess., p. 1114; *RD,* 18th Cong., 2d sess., pp. 623, 696–697; Jefferson to Albert Gallatin, December 26, 1820, and Jefferson to Jared Sparks, February 4, 1824, in *The Writings of Thomas Jefferson,* ed. Paul Leicester Ford (New York: G. P. Putnam's Sons, 1892–1899), 10:178, 290–293; Madison to Robert Evans, June 5, 1819, and Madison to R. R. Gurley, December 28, 1831, in *The Writings of James Madison,* ed. Gaillard Hunt (New York: G. P. Putnam's Sons, 1900–1910), 8:442–443, and 9:469–470.

22 Clay to Francis Brooke, October 4, 1831, *Clay Correspondence,* p. 315; *RD,* 22d Cong., 1st sess., pp. 1114–1115. In Clay's as in other distribution proposals, population was computed according to the constitutional formula for determining congressional representation, counting a slave as three-fifths of a person.

23 *St. Louis Beacon,* June 14, 1832; *Western Sun,* June 23, 1832; *Illinois Advocate,* June 12 and July 10, 1832; *Frankfort* (Kentucky) *Argus,* reprinted in

Washington *Globe,* June 30, 1832. See also Indianapolis *Indiana Democrat,* April 28, 1832; *Globe,* May 28, June 7, 16, 22, 30, 1832; [W. J. Dunnica ?] to Clay, June 8, 1832, Clay papers, LC.

24 Tipton to Noah Noble, April 15 and December 18, 1832, *Tipton Papers,* 2:585, 753; *St. Louis Beacon,* May 10 and June 14, 1832.

25 Springfield, Illinois, *Sangamo Journal,* May 17, 1832; *Indiana Journal,* May 5 and 12, 1832.

26 *RD,* 22d Cong., 1st sess., pp. 1094–1119, 1129, 1132–1154, 1156–1164.

27 *RD,* 22d Cong., 1st sess., pp. 592, 595, 1091–1092, 1164–1165.

28 *RD,* 22d Cong., 1st sess., pp. 1165–1174; *Senate Journal,* 22d Cong., 1st sess., pp. 385–392.

29 *Charleston* (South Carolina) *Mercury,* May 3, 1832; James Hammond memorandum, March 18, 1831, and James Hamilton Jr. to James Hammond, June 11, 1831, in the *American Historical Review* 6 (July 1901):742–747; South Carolina congressional delegation address in the Vicksburg (Mississippi) *Advocate & Register,* August 23, 1832; *RD,* 22d Cong., 1st sess., pp. 1151, 1161; Edward Stanwood, *American Tariff Controversies in the Nineteenth Century* (Boston: Houghton, Mifflin & Co., 1903), 1:374–382.

30 *RD,* 22d Cong., 1st sess., pp. 3852–3853; *House Journal,* 22d Cong., 1st sess., pp. 1077–1081.

31 *RD,* 22d Cong., 1st sess., pp. 2200–2201, 2233–2234, 2259–2273, 647, 684; *House Journal,* 22d Cong., 1st sess., pp. 546–547. Petitions and memorials are in ASP *Public Lands,* 6:22–23, 290, 395; *United States Telegraph,* February 18 and 21, 1832; *Illinois Advocate,* January 13, 1832.

32 Thomas Hart Benton, *Thirty Years' View* (New York: D. Appleton & Co., 1854), 1:275; *RD,* 22d Cong., 1st sess., pp. 1293–1296.

33 *Niles' Weekly Register* 43 (September 22, 1832):51; Tristam Burges and Asher Robbins, *A Statement of Some Leading Principles and Measures Adopted by General Jackson in His Administration of the National Government* (Providence: William Marshall & Co., 1832); *Niles' Weekly Register* 43 (September 22, 1832):51, and 42 (July 21, 1832):369.

34 Hendricks circulars in *Indiana Magazine of History* 71 (June and December, 1975):165–166, 333–334, 341–342; McCarty circular in *Indiana Democrat,* April 6, 1833.

35 Theodore Frelinghuysen speech in Columbus *Ohio State Journal,* September 15, 1832; George Poindexter letter in Vicksburg *Advocate & Register,* August 30, 1832.

36 Jonathan Pugh address in *Sangamo Journal,* July 5, 1832; Thomas Ewing to Tipton, September 9, 1832, in *Tipton Papers,* 2:704–705. See also the Columbia *Missouri Intelligencer,* October 13, 1832; Vicksburg *Advocate & Register,* July 26 and August 2, 1832; *Indiana Journal,* October 6, 1832; St. Louis *Missouri Republican,* August 4, 1832.

37 *Illinois Advocate,* October 23, 1832; *Globe,* April 19 and August 17, 1832; Hill speech in *Niles' Weekly Register* 43 (September 1, 1832):10. On National Republican use of the issue see the *National Intelligencer,* October 4, 1832; *Ohio State Journal,* August 25 and September 15, 1832; *Missouri Intelligencer,*

October 27, 1832; C. B. Goddard to Thomas Ewing, August 30, 1832, and G. Browning to Ewing, September 24, 1832, Ewing papers, LC.

38 Poindexter letter in *Woodville Republican*, February 2, 1833; Poindexter letters in Vicksburg *Advocate & Register*, July 26 and September 13, 1832; Plummer letter in *Advocate & Register*, November 28, 1832; Indiana *Governors Messages*, 5:145–148, 157–171; *Tipton Papers*, 2:745, 787; *Indiana Democrat*, January 12, 1833; *Indiana Journal*, May 19, December 8 and 12, 1832, January 2, 1833.

39 Richardson, *Messages and Papers*, 2:600–601. An earlier draft by Andrew Jackson Donelson is in the Jackson papers, LC.

40 *Memoirs of John Quincy Adams*, ed. Charles Francis Adams (Philadelphia: J. B. Lippincott & Co., 1874–1877), 8:503 (hereafter cited as *Adams Memoirs*).

41 *Louisville Public Advertiser*, reprinted in the Jefferson City, Missouri, *Jeffersonian Republican*, January 12, 1833; *National Intelligencer*, December 8, 1832. For other reactions pro and con, see Archibald Yell to James Polk, December 16, 1832, *Correspondence of James K. Polk*, ed. Herbert Weaver et al. (Nashville: Vanderbilt University Press, 1969–), 1:577; Roswell Colt to Nicholas Biddle, December 8, 1832, in *The Correspondence of Nicholas Biddle Dealing with National Affairs*, ed. Reginald C. McGrane (Boston: Houghton Mifflin Co., 1919), p. 199.

42 Tennessee *Session Laws*, September 1831 sess., p. 138.

43 Resolutions are in ASP *Public Lands*, 6:301, 614; Delaware *Session Laws*, January 1833 sess., p. 296; Maryland *Session Laws*, December 1832 sess., resolution no. 28; New Jersey *Session Laws*, October 1832 sess., p. 170. Debate and proceedings are in Delaware *House Journal*, January 1833 sess., p. 203; Maryland *House Journal*, December 1832 sess., pp. 212–213, 221–222, 341–345, 415, and *Senate Journal*, December 1832 sess., pp. 168, 188; New Jersey *House Journal*, October 1832 sess., pp. 108–110, and *Legislative Council Journal*, October 1832 sess., p. 214; Pennsylvania *House Journal*, December 1832 sess., pp. 347, 367–368, 385–386, 441, 449–451, 475–476, 500. Maryland party affiliations are from *Niles' Weekly Register* 43 (October 13, 1832):101–102.

44 Vermont resolutions in ASP *Public Lands*, 6:604; *Resolves of the General Court of the Commonwealth of Massachusetts*, January 1833 sess., pp. 470–491; New Hampshire *House Journal*, November 1832 sess., pp. 184–185. The New Hampshire roll call closely matched a vote earlier the same day demanding the resignation of National Republican senator Samuel Bell for misrepresenting his constituents (*House Journal*, pp. 175–178).

45 State resolutions are in ASP *Public Lands*, 6:606, 608–609, 612–614. Debate and proceedings are in Alabama *Senate Journal*, November 1832 sess., pp. 11–13; Illinois *House Journal*, December 1832 sess., p. 246; *The Messages and Proclamations of the Governors of the State of Missouri*, ed. Buel Leopard and Floyd Shoemaker (Columbia: The State Historical Society of Missouri, 1922), 1:176–181; *Missouri Intelligencer*, December 15, 1832; Missouri *Senate Journal*, November 1832 sess., pp. 133, 150, 154, 182–183, 186, 197, and *House Journal*, November 1832 sess., pp. 55, 234.

On Indiana, see Indiana *Governors Messages*, 5:145–148; Indiana *House Journal*, December 1832 sess., pp. 47, 61, 68, 72, 84–85, 89, 93–94, 106–109, 116, 127–128, 136–149, 168–172, 178–180, 203, 211–212; Indianapolis *Indiana Journal*, December 5, 1832 through January 16, 1833; *Indiana Democrat*, January 2 and 16, 1833. Indiana party affiliations are from *A Biographical Directory of the Indiana General Assembly* (Indianapolis: Indiana Historical Bureau, 1980), pp. 459–460.

46 William Doherty in *Ohio State Journal*, February 25, 1833; George Dunn in the *Indiana Journal*, December 29, 1832. On Ohio, see the Ohio *Senate Journal*, December 1832 sess., pp. 287–288, 491, 631–632, 646, 648–649, 652. Ohio party affiliations are from electoral data in *Ohio State Journal*, October 27, 1831 and October 20, 1832. On Kentucky, see the Lexington *Kentucky Gazette*, January 12 and 19, February 2 and 16, 1833; *Niles' Weekly Register* 43 (February 9, 1833):399; Washington *Globe*, March 23, 1833.

47 Alabama legislature in House Document 141, 22d Cong., 2d sess.; South Carolina congressional delegation address in Vicksburg *Advocate & Register*, August 23, 1832. State anti-tariff resolutions are in Senate Documents 33, 71, 103, and 105, 20th Cong., 2d sess., and House Report 300, 21st Cong., 1st sess.; Louisiana resolutions are in *Niles' Weekly Register* 38 (May 8, 1830):203.

48 North Carolina *House Journal*, November 1831 sess., pp. 157–158, 202, 218; *Senate Journal*, November 1831 sess., p. 94.

49 Benton letter in the *Missouri Intelligencer*, February 16, 1833. The *Sangamo Journal* (March 2, 1833) sarcastically commented: "The abundant success which has attended his efforts already on this question, must be a great stimulant to future exertion."

50 *RD*, 22d Cong., 2d sess., p. 229.

51 Michael Hoffman to Azariah Flagg, December 18, 1832, Martin Van Buren papers, LC; *Senate Journal*, 22d Cong., 2d sess., pp. 127–129. Debate and roll calls on distribution are in *RD*, 22d Cong., 2d sess., pp. 5–6, 61–98, 104–119, 122–174, 193–235; *Senate Journal*, 22d Cong., 2d sess., pp. 81, 123–138.

52 *RD*, 22d Cong., 2d sess., pp. 462–473, 477–478, 688, 1772, 1810–1811, 1903–1904; Stanwood, *American Tariff Controversies*, 1:390–410; Merrill D. Peterson, *Olive Branch and Sword: The Compromise of 1833* (Baton Rouge: Louisiana State University Press, 1982), chapter 2.

53 *Ohio State Journal*, March 23, 1833; *RD*, 22d Cong., 2d sess., pp. 464.

54 *RD*, 22d Cong., 2d sess., p. 465; John Clayton speech, June 15, 1844, and Clay's response, August 22, 1844, in Calvin Colton, *The Life and Times of Henry Clay* (New York: A. S. Barnes & Co., 1846), 2:252–253, 259–260. See also Clayton to Nicholas Biddle, April 1841, Clayton papers, LC.

55 *National Intelligencer*, quoted in *Niles' Weekly Register* 44 (March 9, 1833):18; *Niles' Weekly Register* 44 (March 9, 1833):17; Clay quoted in *Indiana Journal*, March 30, 1833. See also *Adams Memoirs*, 8:522; *Niles' Weekly Register* 44 (March 2, 1833):1; *Indiana Journal*, February 9, 1833; *Sangamo Journal*, February 16, 1833.

56 *National Intelligencer,* January 5 and February 5, 1833; Lexington *Kentucky Gazette,* February 9, 1833; *Niles' Weekly Register* 43 (February 16, 1833):403, and 44 (March 2, 1833):3; *Globe,* January 22 and 28, February 28, 1833; Churchill Cambreleng to Martin Van Buren, February 5, 1833, Van Buren papers, LC.

57 *Ohio State Journal,* March 23, 1833; *National Intelligencer,* March 14 and 19, 1833; *United States Telegraph,* March 9 and 19, 1833.

58 Madison to Clay, June 1833, *Writings of James Madison,* 9:515–516; *Missouri Intelligencer,* April 13, 1833; Benton, *Thirty Years' View,* 1:364–365; Jackson to Martin Van Buren, July 30, 1833, *Jackson Correspondence,* 5:144.

59 *Address of John Quincy Adams to His Constituents* (Boston: J. H. Eastburn, 1842), pp. 21–23, 41, 51–52; *RD,* 24th Cong., 1st sess., pp. 50, 394; Clay to Nicholas Biddle, March 4, 1833, Clay papers, LC.

60 *Charleston Mercury,* May 3, 1832, and March 8, 1833; *Globe,* March 16, 1833; *United States Telegraph,* March 5, 1833.

61 *RD,* 22d Cong., 2d sess., p. 809. Compare the March 1 roll call with earlier roll calls in *Senate Journal,* 22d Cong., 2d sess., pp. 131–132.

62 *RD,* 22d Cong., 2d sess., pp. 1904–1921; *House Journal,* 22d Cong., 2d sess., pp. 453–461.

63 Washington *Globe,* March 16, 1833. Peterson, *Olive Branch and Sword,* pp. 82–83, denies that distribution was any part of the compromise. But Peterson looked for evidence of a bargain in the wrong places—in the Senate's passage of distribution, which happened *before* Clay introduced his tariff, and in Southern votes for distribution in the House of Representatives, rather than in the absence of Southern votes against it.

64 Lucas Elmendorf to Martin Van Buren, April 8, 1833, and Jackson to Van Buren, April 25, 1833, Van Buren papers, LC.

65 Jackson to Hugh Lawson White, March 24, 1833, and Jackson to unknown correspondent, March 24, 1833, *Jackson Correspondence,* 5:46–48.

66 Richardson, *Messages and Papers,* 3:56–59.

67 Mangum to David L. Swain, December 22, 1833, *The Papers of Willie Person Mangum,* ed. Henry Thomas Shanks (Raleigh, N.C.: State Department of Archives and History, 1950–1956), 2:53–54.

7. The vortex of party, 1833–1837

1 Clay to Francis Brooke, May 30, 1833, *The Works of Henry Clay,* vol. 4: *Private Correspondence,* ed. Calvin Colton (New York: G. P. Putnam's Sons, 1904), pp. 361–362; Vandalia *Illinois Advocate,* July 20, April 27, April 13, 1833; Louisville *Public Advertiser,* reprinted in the Indianapolis *Indiana Democrat,* August 3, 1833.

2 James D. Richardson, ed., *A Compilation of the Messages and Papers of the Presidents, 1789–1897* (Washington: GPO, 1896–1899), 3:56–69; Washington *Globe,* June 24 and 25, July 6, 1833.

3 Richardson, *Messages and Papers,* 3:67; Washington *Globe,* June 27, 1833.

4 Richardson, *Messages and Papers*, 3:66.

5 *Globe*, June 29, 1833; see also issue of June 24, 1833.

6 *Globe*, June 29, 1833; see also issues of July 3 and 12, 1833. The *Globe* series was widely reprinted and its arguments quickly adopted by Jacksonians everywhere. The strong similarities between the *Globe* articles and Jackson's message indicate that they both came from the same source.

7 Jefferson City *Jeffersonian Republican*, December 21, 1833; *Illinois Advocate*, December 28, 1833, and February 1, 1834; *Autobiography of Martin Van Buren*, ed. John C. Fitzpatrick, Annual Report of the American Historical Association for the Year 1918, vol. 2 (Washington: GPO, 1920), pp. 742–744; Joseph Hopkinson to Webster, December 27, 1833, in *The Papers of Daniel Webster: Correspondence*, ed. Charles M. Wiltse et al. (Hanover: University Press of New England, 1974–), 3:296.

8 *Senate Journal*, 23d Cong., 1st sess., pp. 38–39; *RD*, 23d Cong., 1st sess., p. 43.

9 *Senate Journal*, 23d Cong., 1st sess., pp. 37, 42–43; *RD*, 23d Cong., 1st sess., pp. 14–18, 24, 44, 1599–1606; committee reports and state memorials are in ASP *Public Lands*, 6:638, 640–642, 657, 939, and 7:153–161.

10 *The Messages and Proclamations of the Governors of the State of Missouri*, ed. Buel Leopard and Floyd Shoemaker (Columbia: The State Historical Society of Missouri, 1922), 1:252–254; *House Journal*, 23d Cong., 1st sess., pp. 761–762, 768, 770–772; *RD*, 23d Cong., 1st sess., pp. 4521–4522, 4537.

11 *House Journal*, 23d Cong., 1st sess., pp. 751–752; *RD*, 23d Cong., 1st sess., pp. 824, 4469–4481.

12 *Niles' Weekly Register* 45 (September 21, 1833): 49, and 45 (August 31, 1833):1; *Senate Journal*, 23d Cong., 1st sess., p. 197.

13 *The Diary of Philip Hone*, ed. Allan Nevins (New York: Dodd, Mead & Co., 1936), p. 110; Hendricks circular in *Indiana Magazine of History* 71 (December 1975):344–348.

14 On Western support for the Bank, see John M. McFaul, *The Politics of Jacksonian Finance* (Ithaca: Cornell University Press, 1972), pp. 45–48.

15 On Southern Whiggery, see Charles Grier Sellers, Jr., "Who Were the Southern Whigs?" *American Historical Review* 59 (January 1954):335–346.

16 Richard B. Latner, *The Presidency of Andrew Jackson* (Athens: University of Georgia Press, 1979), chap. 7. Their refusal to vote for Benton's expunging resolution cost Mangum of North Carolina and Tyler and Benjamin Leigh of Virginia their seats in the Senate.

17 Dallas to Bedford Brown, December 8, 1833, *Papers of the Historical Society of Trinity College*, Duke University, 6 (1906):70–71.

18 Robert V. Remini, *Andrew Jackson and the Bank War* (New York: W. W. Norton & Co., 1967), pp. 166, 15; *RD*, 23d Cong., 1st sess., pp. 75, 59.

19 Ohio resolutions are in ASP *Public Lands*, 6:654, and Senate Document 146, 23d Cong., 2d sess. For debate and proceedings, see Ohio *Senate Journal*, December 1833 sess., pp. 214–215, 252–253, 256–257, 264–269; Ohio *House Journal*, December 1833 sess., pp. 251–253; Ohio *Senate Journal*, December 1834 sess., pp. 549–552; Ohio *House Journal*, December 1834

sess., pp. 134, 229–233, 237–239, 241–243, 716–718. Party identifications for legislators are from the *Ohio State Journal*, October 25, 1834. The original Ohio resolutions may have been prompted from Washington (Sackett Reynolds to Micajah T. Williams, December 16, 1833, Williams papers, OHS [microfilm ed., roll 2, frame 598]). That legislators were responding to distribution according to party imperatives rather than on its merits is shown by the fact that the same Democratic legislature which denounced Clay's bill later quietly approved a resolution requesting distribution for school support (ASP *Public Lands*, 6:969).

20 Missouri resolutions are in Senate Document 284, 24th Cong., 1st sess.; proceedings are in Missouri *Senate Journal*, November 1834 sess., pp. 185–189; Missouri *House Journal*, November 1834 sess., pp. 245–248.

Kentucky resolutions are in ASP *Public Lands*, 8:657; proceedings are in Kentucky *House Journal*, December 1835 sess., pp. 152–153, 176–178; Kentucky *Senate Journal*, December 1835 sess., pp. 180, 229–232, 235–236. The expunging question (whether to instruct United States senators to vote for Benton's resolution expunging the censure of Jackson from the Senate journal) was agitated in many state legislatures. It was a pure party question—in fact, a definer of party—and may be safely used to determine party makeup in the legislatures as well as in the United States Senate. In the Kentucky senate all the expungers were against distribution, all the anti-expungers for it. In the Kentucky house there was no vote on expunging, but cross-tabulating the vote on distribution with a resolution nominating William Henry Harrison for president shows that Harrison was supported by 55 distribution men and opposed by 9 distribution men and 29 distribution opponents. (Kentucky *House Journal*, December 1835 sess., pp. 335–340).

Vermont resolutions are in *RD*, 23d Cong., 2d sess., pp. 1415–1416; proceedings are in Vermont *General Assembly Journal*, October 1834 sess., pp. 203, 224–225.

New Hampshire resolutions are in House Document 112, 24th Cong., 2d sess.; proceedings are in New Hampshire *House Journal*, November 1836 sess., pp. 305–307, and New Hampshire *Senate Journal*, November 1836 sess., p. 149. Party identifications for legislators are from Concord *New Hampshire Patriot and State Gazette*, March 14, 21, and 28, 1836.

21 William S. Hoffmann, "The Downfall of the Democrats: the Reaction of North Carolinians to Jacksonian Land Policy," *North Carolina Historical Review* 33 (April 1956):166–180. Legislative proceedings are in North Carolina *Senate and House of Commons Journals*, November 1834 sess., pp. 84, 110, 135–136, 189, 222–223, 238–241, 244–245, 262–264, and November 1835 sess., pp. 29, 47, 51, 58–59, 66–67, 69–72, 99–101, 109, 137–141, 143–146, 192–195. See also Thomas Edward Jeffrey, "The Second Party System in North Carolina, 1836–1860" (Ph.D. diss., Catholic University of America, 1976), chap. 2; contemporary confirmation in letters of North Carolina Democrats to Martin Van Buren, *North Carolina Historical Review* 15 (January and April, 1938):69, 76, 135. On Whig use of the issue see *Niles'*

Weekly Register 48 (May 9, 1835):175–176; correspondence in *The Papers of Willie Person Mangum*, ed. Henry Thomas Shanks (Raleigh, N.C.: State Department of Archives and History, 1950–1956), 2:53–54, 273–274, 413–414 (hereafter cited as *Mangum Papers*); *The Papers of Thomas Ruffin*, ed. J. G. de Roulhac Hamilton (Raleigh: North Carolina Historical Commission, 1918–1920), 2:120–121.

22 New Hampshire resolutions are in House Document 112, 24th Cong., 2d sess. Maryland resolutions are in ASP *Public Lands*, 8:609; proceedings are in Maryland *House Journal*, December 1835 sess., pp. 431–436, 657–660. For other state legislative action on the land issue, see New York *Assembly Journal*, January 1836 sess., pp. 212–213, 713–715; Pennsylvania resolutions in ASP *Public Lands*, 8:555; proceedings in Pennsylvania *House Journal*, December 1835 sess., pp. 65–66, 216, 223–225, 725–728, 805–806, and Pennsylvania *Senate Journal*, December 1835 sess., pp. 463–464, 490, 501–503. Party identifications for Pennsylvania legislators are from Charles McCool Snyder, *The Jacksonian Heritage* (Harrisburg: Pennsylvania Historical and Museum Commission, 1958), p. 79. Indiana resolutions are in ASP *Public Lands*, 6:939; proceedings are in Indiana *House Journal*, December 1833 sess., pp. 506–507, and Indiana *Senate Journal*, December 1833 sess., pp. 34, 77, 96, 99, 294–301, 365. See also *Governors Messages and Letters*, vol. 38 of the Indiana Historical Collections (Indianapolis: Indiana Historical Bureau, 1958), 5:276–285. Party identifications for legislators are from *A Biographical Directory of the Indiana General Assembly* (Indianapolis: Indiana Historical Bureau, 1980).

23 ASP *Public Lands*, 6:628–630, 7:329, 8:8,10.

24 Paul W. Gates, *History of Public Land Law Development* (Washington: GPO, 1968), chap. 8. In only one year of the boom (1834) did the average federal selling price exceed $1.30 per acre, and then not by much.

25 Committee reports are in ASP *Public Lands*, 8:330–332, 408–413, 877–885; debate on Benton's fortification resolutions is in *RD*, 24th Cong., 1st sess., pp. 52–55, 106–578.

26 Roll calls are in *Senate Journal*, 24th Cong., 1st sess., pp. 219–221, 313, 316–319, 330–331; debate is in *RD*, 24th Cong., 1st sess., pp. 48–52, 471, 810–833, 848–877, 1172–1177, 1187–1198, 1212–1248, 1254, 1279–1286, 1288–1313, 1318–1374, 1396.

27 *Senate Journal*, 24th Cong., 1st sess., pp. 313–314. On Webster, see Peter J. Parish, "Daniel Webster, New England, and the West," *Journal of American History* 54 (December 1967):524–549.

28 *RD*, 24th Cong., 1st sess., pp. 1028–1032.

29 *House Journal*, 24th Cong., 1st sess., pp. 641–643, 648–649, 781–782, 863–864, 870–872, 966–967, 1023–1024. Debate is in *RD*, 24th Cong., 1st sess., pp. 2892–2917, 2989–2996, 3095, 3201, 3231, 3359–3363, 3495–3496, 3548–3553, 3580–3593, 3617–3630, 3679–3686, 3718–3719, 3820–3863, 4177–4186, 4195–4196, 4322–4328.

30 *RD*, 24th Cong., 1st sess., pp. 1577, 1810; *Senate Journal*, 24th Cong., 1st sess., pp. 434, 437, 441, 445, 447–448.

31 Thomas Hart Benton, *Thirty Years' View* (New York: D. Appleton & Co., 1854), 1:649–658; veto draft, and Taney to Jackson, June 27, 1836, in *Correspondence of Andrew Jackson*, ed. John Spencer Bassett (Washington: Carnegie Institution, 1926–1935), 5:404–412; *House Journal*, 24th Cong., 1st sess., pp. 1043–1044, 1051–1052, 1067–1072. See also Washington *Globe*, reprinted in *Niles' Weekly Register* 50 (June 25, 1836):281.

32 Van Buren to Sherrod Williams, and Harrison to Williams, in *Niles' Weekly Register* 51 (September 10, 1836):23–27; White speech in *RD*, 24th Cong., 1st sess., pp. 4641–4653. On the distribution issue in White's candidacy, see *Mangum Papers*, 2:383, 391, 414, 441, 445–447, 451; *The Papers of William Alexander Graham*, ed. J. G. de Roulhac Hamilton et al. (Raleigh, N.C.: State Department of Archives and History, 1957–), 1:443–445; *Correspondence of James K. Polk*, ed. Herbert Weaver et al. (Nashville: Vanderbilt University Press, 1969–), 3:629, 633, 640, 658.

33 Joel H. Silbey, "Election of 1836," in *History of American Presidential Elections*, ed. Arthur M. Schlesinger, Jr. (New York: Chelsea House, 1971), pp. 577–640.

34 ASP *Public Lands*, 8:893–896.

35 Richardson, *Messages and Papers*, 3:249.

36 Ibid., pp. 249–250; text of the circular in *RD*, 24th Cong., 2d sess., appendix pp. 107–108. On Benton's introduction of the Specie Circular in the Senate and its rejection there, see *Senate Journal*, 24th Cong., 1st sess., pp. 306, 308.

37 *RD*, 24th Cong., 2d sess., p. 41.

38 Richardson, *Messages and Papers*, 3:250. On pre-emption in the Senate, see *Senate Journal*, 24th Cong., 1st sess., pp. 410, 419.

39 *Senate Journal*, 24th Cong., 2d sess., p. 76; debate and proceedings in *RD*, 24th Cong., 2d sess., pp. 204, 377–380, 419–428, 512–513, 529–530, 534–562, 644–669, 671–690, 692–696, 701–706, 726–737, 739–777, 780–794, 2190–2191; roll calls on Calhoun's proposition are in *Senate Journal*, 24th Cong., 2d sess., pp. 223–224, 232, 240.

40 Benton in *RD*, 24th Cong., 2d sess., p. 681; Senate proceedings in *Senate Journal*, 24th Cong., 2d sess., pp. 130–233, including graduation roll calls on pp. 130, 145, 157–158, 194–195; House proceedings in *RD*, 24th Cong., 2d sess., pp. 2091–2092, and *House Journal*, 24th Cong., 2d sess., pp. 561–562.

41 Lauchlin Bethune circular in Washington *Globe*, April 4, 1833; Adams in *RD*, 22d Cong., 2d sess., appendix pp. 46–48; Richardson, *Messages and Papers*, 3:384.

42 Richardson, *Messages and Papers*, 3:384–389, 496, 536–537. *Senate Journal*, 25th Cong., 2d sess., pp. 191, 356; 25th Cong., 3d sess., p. 134; 26th Cong., 1st sess., pp. 316–317, 329–330, 334, 337; 26th Cong., 2d sess., p. 156. *House Journal*, 25th Cong., 2d sess., pp. 357–358, 364–365, 1099–1101; 26th Cong., 1st sess., pp. 1031–1032, 1035–1036.

43 Richardson, *Messages and Papers*, 4:47–48. For a detailed treatment of the

events of 1841–1842, see George M. Stephenson, *The Political History of the Public Lands, from 1840 to 1862* (Boston: Richard G. Badger, 1917), chap. 3.
44 The evolution of the land issue in the 1850s is treated in detail in Stephenson, *Political History of the Public Lands*, chaps. 7–15.
45 Allan G. Bogue, "Senators, Sectionalism, and the 'Western' Measures of the Republican Party," in David M. Ellis, ed., *The Frontier in American Development* (Ithaca: Cornell University Press, 1969); Paul W. Gates, "Western Opposition to the Agricultural College Act," *Indiana Magazine of History* 37 (March 1941):103–136; John Y. Simon, "The Politics of the Morrill Act," *Agricultural History* 37 (April 1963):103–111.

8. The public lands and the party system

1 On the Whig ethos, see Daniel Walker Howe, *The Political Culture of the American Whigs* (Chicago: University of Chicago Press, 1979); Major L. Wilson, *Space, Time, and Freedom* (Westport, Conn.: Greenwood Press, 1974), chap. 3.
2 Wilson, *Space, Time, and Freedom*; Marvin Meyers, *The Jacksonian Persuasion* (Stanford: Stanford University Press, 1960).
3 On local party formation, see Harry L. Watson, *Jacksonian Politics and Community Conflict* (Baton Rouge: Louisiana State University Press, 1981). On state legislatures, see Rodney O. Davis, "Partisanship in Jacksonian State Politics: Party Divisions in the Illinois Legislature, 1834–1841" in *Quantification in American History: Theory and Research*, ed. Robert P. Swierenga (New York: Atheneum, 1970), pp. 149–162; Herbert Ershkowitz and William G. Shade, "Consensus or Conflict? Political Behavior in the State Legislatures During the Jacksonian Era," *Journal of American History* 58 (December 1971):591–621; Peter Levine, "State Legislative Parties in the Jacksonian Era: New Jersey, 1829–1844," *Journal of American History* 62 (December 1975):591–608. On state banking controversies, see William Gerald Shade, *Banks or No Banks* (Detroit: Wayne State University Press, 1972); James Roger Sharp, *The Jacksonians versus the Banks* (New York: Columbia University Press, 1970).
4 Oliver H. Smith, *Early Indiana Trials and Sketches* (Cincinnati: Moore, Wilstach, Keys & Co., 1858), p. 80. See also the circular of state senator Elisha Embree in *Indiana Magazine of History* 32 (March 1936):68–69.
5 William Fort to Lewis F. Linn, September 16, 1836, and S. Milton Skinner to Moses Y. Tilden, January 3, 1837, Van Buren papers, LC.
6 Thomas B. Alexander et al., "The Basis of Alabama's Ante-Bellum Two-Party System," *Alabama Review* 19 (October 1966):243–276; John Vollmer Mering, *The Whig Party in Missouri* (Columbia: University of Missouri Press, 1967), chap. 6; Watson, *Jacksonian Politics and Community Conflict*; Donald B. Cole, *Jacksonian Democracy in New Hampshire, 1800–1851* (Cambridge: Harvard University Press, 1970), pp. 158–159; Everett William Kindig, "Western Opposition to Jackson's 'Democracy': The Ohio Valley as a Case Study, 1827–1836" (Ph.D. diss., Stanford University, 1974); Donald J. Ratcliffe,

"Politics in Jacksonian Ohio: Reflections on the Ethnocultural Interpretation," *Ohio History* 88 (Winter 1979):5–36; Sharp, *Jacksonians versus the Banks*, pp. 325–326.

7 For a radically different view, see Michael F. Holt, *The Political Crisis of the 1850s* (New York: John Wiley & Sons, 1978). According to Holt the blurring of party identities was the cause, not the product, of the rise of the slavery controversy. Holt sees no essential difference between the strains imposed upon a national party by the slavery issue and those imposed by other sectional questions. Underlying his work is the assumption, strangely akin to Richard P. McCormick's, that issues were never more than counters manipulated by politicians for personal and partisan advantage.

8 Roy M. Robbins, *Our Landed Heritage*, 2d rev. ed. (Lincoln: University of Nebraska Press, 1976); Paul W. Gates, "The Role of the Land Speculator in Western Development" and "Land Policy and Tenancy in the Prairie Counties of Indiana," in Gates, *Landlords and Tenants on the Prairie Frontier* (Ithaca: Cornell University Press, 1973), pp. 48–71, 108–139; Paul W. Gates, *History of Public Land Law Development* (Washington: GPO, 1968).

9 Robert P. Swierenga, "Land Speculation and its Impact on American Economic Growth and Welfare: A Historiographical Review," *Western Historical Quarterly* 8 (July 1977):283–302; Robert P. Swierenga, *Pioneers and Profits: Land Speculation on the Iowa Frontier* (Ames: Iowa State University Press, 1968); Allan G. Bogue, *From Prairie to Corn Belt* (Chicago: University of Chicago Press, 1963), pp. 38–46; Allan G. Bogue, "The Iowa Claim Clubs: Symbol and Substance," in *The Public Lands*, ed. Vernon Carstensen (Madison: University of Wisconsin Press, 1963), pp. 47–69; Thomas LeDuc, "Public Policy, Private Investment, and Land Use in American Agriculture, 1825–1875," *Agricultural History* 37 (January 1963):3–9; John D. Haeger, *The Investment Frontier* (Albany: State University of New York Press, 1981).

10 Gates, *History of Public Land Law Development*, chap. 8; Bogue, "Iowa Claim Clubs"; Everett Dick, *The Lure of the Land* (Lincoln: University of Nebraska Press, 1970), chap. 5; Herman Bowmar to Martin Van Buren, August 29, 1836, Van Buren papers, LC.

11 Paul K. Conkin, *Prophets of Prosperity* (Bloomington: Indiana University Press, 1980), chap. 9; Harry R. Stevens, "Did Industrial Labor Influence Jacksonian Land Policy?" *Indiana Magazine of History* 43 (June 1947): 159–167; Helene Sara Zahler, *Eastern Workingmen and National Land Policy, 1829–1862* (New York: Columbia University Press, 1941).

12 Meyers, *Jacksonian Persuasion*, chaps. 6 and 7; Thomas P. Abernethy, *The South in the New Nation, 1789–1819* (Baton Rouge: Louisiana State University Press, 1961), pp. 453–455.

13 Malcolm J. Rohrbough, *The Land Office Business* (New York: Oxford University Press, 1968), p. 297. For a provocative critique of federal land policy, see Thomas LeDuc, "History and Appraisal of U.S. Land Policy to 1862," in *Land Use Policy and Problems in the United States*, ed. Howard W. Ottoson (Lincoln: University of Nebraska Press, 1963), pp. 3–27.

BIBLIOGRAPHY

1. Government documents

A. Federal

Journal of the House of Representatives of the United States, 1815–842.

Journal of the Senate of the United States, 1815–1842.

American State Papers: Documents, Legislative and Executive, of the Congress of the United States, 1789–1838. 38 vols., arranged by subject matter. Washington: Gales & Seaton, 1832–1861.

House Documents, 1817–1837.

House Reports, 1819–1837.

Senate Documents, 1817–1837.

The Public Statutes at Large of the United States of America. Vols. 1–4. Boston: Little and Brown, 1845–1848.

Annals of Congress (also titled *Debates and Proceedings in the Congress of the United States, 1789–1824*). 42 vols. Washington: Gales & Seaton, 1834–1856.

Register of Debates in Congress, 1825–1837. 29 vols. Washington: Gales & Seaton, 1825–1837.

Carter, Clarence Edwin, ed. *The Territorial Papers of the United States.* 26 vols. Washington: GPO, 1934–1962.

Ford, Worthington Chauncey, et al., eds. *Journals of the Continental Congress, 1774–1789.* 34 vols. Washington: GPO, 1904–1937.

Richardson, James D., ed. *A Compilation of the Messages and Papers of the Presidents, 1789–1897.* 10 vols. Washington: GPO, 1896–1899.

Royce, Charles. *Indian Land Cessions in the United States.* Eighteenth Annual Report of the Bureau of American Ethnology, part 2. Washington: GPO, 1899.

B. State

Legislative journals (variously titled).

Session law volumes (variously titled).

The Governors' Letter-Books, 1818–1834. Collections of the Illinois State Historical Library, vol. 4. Springfield: Illinois State Historical Library, 1909.

247

Governors Messages and Letters, vols. 3–5. Indiana Historical Collections, vols. 12, 34, and 38. Edited by Logan Esarey et al. Indianapolis: Indiana Historical Commission, 1924, and Indiana Historical Bureau, 1954, 1958.
Messages of the Governors of Michigan, vol. 1. Edited by George N. Fuller. Lansing: The Michigan Historical Commission, 1925.
The Messages and Proclamations of the Governors of the State of Missouri, vol. 1. Edited by Buel Leopard and Floyd Shoemaker. Columbia: The State Historical Society of Missouri, 1922.
State of New York. Messages from the Governors, vol. 3. Edited by Charles Z. Lincoln. Albany: J. B. Lyon Co., 1909.

2. Manuscript collections

Ethan Allen Brown papers, Ohio Historical Society
Henry Clay papers, Library of Congress
John M. Clayton papers, Library of Congress
John Jordan Crittenden papers, Library of Congress
Thomas Ewing papers, Library of Congress
Thomas Ewing papers, University of Notre Dame Archives
Albert Gallatin papers, New York Historical Society
Duff Green letterbooks, Library of Congress
Duff Green papers, Southern Historical Collection, University of North Carolina Library
Charles Hammond papers, Ohio Historical Society
Andrew Jackson papers, Library of Congress
Virgil Maxcy correspondence in the Galloway–Maxcy–Markoe papers, Library of Congress
Duncan McArthur papers, Library of Congress
Short family papers, Library of Congress
Benjamin Tappan papers, Library of Congress
Martin Van Buren papers, Library of Congress
Micajah T. Williams papers, Ohio Historical Society

3. Newspapers

Washington, D.C.
National Intelligencer, 1817–1833
National Journal, 1826–1830
United States Telegraph, 1827–1833
Globe, 1830–1833

Alabama
Huntsville *Democrat*, 1823–1831
Huntsville *Southern Advocate*, 1825–1832
Montgomery *Alabama Journal*, 1825–1832

Illinois
Edwardsville *Illinois Advocate*, 1831–1832, continued by Vandalia *Illinois Advocate*, 1832–1834
Edwardsville Spectator, 1819–1826
Kaskaskia *Western Intelligencer*, 1817–1818, continued by Kaskaskia *Illinois Intelligencer*, 1818–1820, continued by Vandalia *Illinois Intelligencer*, 1820–1831
Shawneetown *Illinois Gazette*, 1819–1830
Springfield *Sangamon Journal*, 1831–1832, continued by Springfield *Sangamo Journal*, 1832–1834

Indiana
Charlestown *Indiana Intelligencer*, 1821–1825
Corydon *Indiana Gazette*, 1817–1824, continued by Bloomington *Indiana Gazette*, 1824–1825
Indianapolis Gazette, 1822–1829, continued by Indianapolis *Indiana State Gazette*, 1829–1830, continued by Indianapolis *Indiana Democrat*, 1830–1833
Indianapolis *Indiana Journal*, 1825–1833
Vincennes *Western Sun*, 1815–1832

Louisiana
Baton Rouge Gazette, 1827–1834
New Orleans *Louisiana Advertiser*, 1820, 1826–1828

Mississippi
Natchez *Mississippi Republican*, 1818–1823
Natchez *Mississippi State Gazette*, 1818–1825, continued by *Natchez Gazette*, 1825–1827, continued by *Mississippi Statesman and Natchez Gazette*, 1827, continued by Natchez *Statesman and Gazette*, 1827–1829
Natchez *Mississippi Statesman*, 1826–1827 (merged with *Natchez Gazette*)
Vicksburg *Advocate & Register*, 1831–1834
Woodville Republican, 1823–1830, continued by Woodville *Mississippi Democrat*, 1831, continued by *Woodville Republican*, 1833–1834

Missouri
Franklin *Missouri Intelligencer*, 1819–1826, continued by Fayette *Missouri Intelligencer*, 1826–1830, continued by Columbia *Missouri Intelligencer*, 1830–1833
Jackson *Independent Patriot*, 1820–1826
Jackson *Missouri Herald*, 1819–1820
Jefferson City *Jeffersonian Republican*, 1831–1834
St. Charles *Missourian*, 1820–1822
St. Louis Beacon, 1829–1832
St. Louis Enquirer, 1819–1824
St. Louis *Missouri Gazette*, 1819–1822
St. Louis *Missouri Republican*, 1822–1828

Ohio
Chillicothe *Scioto Gazette*, 1818–1821, continued by Chillicothe *Supporter and Scioto Gazette*, 1821–1827, continued by Chillicothe *Scioto Gazette*, 1827–1829
Chillicothe *Supporter*, 1817–1821 (merged with *Scioto Gazette*)
Cincinnati *Inquisitor Advertiser*, 1818–1822
Cincinnati *Western Spy*, 1817–1822
Columbus *Gazette*, 1817–1825, continued by Columbus *Ohio State Journal*, 1825–1833
Lebanon *Western Star*, 1828

4. Periodicals

American Quarterly Review, 1827–1837
Niles' Weekly Register, 1817–1837
North American Review, 1815–1833
Western Monthly Review, 1827–1830

5. Pamphlets

Adams, John Quincy. *Address of John Quincy Adams to His Constituents*. Boston: J. H. Eastburn, 1842.
Benton, Thomas Hart. *Mr. Benton's Speeches on the Public Lands*. Washington: Green & Jarvis, 1828.
Burges, Tristam, and Asher Robbins. *A Statement of Some Leading Principles and Measures Adopted by General Jackson in His Administration of the National Government*. Providence: William Marshall & Co., 1832.
[Maxcy, Virgil]. *The Maryland Resolutions, and the Objections to Them Considered*. Baltimore: E. J. Coale & Co., 1822.

6. Published correspondence, diaries, memoirs, and autobiographies

Adams, John Quincy. *Memoirs of John Quincy Adams*. Edited by Charles Francis Adams. 12 vols. Philadelphia: J. B. Lippincott & Co., 1874–1877.
Adams, John Quincy. "Letters of John Quincy Adams to Alexander Hamilton Everett, 1811–1837." *American Historical Review* 11 (January 1906):332–354.
Adams, John Quincy. "Ten Unpublished Letters of John Quincy Adams, 1796–1837." Edited by Edward H. Tatum, Jr. *The Huntington Library Quarterly* 4 (April 1941):371–388.
Anderson, Richard Clough, Jr. *The Diary and Journal of Richard Clough Anderson, Jr.* Edited by Alfred Tischendorf and E. Taylor Parks. Durham: Duke University Press, 1964.
Austin, Moses, and Stephen F. Austin. *The Austin Papers*. Annual Report of the American Historical Association for the Year 1919, vol. 2. Edited by Eugene C. Barker. Washington: GPO, 1924.

Badollet, John, and Albert Gallatin. *The Correspondence of John Badollet and Albert Gallatin.* Edited by Gayle Thornbrough. Indianapolis: Indiana Historical Society, 1963.

Benton, Thomas Hart. *Thirty Years' View.* Vol. 1. New York: D. Appleton & Co., 1854.

Biddle, Nicholas. *The Correspondence of Nicholas Biddle Dealing with National Affairs.* Edited by Reginald C. McGrane. Boston: Houghton Mifflin Co., 1919.

Birkbeck, Morris. *Letters from Illinois.* Originally published 1818. New York: Da Capo Press, 1970.

Birkbeck, Morris. *Notes on a Journey in America, from the Coast of Virginia to the Territory of Illinois.* London: Severn & Co., 1818.

Brown, Bedford. "Selections from the Correspondence of Bedford Brown." Edited by William K. Boyd. *Papers of the Historical Society of Trinity College, Duke University.* Vol. 6 (1906), pp. 66–92.

Brown, Bedford, and others. "Unpublished Letters from North Carolinians to Van Buren." Edited by Elizabeth Gregory McPherson. *North Carolina Historical Review* 15 (January 1938):53–81.

Brown, James. "Letters of James Brown to Henry Clay, 1804–1835." Edited by James A. Padgett. *Louisiana Historical Quarterly* 24 (October 1941): 921–1177.

Buchanan, James. *The Works of James Buchanan.* Edited by John Bassett Moore. 12 vols. Philadelphia: J. B. Lippincott Co., 1908–1911.

Calhoun, John C. *The Papers of John C. Calhoun.* Edited by Robert L. Meriwether et al. 15 vols. to date. Columbia: University of South Carolina Press, 1959– .

Clay, Henry. *The Papers of Henry Clay.* Edited by James F. Hopkins et al. 7 vols. to date. Lexington: University of Kentucky Press, 1959– .

Clay, Henry. *Private Correspondence. The Works of Henry Clay,* vol. 4. Edited by Calvin Colton. New York: G. P. Putnam's Sons, 1904.

Coles, Edward. "Letters of Governor Edward Coles Bearing on the Struggle of Freedom and Slavery in Illinois." *Journal of Negro History* 3 (April 1918):158–195.

Coles, Edward. *Sketch of Edward Coles, Second Governor of Illinois, and of the Slavery Struggle of 1823–4.* By Elihu B. Washburne. Chicago: Jansen, McClurg & Company, 1882.

Cunningham, Noble E. Jr., ed. *Circular Letters of Congressmen to Their Constituents, 1789–1829.* 3 vols. Chapel Hill: University of North Carolina Press, 1978.

Dike, Nathaniel. "Nine Letters of Nathaniel Dike on the Western Country, 1816–1818." Edited by Dwight L. Smith. *Ohio Historical Quarterly* 67 (July 1958):189–220.

Edwards, Ninian. *The Edwards Papers.* Chicago Historical Society Collections, vol. 3. Edited by Elihu B. Washburne. Chicago: Fergus Printing Co., 1884.

Edwards, Ninian. *History of Illinois from 1778 to 1833; and Life and Times of*

Ninian Edwards. By Ninian Wirt Edwards. Springfield: Illinois State Journal Co., 1870.

Fairfield, John. *The Letters of John Fairfield.* Edited by Arthur G. Staples. Lewiston, Maine: Lewiston Journal Company, 1922.

Flint, Timothy. *Recollections of the Last Ten Years.* Boston: Cummings, Hilliard, & Co., 1826.

Ford, Thomas. *A History of Illinois.* Originally published 1847. Edited by Milo Quaife. Chicago: R. R. Donnelley & Sons, 1945.

Gallatin, Albert. *The Writings of Albert Gallatin.* Edited by Henry Adams. 3 vols. Philadelphia: J. B. Lippincott & Co., 1879.

Graham, William Alexander. *The Papers of William Alexander Graham.* Edited by J. G. de Roulhac Hamilton et al. 6 vols to date. Raleigh, N.C.: State Department of Archives and History, 1957– .

Hammond, James H., and others. "Letters on the Nullification Movement in South Carolina, 1830–1834." *American Historical Review* 6 (July 1901):736–765.

Hendricks, William. "William Hendricks' Political Circulars to his Constituents." Edited by Frederick D. Hill. *Indiana Magazine of History* 70 (December 1974):296–344; 71 (June and December 1975):124–180, 319–374.

Hone, Philip. *The Diary of Philip Hone.* Edited by Allan Nevins. New York: Dodd, Mead & Co., 1936.

Houston, Sam. *The Writings of Sam Houston.* Edited by Amelia W. Williams and Eugene C. Barker. 8 vols. Austin: University of Texas Press, 1938–1943.

Jackson, Andrew. *Correspondence of Andrew Jackson.* Edited by John Spencer Bassett. 7 vols. Washington: Carnegie Institution, 1926–1935.

Jefferson, Thomas. *The Writings of Thomas Jefferson.* Edited by Paul Leicester Ford. 10 vols. New York: G. P. Putnam's Sons, 1892–1899.

Jennings, Jonathan. "Unedited Letters of Jonathan Jennings." Edited by Dorothy Riker. *Indiana Historical Society Publications* 10 (1933):147–278.

Jennings, Jonathan. "Some Additional Jennings Letters." *Indiana Magazine of History* 39 (September 1943):279–295.

Johnson, Richard M. "The Letters of Colonel Richard M. Johnson of Kentucky." Edited by James A. Padgett. *The Register of the Kentucky State Historical Society* 39 (1941):22–46, 172–188, 260–277, 358–367; 40 (January 1942): 69–91.

King, Rufus. *The Life and Correspondence of Rufus King.* Edited by Charles R. King. 6 vols. New York: G. P. Putnam's Sons, 1894–1900.

Lucas, J. B. C. *Letters of Hon. J. B. C. Lucas.* Edited by John B. C. Lucas. St. Louis: n.p., 1905.

Madison, James. *Letters and Other Writings.* 4 vols. Philadelphia: J. B. Lippincott & Co., 1865.

Madison, James. *The Writings of James Madison.* Edited by Gaillard Hunt. 9 vols. New York: G. P. Putnam's Sons, 1900–1910.

Mangum, Willie P. *The Papers of Willie Person Mangum.* Edited by Henry Thomas Shanks. 5 vols. Raleigh, N.C.: State Department of Archives and History, 1950–1956.

Mason, Jeremiah. *Memoir, Autobiography, and Correspondence of Jeremiah Mason.* Edited by G. J. Clark. Kansas City: Lawyer's International Publishing Co., 1917.

Monroe, James. *The Writings of James Monroe.* Edited by Stanislaus Murray Hamilton. 7 vols. New York: G. P. Putnam's Sons, 1898–1903.

Plumer, William, Jr. *The Missouri Compromises and Presidential Politics, 1820–1825, From the Letters of William Plumer, Junior.* Edited by Everett Somerville Brown. St Louis: Missouri Historical Society, 1926.

Plumer, William, Jr. "Reminiscences of Daniel Webster." *The Writings and Speeches of Daniel Webster,* vol. 17. Edited by Fletcher Webster. Boston: Little, Brown, & Co., 1903.

Polk, James K. *Correspondence of James K. Polk.* Edited by Herbert Weaver et al. 6 vols. to date. Nashville: Vanderbilt University Press, 1969– .

Reynolds, John. *My Own Times.* Chicago: Chicago Historical Society, 1879.

Roberts, Jonathan. "Memoirs of a Senator from Pennsylvania." Edited by Philip S. Klein. *Pennsylvania Magazine of History and Biography* 62 (July 1938):361–409.

Robertson, George. *An Outline of the Life of George Robertson, Written by Himself.* Lexington, Ky.: Transylvania Printing & Publishing Co., 1876.

Ruffin, Thomas. *The Papers of Thomas Ruffin.* Edited by J. G. de Roulhac Hamilton. 4 vols. Raleigh: North Carolina Historical Commission, 1918–1920.

Smith, Oliver H. *Early Indiana Trials and Sketches.* Cincinnati: Moore, Wilstach, Keys & Co., 1858.

Tipton, John. *The John Tipton Papers.* Indiana Historical Collections, vols. 24–26. Edited by Nellie Armstrong Robertson and Dorothy Riker. Indianapolis: Indiana Historical Bureau, 1942.

Trimble, Allen. "Selections from the Papers of Governor Allen Trimble." *Old Northwest Genealogical Quarterly* 10 (July and October, 1907):259–274, 301–342; 11 (January and April 1908):14–37, 130–151.

Tyler, John. *The Letters and Times of the Tylers.* By Lyon G. Tyler. 3 vols. Richmond, Va.: Whittet & Shepperson, 1884–1896.

Van Buren, Martin. *Autobiography of Martin Van Buren.* Annual Report of the American Historical Association for the Year 1918, vol. 2. Edited by John C. Fitzpatrick. Washington: GPO, 1920.

Webster, Daniel. *The Papers of Daniel Webster: Correspondence.* Edited by Charles Wiltse et al. 5 vols. to date. Hanover: University Press of New England, 1974– .

7. Secondary works

Abernethy, Thomas P. *The South in the New Nation, 1789–1819.* Baton Rouge: Louisiana State University Press, 1961.

Alexander, Thomas B. *Sectional Stress and Party Strength.* Nashville: Vanderbilt University, 1967.

Alexander, Thomas B., et al. "The Basis of Alabama's Ante-Bellum Two-Party System." *Alabama Review* 19 (October 1966):243–276.

Ambler, Charles Henry. *Sectionalism in Virginia from 1776 to 1861*. Chicago: University of Chicago Press, 1910.

Bemis, Samuel Flagg. *John Quincy Adams and the Union*. New York: Alfred A. Knopf, 1956.

Benson, Lee. *The Concept of Jacksonian Democracy: New York as a Test Case*. Princeton: Princeton University Press, 1961.

Berry, Thomas Senior. *Western Prices Before 1861*. Cambridge, Mass.: Harvard University Press, 1943.

Bogue, Allan G. *From Prairie to Corn Belt*. Chicago: University of Chicago Press, 1963.

Bogue, Allan G., and Mark Paul Marlaire. "Of Mess and Men: The Boardinghouse and Congressional Voting, 1821–1842." *American Journal of Political Science* 19 (May 1975):207–230.

Buck, Solon Justus. *Illinois in 1818*. Sesquicentennial edition. Urbana: University of Illinois Press, 1967.

Buley, R. Carlyle. *The Old Northwest*. 2 vols. Indianapolis: Indiana Historical Society, 1950.

Carstensen, Vernon, ed. *The Public Lands*. Madison: University of Wisconsin Press, 1963.

Chambers, William Nisbet. *Old Bullion Benton*. Boston: Little, Brown & Co., 1956.

Cole, Donald B. *Jacksonian Democracy in New Hampshire, 1800–1851*. Cambridge, Mass.: Harvard University Press, 1970.

Colton, Calvin. *The Life and Times of Henry Clay*. 2 vols. New York: A. S. Barnes & Co., 1846.

Conkin, Paul K. *Prophets of Prosperity*. Bloomington: Indiana University Press, 1980.

Davis, Rodney O. "Partisanship in Jacksonian State Politics: Party Divisions in the Illinois Legislature, 1834–1841." In *Quantification in American History: Theory and Research*, ed. Robert P. Swierenga, pp. 149–162. New York: Atheneum, 1970.

Dick, Everett. *The Lure of the Land*. Lincoln: University of Nebraska Press, 1970.

Donaldson, Thomas. *The Public Domain*. Washington: GPO, 1884.

Ellis, David M., ed. *The Frontier in American Development*. Ithaca: Cornell University Press, 1969.

Ershkowitz, Herbert, and William G. Shade. "Consensus or Conflict? Political Behavior in the State Legislatures During the Jacksonian Era." *Journal of American History* 58 (December 1971): 591–621.

Formisano, Ronald P. *The Birth of Mass Political Parties: Michigan, 1827–1861*. Princeton: Princeton University Press, 1971.

Formisano, Ronald P. "Toward a Reorientation of Jacksonian Politics: A Review of the Literature." *Journal of American History* 63 (June 1976):42–65.

Fox, Stephen C. "Politicians, Issues, and Voter Preference in Jacksonian Ohio: A Critique of an Interpretation." *Ohio History* 86 (Summer 1977):155–170.

Freehling, William W. *Prelude to Civil War*. New York: Harper & Row, 1966.

Gates, Paul W. *History of Public Land Law Development*. Washington: GPO, 1968.

Gates, Paul W. *Landlords and Tenants on the Prairie Frontier*. Ithaca: Cornell University Press, 1973.

Gates, Paul W. "Pressure Groups and Recent American Land Policies." *Agricultural History* 55 (April 1981):103–127.

Gates, Paul W. "Western Opposition to the Agricultural College Act." *Indiana Magazine of History* 37 (June 1941):103–136.

Gray, Lewis Cecil. *History of Agriculture in the Southern United States to 1860*. 2 vols. Washington: Carnegie Institution, 1933.

Haeger, John D. *The Investment Frontier*. Albany: State University of New York Press, 1981.

Harrison, Joseph Hobson. "The Internal Improvement Issue in the Politics of the Union, 1783–1825." Ph.D. diss., University of Virginia, 1954.

Hibbard, Benjamin Horace. *A History of the Public Land Policies*. New York: MacMillan Company, 1924.

Hoffman, William S. "The Downfall of the Democrats: the Reaction of North Carolinians to Jacksonian Land Policy." *North Carolina Historical Review* 33 (April 1956):166–180.

Holt, Michael F. *The Political Crisis of the 1850s*. New York: John Wiley & Sons, 1978.

Howe, Daniel Walker. *The Political Culture of the American Whigs*. Chicago: University of Chicago Press, 1979.

Hulburt, Archer Butler. *The Cumberland Road*. Historic Highways of America, vol. 10. Cleveland, Ohio: Arthur H. Clark Co., 1904.

Jeffrey, Thomas Edward. "The Second Party System in North Carolina, 1836–1860." Ph.D. diss., Catholic University of America, 1976.

Jensen, Merrill. *The New Nation*. New York: Alfred A. Knopf, 1950.

Kelley, Robert. *The Cultural Pattern in American Politics: The First Century*. New York: Alfred A. Knopf, 1979.

Kindig, Everett William. "Western Opposition to Jackson's 'Democracy': The Ohio Valley as a Case Study, 1827–1836." Ph.D. diss., Stanford University, 1974.

Kousser, Morgan. "The 'New Political History': A Methodological Critique." *Reviews in American History* 4 (March 1976):1–14.

Latner, Richard B. *The Presidency of Andrew Jackson*. Athens: University of Georgia Press, 1979.

Latner, Richard B., and Peter Levine. "Perspectives on Antebellum Pietistic Politics." *Reviews in American History* 4 (March 1976):15–24.

LeDuc, Thomas. "Public Policy, Private Investment, and Land Use in American Agriculture, 1825–1875." *Agricultural History* 37 (January 1963):3–9.

Levine, Peter. "State Legislative Parties in the Jacksonian Era: New Jersey, 1829–1844." *Journal of American History* 62 (December 1975):591–608.

McCandless, Perry. *A History of Missouri, 1820 to 1860*. The Missouri Sesquicentennial Edition, vol. 2. Columbia: University of Missouri Press, 1972.

McCormick, Richard L. "Ethno-Cultural Interpretations of Nineteenth-

Century American Voting Behavior." *Political Science Quarterly* 89 (June 1974):351–377.

McCormick, Richard P. *The Second American Party System: Party Formation in the Jacksonian Era.* Chapel Hill: University of North Carolina Press, 1966.

McCormick, Richard P. "New Perspectives on Jacksonian Politics." *American Historical Review* 65 (January 1960):288–301.

McFaul, John M. *The Politics of Jacksonian Finance.* Ithaca: Cornell University Press, 1972.

Mering, John Vollmer. *The Whig Party in Missouri.* Columbia: University of Missouri Press, 1967.

Meyers, Marvin. *The Jacksonian Persuasion.* Stanford: Stanford University Press, 1960.

Moore, Glover. *The Missouri Controversy.* Lexington: University of Kentucky Press, 1953.

Nielsen, George R. "The Indispensable Institution: The Congressional Party During the Era of Good Feelings." Ph.D. diss., University of Iowa, 1968.

Ottoson, Howard W., ed. *Land Use Policy and Problems in the United States.* Lincoln: University of Nebraska Press, 1963.

Parish, Peter J. "Daniel Webster, New England, and the West." *Journal of American History* 54 (December 1967):524–549.

Peterson, Merrill D. *Olive Branch and Sword: The Compromise of 1833.* Baton Rouge: Louisiana State University Press, 1982.

Philbrick, Francis S. *The Rise of the West.* New York: Harper & Row, 1965.

Phillips, Ulrich Bonnell. *Georgia and State Rights.* Annual Report of the American Historical Association for the Year 1901, vol. 2. Washington: GPO, 1902.

Ratcliffe, Donald J. "Politics in Jacksonian Ohio: Reflections on the Ethnocultural Interpretation." *Ohio History* 88 (Winter 1979):5–36.

Ratcliffe, Donald J. "The Role of Voters and Issues in Party Formation: Ohio, 1824." *Journal of American History* 59 (March 1973):847–870.

Remini, Robert V. *Andrew Jackson and the Bank War.* New York: W. W. Norton & Co., 1967.

Remini, Robert V. *The Election of Andrew Jackson.* Philadelphia: J. B. Lippincott Company, 1963.

Remini, Robert V. *Martin Van Buren and the Making of the Democratic Party.* New York: Columbia University Press, 1959.

Robbins, Roy M. *Our Landed Heritage.* 2d rev. ed. Lincoln: University of Nebraska Press, 1976.

Rohrbough, Malcolm J. *The Land Office Business.* New York: Oxford University Press, 1968.

Scheiber, Harry N. *Ohio Canal Era.* Athens: Ohio University Press, 1969.

Schlesinger, Arthur M., Jr. *The Age of Jackson.* Boston: Little, Brown & Co., 1945.

Sellers, Charles Grier, Jr. "Who Were the Southern Whigs?" *American Historical Review* 59 (January 1954):335–346.

Shade, William Gerald. *Banks or No Banks*. Detroit: Wayne State University Press, 1972.

Shalhope, Robert E. "Jacksonian Politics in Missouri: A Comment on the McCormick Thesis." *Civil War History* 15 (September 1969):210–225.

Sharp, James Roger. *The Jacksonians versus the Banks*. New York: Columbia University Press, 1970.

Silbey, Joel H. *The Shrine of Party*. Pittsburgh: University of Pittsburgh Press, 1967.

Silbey, Joel H. "Election of 1836." In *History of American Presidential Elections*, ed. Arthur M. Schlesinger, Jr., pp. 577–640. New York: Chelsea House, 1971.

Simon, John Y. "The Politics of the Morrill Act." *Agricultural History*, 37 (April 1963):103–111.

Smith, Elbert B. *Magnificent Missourian*. Philadelphia: J. B. Lippincott Company, 1958.

Snyder, Charles McCool. *The Jacksonian Heritage*. Harrisburg: Pennsylvania Historical and Museum Commission, 1958.

Stanwood, Edward. *American Tariff Controversies in the Nineteenth Century*. Vol. 1. Boston: Houghton, Mifflin & Co., 1903.

Stephenson, George M. *The Political History of the Public Lands, from 1840 to 1862*. Boston: Richard G. Badger, 1917.

Stevens, Harry R. "Did Industrial Labor Influence Jacksonian Land Policy?" *Indiana Magazine of History* 43 (June 1947):159–167.

Swierenga, Robert P. *Pioneers and Profits: Land Speculation on the Iowa Frontier*. Ames: Iowa State University Press, 1968.

Swierenga, Robert P. "Land Speculation and its Impact on American Economic Growth and Welfare: A Historiographical Review." *Western Historical Quarterly* 8 (July 1977):283–302.

Swift, Fletcher Harper. *A History of Public Permanent Common School Funds in the United States*. New York: Henry Holt & Co., 1911.

Sydnor, Charles S. *The Development of Southern Sectionalism, 1819–1848*. Baton Rouge: Louisiana State University Press, 1948.

Treat, Payson Jackson. *The National Land System, 1785–1820*. New York: E. B. Treat & Co., 1910.

Tregle, Joseph George, Jr. "Louisiana and the Tariff, 1816–1846." *Louisiana Historical Quarterly* 25 (January 1942):24–148.

Turner, Frederick Jackson. *Rise of the New West*. The American Nation Series, vol. 14. New York: Harper & Brothers, 1906.

Turner, Frederick Jackson. *The United States, 1830–1850*. New York: Henry Holt & Co., 1935.

Van Deusen, Glyndon G. *The Life of Henry Clay*. Boston: Little, Brown & Co., 1937.

Ward, John William. *Andrew Jackson: Symbol for an Age*. New York: Oxford University Press, 1955.

Watson, Harry L. *Jacksonian Politics and Community Conflict*. Baton Rouge: Louisiana State University Press, 1981.

Weiner, Alan S. "John Scott, Thomas Hart Benton, David Barton and the Presidential Election of 1824: A Case Study in Pressure Politics." *Missouri Historical Review* 60 (July 1966):460–494.

Weisenburger, Francis P. *The Passing of the Frontier. The History of the State of Ohio*, vol. 3. Columbus: Ohio State Archaeological and Historical Society, 1941.

Wellington, Raynor G. *The Political and Sectional Influence of the Public Lands, 1828–1842*. Cambridge, Mass: Riverside Press, 1914.

Wilson, Major L. *Space, Time, and Freedom*. Westport, Conn.: Greenwood Press, 1974.

Wright, James E. "The Ethnocultural Model of Voting: A Behavioral and Historical Critique." *American Behavioral Scientist* 16 (May-June 1973):653–674.

Young, James Sterling. *The Washington Community, 1800–1828*. New York: Columbia University Press, 1966.

Young, Jeremiah Simeon. *A Political and Constitutional Study of the Cumberland Road*. Chicago: University of Chicago Press, 1904.

Zahler, Helene Sara. *Eastern Workingmen and National Land Policy, 1829–1862*. New York: Columbia University Press, 1941.

INDEX

DESIGNED BY MIKE JAYNES
COMPOSED BY MODERN TYPOGRAPHERS, INC.
DUNEDIN, FLORIDA
MANUFACTURED BY CUSHING-MALLOY, INC.
ANN ARBOR, MICHIGAN
TEXT AND DISPLAY LINES ARE SET IN BASKERVILLE

Library of Congress Cataloging in Publication Data

Feller, Daniel, 1950–
The public lands in Jacksonian politics.

Bibliography: p. 247–258
Includes index.
1. United States—Public lands—History—19th century.
2. United States—Politics and government—1829–1837.
3. United States—History—1815–1861. 4. Jackson, Andrew,
1767–1845. I. Title.
HD197.F45 1984   333.1'0973   84-40149
ISBN 0-299-09850-8